Carrie Bailee was born in Canada and now lives in Melbourne with her two daughters. She is a spoken-word performer, poet, blogger, advocate and speaker. For more information, go to her website: flyingonbrokenwings.com.

For Diane,

In our darkest hours, our deepest insights can be gained ♡

Bailee xx

FLYING
ON
BROKEN
WINGS

CARRIE BAILEE

AFFIRM press

Published by Affirm Press in 2014
28 Thistlethwaite Street, South Melbourne, VIC 3205
www.affirmpress.com.au

National Library of Australia Cataloguing-in-Publication
entry available for this title at www.nla.gov.au.
Title: Flying on Broken Wings / Carrie Bailee, author.
ISBN: 9781922213297 (paperback)

Cover design by Josh Durham/Design by Committee
Cover photography by Adam Haddrick
Typeset in Bembo 12.75/16 by J&M Typesetting
Proudly printed in Australia by Griffin Press

This project has been assisted by the Australian Government
through the Australia Council, its arts funding and advisory body.

*Some names have been changed to protect the identity of individuals. All accounts
of trials are recollections and recreations and not taken directly from transcripts.*

I dedicate this book with love to my beautiful daughters, to the memory of my mother, and to every soul who ever believed they were too broken to fly.

Prologue

MY BIRTH MOTHER sat in the waiting room of the abortion clinic. She was seventeen years old. Looking around the room, she no doubt connected with many of the young women who had come in for similar reasons. The only support she had from my birth father was the money to pay for the termination. Her parents were ashamed and feared for her future.

The nurse called her name, but she didn't hear. They called her a second time. She heard but didn't respond. When they called her name a third and final time, she rose from her seat and ran out the door.

For this, I am grateful. Months later I was given up for adoption.

When I trace back in time and track my life up until this point, the 'coincidental' moments I've experienced and the number of times the universe has divinely intervened, guiding me toward an experience or a certain person who could help me along my journey, I am quite certain some may find it hard to believe. But then again, you would probably find my lowest points, when I had no one there to step into the darkness and offer a hand to lift me out, hard to believe as well.

It has been said that tragedy befalls us all at some point. We each face trauma and loss of some kind at least once in our lifetime. What I have come to know is that during our darkest hours, our deepest insights can be gained. And from our most desperate moments emerge the lessons of hope and resilience. No matter the trauma, the ability to overcome and rise to the greatest of heights is a possibility. In all honesty, I can't say for certain why I am not crazy or dead. Why others in situations similar to mine failed in pursuit of their dreams, never having found a way to get beyond merely surviving because what they carried grew too heavy to bear.

Every single one of us is a little broken in some way. Perhaps I can be a reminder for everyone: no matter how damaged we may be, it is possible to rise above our past and make that flight on broken wings.

2013 – The Year of Courage

Standing alone on stage, I was in a room filled with people waiting to hear my story. My nerves almost got the better of me, and then I remembered why I was there. Maybe rock bottom was where I had to plummet, to summon the strength to step into my power and realise that I did have an important message to bestow upon others. I wanted to demonstrate what was possible when people invested their time, love and encouragement in individuals who would otherwise get lost in the system. The ones put in the 'broken beyond repair' category that society deems irredeemable. I walked toward the microphone and looked out at the audience for the first time.

The room was packed, and yet the silence was deafening. Faces stared intently and waited for me to begin my story. I knew what I had been through in life was both fascinating and uncomfortable for many to listen to. That's why I decided capturing it in a poem would be my safest bet. Tackle the unimaginable with creativity and somehow manage to portray beauty, grace and hope while taking the audience on a confronting journey many might otherwise shy away from. Scared though I was to go public with something so personal, if I could stand up, own my story and struggles, and deliver a message that inspired, I figured it was worth it.

As I reached for the mic, I noticed my hands were trembling. I hoped my nerves were only visible to me. I looked out into the audience again, locking eyes with my support group. My daughters sat proudly in the front row, next to my best friend of seventeen years. Deanne told me she would be unable to make it due to her rodeo commitments, which meant she would be located two hours southwest of Melbourne with a horse float. And it would be a little difficult to park a float in the city. However, she had driven back to Bendigo, dropped off the horses and jumped in her car to make the two-hour trip back to my event in Melbourne. I'd been quite composed until I saw her walk through the door. Next to Deanne was Dr Driscoll, the psychiatrist who helped me when I first came to Australia. Other friends were scattered in the audience as well.

I was unsure of how long I'd been standing there, but I'd scanned the room at least ten times, looking for familiar faces. Taking one final deep breath, I closed my eyes for a moment to centre myself, grabbed the mic and began to recite my spoken-word poem.

SOLD

I never knew what happened to me had a name
And I never knew existing words I could utter to describe to
*   another soul what had been done to mine*
I never dreamed that the insanity of humanity based on my
*   reality as a child could also be the reality for millions of*
*   others right now*
I also never dreamed I would one day take something so dark
Use it to ignite a spark
And shed light on a fight nobody wishes to know about
But we all know that evil thrives in darkness
Placing a line in the sand, taking your hand in my hand,
*   I'm asking you to journey with me*
I can drop one sentence with ten words
But will never adequately capture the horror of my childhood
I was nine years old when I was first sold
I can paint you a picture with a broken brush that bleeds
*   misery*
And yet place it on canvas and each stroke shines eternal and
*   inspires hope*
Speaking to the possibility of achieving that Happily Ever
*   After despite any beginning*
Through the depths of despair would you follow me there?
If I showed you my scars could you still see the stars
In my eyes beyond the tears that I cry sometimes?
Cos there are days when it just hurts to be me
And people aren't so good with pain. Cos people aren't so
*   good with helpless*
You recognise this early in life and master the masking of
*   your own private hell*
Protecting people from the depths of your pain so that they
*   can stay comfortably shallow*

*While you continue to drown in your imperfections and
    never tell*
I remember as a child wondering what it felt like to be alive
*If the burden weighing me down and making me believe I
    was worthless had a name …*
I'm guessing it's SHAME
*It is the paralysing equaliser placing predator and prey in the
    same common experience*
With the same feelings of helplessness and fear
It is the untold lie creating predestined tears
Blazing trails into the flesh of your cheeks like acid
But no matter the pain, conditioned to remain placid
Placing restrictions on dreams as it welcomes defeat
The world passing you by while you stare at your feet
And ponder the monetary value of a child's soul
SOLD. I was nine years old …

1

AS A CHILD, I would always count the stairs as I took them – a habit I have yet to break completely. There were twelve steps to the bottom of that basement, and I will remember that walk for as long as I live. No matter where I was when I was down there, anytime I glanced upon the last step, I saw angels watching me. Perhaps it was only a child's imagination, maybe it was something more. But that image became the miracle I needed to get me through some of the darkest years of my life. Whatever the explanation, there were always angels, and the love that flowed through their tears rained down upon me, guiding me through a measure of time when I otherwise may have fallen. If I had nothing else in life, I had this – and it carried me.

Growing up, my mother always told me that good things come to those who wait.

'Wait for what, Mom?' I would ask, gazing into her green eyes and watching the auburn in her hair dance in the summer sun.

She would glance down at me and shake her head, while we both watched a trail of sticky chocolate ice-cream steadily making tracks toward my elbow.

'Carrie, we all must wait for the right time to do what

needs to be done.'

I hadn't a clue what she meant by that, but I somehow understood that the meaning would become clear in time and I would have to wait until I acquired a certain level of maturity to view the situation from a far less innocent perspective.

I was born on a small island on Canada's eastern seaboard, but my life didn't really begin until September of 1996, one month before my twenty-first birthday, in front of the international departures gate. Yes, I'd been alive for two decades, but I couldn't help feeling I hadn't lived until then. Standing beside me at the airport were the three people who mattered most in my life: Tami, the woman who had taken me in off the streets as a fifteen-year-old runaway; my inconsolable younger sister, Jillian; and my mother. Despite having a very different relationship with all three, each face was a mirror image of worry. That past year had probably been my least stable, and I knew if I had to breathe the air of my Canadian city another minute, it might as well have been carbon monoxide. I tried my best to hide my joy and look as depressed as they did.

My sister Jillian was a heaving mess, and as I leaned over to give her a hug, I whispered into her ear that it would be okay and she would see me again. She only cried more.

The tears in Tami's eyes reminded me of everything we had been through together. I owed this woman my life. As detached as I was in that moment, leaving her behind proved to be most difficult for me.

'You look after yourself, my Carrie-kid.' Tami hugged me.

I felt so safe and protected being held by this woman; wrapped in her arms, everything else in my world became irrelevant. For a few seconds, I didn't think I could let her go.

'I love you, Tami.'

'I love you too, baby girl.'

Turning to Mom, I fought back tears and held my breath for the duration of our farewell.

'You call me as soon as you get there, okay, sweetie?'

'Yes, Mom, I promise.'

I had never seen my mother cry, but this time she came pretty close. A lifetime of pain swam in her eyes. Although I knew her current situation was the best it had ever been, I couldn't help drowning in guilt and sorrow as I remembered the hell I'd put her through during my teen years. Leaving her after all we'd been through together ripped at my soul. She had always put her children's needs before her own, going without so that Jillian and I would not have to. I hoped she knew I didn't blame her for what had happened to me.

'I love you, Mom,' I told her, folding myself into her arms.

'Promise me you'll remember to eat?'

'I promise.'

'And, Carrie,' she said, 'anytime you want to come home, you just let me know, okay?'

'I will, Mom.' I gave her one last hug.

The time had come to head through customs and leave the three most important people in my life. I bit my lip, trying hard to contain my excitement. Throwing my backpack over my shoulder, I turned and walked away from the only life I'd known, drawing strength from the knowledge that in doing so I was creating an opportunity to change a destiny that had once seemed carved in stone.

I glanced back at my mother; it was hard not to run back and try to save her from her own pain, but those impulses were the same childhood habits that had never really gotten me anywhere. Canada was no longer my home, nor, in the truest sense, had it ever been.

I may have been born in a free country but I was so accustomed to living in fear, never having experienced anything else, it felt like a prison to me. Australia offered a second chance to get it right. For nearly twenty-one years I had been denied what most people living in a democracy see as their birthright: freedom.

Before the doors closed completely, I took one last look at the life I was leaving behind. It was in that moment I realised what my mother had meant that day on the park bench all those years before. I had waited, and the time had finally come for me to do what was needed to change the path I once believed I had no choice but to walk.

A soothing calm worked its way to the depths of my soul during the flight. I had read about and watched others find peace in their lives, and as I gazed down at the blue vastness of the South Pacific, I closed my eyes for the first time in days, praying peace would come to me. Every mile covered helped to relax my tightly knotted muscles as the distance from Canada increased. I chose Australia for three reasons: it was warm; its people were relatively English-speaking; and, other than landing on the moon, I could hardly get any further away from Canada.

When the plane finally touched down, even though I had been sitting in the middle of the aircraft, I was one of the first people to disembark. Retrieving my backpack, I bypassed the crowds of people searching for their loved ones and wandered out into a city that neither embraced me nor turned its back. From that point, I was on my own.

Despite Sydney's distinctive tourist attractions, the most compelling feature of the city for me was not the famous Harbour Bridge nor the Sydney Opera House, but the sea of unfamiliar faces. I knew, without a doubt, that not one person there had any connection to my past. So, instead of looking over my shoulder, I held my head high. Fear was absent, and freedom could finally be mine. For the first time in my life I believed I was safe.

The sun began to set between the city skyscrapers, and the beautiful orange rays cast reflections upon the windows, creating a spectacular sight. I stood in the city centre, surrounded by buildings and strangers rushing past, and that magical moment was more than just a sunset for me. It symbolised a dramatic change in my life. When the sun disappeared beyond the horizon, it took with it the grip of my past. For a number of years, I hadn't the ability nor the inclination to imagine a future beyond the struggles inflicted upon me early in life. There were many times as a child that I couldn't see past the hell around me. I was immobilised by fear, and when I was a teenager the pattern repeated itself.

Standing there, it was as if I was awakening to life for the first time. To realise my life was filled with choices was mind-blowing. In that moment I became determined that I would never again be powerless. Camera in hand, I captured the glorious sunset that not only represented how far I had come but how quickly I had done so.

Returning the camera to my backpack, I found the old Polaroid I'd taken from my baby album before I had left. It was the only photo I'd brought along. As I had done so many times before, I stared closely at every square inch of that photograph. In it, I was six weeks old and propped up in a cheap plastic chair, positioned on some sort of work desk. Every time I looked at that photo, I focused on my expression. It was not so much the cuteness of a newborn baby that fascinated me, but my obsession with wondering what, if anything, was going through my mind that day.

In my own limited experience with babies, it seemed to me that all one really saw in their eyes was an enormous amount of innocence. But I was now convinced mine held something different. The eyes of that six-week-old child seemed to reflect a knowing only attained after years of experience. I wondered if it were possible that I had already been aware of, and prepared for, the direction my life would take.

I turned the photo over to read aloud the name I had once been called and the date written there in blue ink.

Jamie. December 8th, 1975.

It was one of two photographs taken by the nuns at the adoption agency. One shot had been given to the teenage girl who had given me up and the other to the woman I had recently left behind at the airport – and the only person I will ever call my mom.

I don't remember anyone ever sitting me down to tell me I was adopted, but it was something I'd always known. I think I was three years old when the word 'adoption' became a concept I could grasp – at least to the extent any three-year-old is able to comprehend the complexities of their existence.

Growing up, I knew very little about my birth mother. The only information I had been given was that she was seventeen years old when she became pregnant with me. How she looked, the smell of her hair and the warmth of her touch had been left up to my imagination.

As a child, I would sit for hours on the front steps of the adoption agency trying to remember that day. The building was on a hill overlooking a local park. It was the very last place my birth mother and I were together. I sat on that porch completely fixated, yet unable to recall a thing. I would just allow my mind to imagine. Sometimes I pictured a young woman rocking her small baby, trying to savour every last moment. Or I envisioned a young girl's devastation as she was torn from her precious child and left in a sobbing, inconsolable heap. Watching helplessly as the nun walked off with a part of her soul, she would let out a pained cry and vow that one day she would find her baby girl again.

Other times, my mind created a scene of indifference. After all, she was just a teenager and perhaps wanted nothing more than to ditch the burden of a baby and head off for a smoke and a movie with friends. Whatever the case, each time I went back to visit that place, I imagined it differently. And although the sequence of events changed a little each time, the ending remained the same.

My longing and yearning for my birth mother comforted me whenever I felt alone or wasn't sure of my place in the world. Despite everything, I always believed my original mother would one day come to rescue me. I'd sit patiently on the steps and study the features of people passing by, hoping to one day see my own face looking back at me. My reasoning was that maybe she, too, would be drawn to the last place she had held me. Maybe it was just a dream a child needed in a world in which hatred and brutality ruled, but it was a dream I clung to tightly.

It was spring when I arrived in Australia. I checked into the closest hostel I could find. After a quick shower, I rummaged through my backpack for a cooler outfit. As I pulled my singlet over my head, I smiled at the thought of my friends back home wearing their scarves and hats and cursing yet another miserable winter. Minus forty degrees is not conducive to comfortable living for anyone.

Stepping out of the hostel the next day, the morning sun hit me and it was bliss. My whole body warmed as I stood on the footpath, face to the sky. It was a beautiful day, and I decided to hike around the hills of Sydney and explore what the city had to offer. With a heavy pack and an empty stomach, I stopped first at a bakery. The sweet smells of coffee and croissants made my mouth water. Fumbling with the unfamiliar coins that I was still getting used to, I paid for breakfast and parked myself under a palm tree in the famous Hyde Park.

Sitting there in awe of the strange vegetation, I ran my hand over the grass and smiled at a lifetime of ignorant misconceptions. Weren't blades of grass the same all over the world? Sinking my hand into the moss-like sponge, I turned around to see peculiar-looking birds with hooked beaks and long flamingo legs edging closer to my breakfast. I took out my diary so that I could sketch my surroundings. My ability to draw fluctuated. At times I struggled like a small child with circles and basic shapes, while at other times my pictures were the work of a talented artist.

The first person to point out the inconsistency of my artistic talents was a social worker I was sent to see in junior high school. The series of events that led me to her had nearly caused me to come undone. Summer break was spent with my mom's relatives, and school had only been back a few days. My anxiety, depression and erratic moods were becoming too difficult to hide. How I managed to slip through the cracks for that long I will never know, but the beginning of grade eight became the end of my flying under the radar. Confrontation found me with my back against the wall. I was a pressure cooker containing years of secrets that was about to explode, had the steam not been safely released – if only a little.

I was changing for gym class on the morning my secret had nearly been revealed. My best friend, Kathryn, noticed bruising and scratch marks on my body, left behind by an assault I had endured over the weekend. She insisted on knowing what had caused them, asking again and again. I broke down and told her the only believable lie I could think of: a boy from a party I had attended had gone too far. There was a struggle, but I managed to get away. Thinking that would be the end of it, I began to relax. She freaked out and wanted to confront him – and also to get her older brothers to beat him up and teach him a lesson.

The room began to spin, and I thought I was going to be sick. In that moment I created the cover story I stuck to for more than a year. The gym teacher was told, as was the school guidance counsellor. The shame held in the truth enabled the lie. My fear of my father's retribution became my motivation. My lie became this: I was raped the week before school started while on holidays visiting relatives. No person on earth would believe the disgusting truth. That is, until I began my Tuesday sessions with Sheila.

We arrived early, twenty minutes before my counselling appointment, in my mother's bright yellow Toyota. Mom was anal when it came to punctuality. Above the door in big bold letters was a sign that screamed *CHILD AND ADOLESCENT SERVICES*. It was so large I was absolutely certain you could see it from space. There we sat – in a fluorescent yellow car – parked in front of the children's services centre that, as luck would have it, connected to the local mental hospital. Leaving the house that morning, I had wanted nothing more than to make myself invisible. Driving there in a car that glowed in the dark wasn't the best start in executing that plan.

'Are you nervous, sweetie?' Mom asked, as her hand landed hard on my knee, offering one of her loving taps that scared me to death.

'No,' I lied.

'Do you need me to come in with you?'

Neither one of us was looking at the other.

'No, thanks, I'm fine to go in by myself.' I thought it best to leave then before she landed me another one of those comforting taps. I opened the passenger door, scanned my surroundings to make certain no one I knew was in the vicinity, and made my way to the appointment I'd been both dreading and secretly looking forward to.

I went inside, glancing back through the door to see if Mom had left. She hadn't, so I waved goodbye. My wave went unnoticed as she was staring off into space, something she did rather frequently. And I was the one in therapy!

'Can I help you?' the receptionist asked.

Much to my dismay, I wasn't invisible after all. I wanted to run but I seemed to have lost sensation in both legs. The embarrassment and shame I felt, I can only attribute to being fourteen years old. Mostly I was just terrified of the unknown and feared judgement if I was to disclose my deepest secrets.

The receptionist waited for my name, but the words just wouldn't come. Fumbling, I managed to reach into my pocket and pull out a crumpled piece of paper with the social worker's name and appointment time on it. She took it and offered a sympathetic smile. I interpreted it as: I'll be seeing you regularly.

'You must be Carrie,' she said gently. 'Take a seat in the waiting room and I'll tell Sheila you're here.'

There were magazines on the table in front of me but, too nervous to read, I sat looking out the window, losing myself in the grey day. I was a terrible liar, but protecting the truth to preserve your life makes you capable of almost anything. Every footstep that echoed in the hallway knotted my stomach and made my palms sweat. Despite my inner turmoil, I tried my best to maintain a cool exterior until my name was called.

'Carrie?'

The woman in the doorway appeared to be in her early thirties – very pretty, with short, dark hair. So much for the old lady with warts and facial stubble I had been expecting.

'Hi, Carrie,' she said. 'I'm Sheila. It's nice to meet you.' She offered me her hand.

I reached out and quickly shook it. As I glanced up from the floor to her face and back down again, I saw her smile at me.

'Would you like to come with me? My room is just along the hallway.'

I visited Sheila regularly for just over a year. During the sessions, she would sometimes ask me about my childhood, in particular my relationship with my father. I would never say much, just that I hated him and that life would carry on just fine if ever he were crushed under something heavy. For whatever reason, she did not press me further, probably believing that, in time, all would be revealed.

I told her how my parents divorced when I was seven and how my mother had left him a few times before that. Sheila once asked me to tell her about one of those times. I thought for a minute and decided upon the most memorable for me: the time we moved to a basement flat just a few houses down from the place we were escaping.

That day had started out like any other, but on this occasion my father, the man who needed control over every detail in his world, would be the one uninformed.

Mom organised for the removalists to arrive not long after my father had gone to work that morning; he probably passed them on the street. I figured she would have them take only the bare minimum. After all, her decision to defy my father's threats was amazing enough in my eyes. But I stood there in disbelief as she ordered the men to remove everything that wasn't attached to a wall. I only wish I could have seen the look of shock on my father's face when he came home that night to find not only his family missing, but also his precious furniture as well.

As I stood in the middle of the commotion, I was drawn to the expression on my mother's face. At first I couldn't place what was different about her, then suddenly it hit me. This was the first time I had seen my mother truly living in the moment. For as long as I had known her, her eyes had had a certain look of detachment to them – as if she was disengaged from reality, living largely in her mind. And although I would never know where she went, I knew then that wherever it was beat the alternative.

With everything loaded onto the truck, my mom took my sister Jillian's hand, and we walked behind the vehicle to our new home. Even though I had hoped for somewhere slightly further away, the minute the three of us were in that basement apartment, it was as if we were a million miles from home. We were safe. It was only a matter of time before my father would track us down but until then we could all breathe that little bit easier.

The only windows in the basement were a small one above the kitchen sink and another in the lounge area, so it was quite dark. The lack of a view didn't bother me. I knew that if we were unable to see out, my father could not see in. I decided then that I would be willing to spend the rest of my life in the dark so long as he could not get to us.

I remember my mother singing Jillian and me a lullaby as she tucked us into bed on that first night in our new home. I loved her for trying to make things as normal for us as possible. Jillian was asleep before the song had even ended, but I stayed awake, staring into the darkness long after Mom left the room. I'm not sure whether the screams and violent banging woke me, but it didn't take me long to realise my father had found us.

'You better open this fucking door, bitch, or I'm gonna break it down.'

My mother came into our room, trying to mask the fear on her face. Getting the two of us out of bed, she didn't speak until she had us safely wedged in the back of a closet behind the hanging clothes.

'Okay, girls, I need you to listen to me. I want you to stay here and don't open the door until I come back to get you, do you understand?'

She kissed me on the forehead, told me that everything would be fine and closed the door, hiding us away. I begged her to be careful, but she had already left. As we sat there in the dark, I pulled Jillian close to me and sang the lullaby Mom had sung to us. The loud noises were growing more ferocious by the second. I was certain my father would get us. All I could do was hold my breath and hope for a miracle.

'Woman, I am going to kill you if you don't let me in,' he shouted, while beating furiously at the door.

They screamed at each other through the door for what seemed like forever. I kept wondering what the neighbours thought was going on. In my limited experience with the outside world, I had already noticed that when it came to domestic violence, you were well and truly on your own. Whenever my father lost his temper, nobody wanted to know us or take the time to help him find it.

'You better get the hell off my property before I call the police,' a voice boomed.

Finally the miracle I had been praying for arrived in the form of our landlord. Not exactly quite what I was wishing for, a little old man with arthritic bones, but we had no alternatives. Had he not come down to try to reason with the madman at our door, the owner would have had a trashed apartment and three bodies to deal with.

'Mind your own goddamn business, buddy,' my father screeched at him.

'I'm only going to warn you once more and then I will call the police.'

The next thing I remember hearing was my father's car tearing out of the driveway and speeding down the road toward his house. My mom must have been speaking to the owner because it was a few minutes before she remembered us stuffed away in that musty closet. She led us back to bed, calmly whispered goodnight and walked out, never attempting to offer an explanation. That would have entailed admitting that something out of the ordinary had just taken place, and by then I could see from her face that she was already a million miles away. I envied her for those holidays she would take in her head. More than anything, I wanted to purchase the same one-way flight to nowhere Mom kept cashing in, but no matter how quickly I packed my bags and whipped out my passport, she would already be gone. It took me some time to realise that travelling light was the key to a speedy exit. Once I'd worked this out, I too became a frequent flyer.

We lasted four months in the darkness of that tiny basement before my mother could no longer endure the living conditions. I don't recall the reunion between my mother and father, although I can only assume it did not go well because we hadn't been back in the family home a month before she filed a restraining order against him, this time forcing him out of the house.

We never again lived as a family of four. It was strange to me the way Mom acted. As if life was no different now that the man she had spent the last fourteen years with had departed. I remember the confusion I felt in the early days over my mother giving no outward indication of her joy to be rid of him and of the hell his presence had caused her. Maybe the years spent with him had utterly destroyed her already broken spirit. At least with him gone, she was no longer his prisoner. That soon became the role I took on – every other weekend.

2

AUSTRALIAN HOSTEL LIFE was beginning to lose its appeal after a week of sleeping with my belongings in the bed with me – the most important documents living under my pillow. I was sharing a room with three British girls. One in particular appeared ignorant about the possibility of a cockroach infestation when food and garbage were left in the room. While she crunched away at her apple, I stayed silent on the top bunk across from her, my anger and resentment building. My decision to move out was made the moment she chucked her apple core across the room in the direction of the bin, which she of course missed, but she remained in bed and apparently drifted off to sleep. Sighing audibly, I crawled from my bunk, picked up her core and placed the whole bin outside the room.

I woke abruptly the next morning, a dream still fresh in my mind. In it, I had died before the opportunity to escape my subconscious had presented itself. I had always heard that you were supposed to wake up before you died in a dream. Not me. I averaged at least one dreamed death a week. It surely wasn't good for the heart.

Hauling myself out of bed, I walked over to the window where the sun's distorted rays spilled through a pane covered in years of grime. The others were still sleeping, and the sloppy one was snoring loudly. I ignored the urge to get the apple core from the bin and shove it in her open mouth. Quickly packing all of my things, I made a mad rush to the door and down the stairs to check out of the run-down hostel. Surely I could find a place to stay that felt more backpacker accommodation and less brothel.

Before leaving Canada, I had worked at a private guesthouse in the mountains. I'd made sure I'd earned enough money to get me through the first three months in Australia. I had been granted a working-holiday visa, which permitted me a year in the country with permission to work but only for twelve weeks at any given company. I had been in Sydney just twelve days and life appeared to be growing more expensive by the minute. I would walk around the supermarkets in a state of shock over the prices. Take fruit, for instance. In Canada, you couldn't grow bananas if your life depended on it. In Australia they grew them, but if I wanted to eat one it would cost twice the price of the ones Canada imported from Mexico, or wherever.

With cheaper fruit motivating my migration, I figured the further north I went the cheaper life would be, and Queensland became my next destination. That evening I hopped on a bus and drifted in and out of consciousness during a bumpy ten-hour drive.

Arriving at the Brisbane bus terminal, I noticed a plague of backpackers congregating outside. I threw my own pack over my shoulder and followed the crowd, ending up at a hostel that provided a free shuttle from the terminal. After settling in to my room, I grabbed my journal and ran downstairs to search for a reasonably quiet spot among the noisy, self-assured backpackers. I felt out of place and totally unsure of myself. Eavesdropping on some of the conversations, I decided I was definitely the greenest member of this select group of travellers. Smiling at my new insecurities, I returned to my writing.

It was then that a woman came through the hostel kitchen like a whirlwind. Her voice was loud, her confidence astounding, and I sat in awe as small knots of people parted ways to allow her space while she put her groceries away.

'Anybody who drinks this,' the woman said, holding up a bottle of Diet Coke, 'I will torture slowly and eventually kill.'

She smiled and began joking around with a few of the guys. I remained in the corner of the room observing this amazonian blonde whose accent bore a striking similarity to mine. With my own confidence building, and the space she had created presenting an opportunity, I surprised myself and approached her.

'Hey, I'm Carrie.'

'Yeah, hey. The name's Paula.' She stuck out her hand. 'You Canadian?'

I nodded, hoping it was the right answer. 'How long you been travelling here?'

'Six months,' she said.

She laughed when I told her I was one day shy of reaching the two-week milestone. She dug one of her Diet Cokes out of the refrigerator and guided me back to where I had been sitting. Pulling a seat up next to mine, she went on to tell me she had recently completed the bar exam in Toronto and intended to practise law at a few firms in Australia before settling into her career.

From the beginning, it was obvious that Paula and I were very different people. A big girl, Paula had a confidence about her that matched her size. I concluded quickly that spending time with her, as outspoken and in control as she was, would help me come out of my little shell – either that, or she'd tire of my company and eat me.

During our third day together, we decided to hire two of the hostel's mountain bikes and set out to see the city. After a couple of hours on an uncomfortable seat, my butt was ready for a rest. We stopped at a park bench overlooking the river. I learned that Paula was adopted as well, and we entered into a discussion about tracking down one's natural family.

'The mom who raised me is the only mom I have, in my opinion,' she said, disagreeing with my view.

Lawyer that she was, her opinion appeared to be the only one that mattered. Feeling as though I was under attack for having my own beliefs, I felt the need to justify myself.

'Hey, that's cool you feel that way, and I'm sure that must make your adopted family really happy. But for my own reasons, I have always wanted to find my mother,' I said.

'Your birth mother,' she corrected. 'So, did you ever end up finding her?'

I looked her straight in the eye and said, 'Yeah, actually, I did find her.'

This was the first time I'd seen my opinionated new friend at a loss for words. It didn't last long.

'So, was meeting her all you dreamed and more?' The sarcasm dripped from each of her words.

Staring out across the river running through Brisbane, I allowed myself to revisit the memories of the past.

'Listen, for a lot of reasons, I felt the need to meet my natural mother. We're not all blessed with a perfect little Brady Bunch home. Maybe you were, and good for you. But don't give me a hard time for following my heart and doing what I had to do.'

Swept up in the passion of my defence, I hadn't noticed the tears tracking steadily down my cheeks. But Paula had.

'Carrie, I'm sorry. I know I can be a real asshole at times. I guess I was just thinking of my mom and how much it would hurt her if I set out to find my birth mother.'

Wiping my face with the back of my hand, I continued to stare at the sun's rays dancing on the water. Paula followed my gaze. We sat there beside each other as I recounted the reunion I'd had with my birth family.

It was actually my adoptive mom who found my birth mother. She gave me the news one afternoon when I got home from school. The timing couldn't have been more bizarre. That same morning, before classes started, I had rung the adoption agency to begin the search myself. I was informed that I could only send in the paperwork after my eighteenth birthday, which was only one month away. I spent the day in a cloud of guilt: I was excited about the prospect, but protective of my adoptive mother's feelings. When I got home from school, Mom was there to greet me. I thought for sure she had found out what I'd been up to earlier that day. She merely smiled and asked me to come into her room as she had something to tell me.

'I found your mother.'

'I'm sorry, what?'

'Your mother,' she repeated. 'I found her for you.'

When Mom signed the adoption agency papers all those years ago, she had seen a document that she wasn't supposed to. It contained minimal information about my birth parents. All she could now remember was that my birth mother's last name was Weston.

For whatever reason, my mother always started from the bottom of lists and worked her way up. She did the same on the morning she went through the phone book, calling every Weston listed. She began each call by politely introducing herself and saying she was looking for her adopted daughter's natural mother. I listened as she relayed the conversation she eventually had with my grandmother.

'I asked her if she had a daughter who was about thirty-four years old. She said that she did, and so I asked if that daughter would have given birth to a baby girl nearly eighteen years ago. She said, yes, on October 25th, 1975, and that the baby's name was Jamie. And then I said, well, her name is Carrie now.'

I could only stare and hope that my jaw would recover from the quick drop. Moments later I learned that I had two full-blood siblings: a brother and a sister. My parents had stayed together after giving me up and kept their two other children.

'Your grandmother is going to phone her daughter Patricia, and I told them that you would call back at six o'clock.'

Patricia. My mother's name was Patricia. I had always wondered. The enormity of what Mom had done for me finally started to sink in. In less than two hours, I would be speaking to the woman I saw most nights in my dreams.

It took an eternity for six o'clock to roll around. I sat for an hour beside the phone that evening and counted the minutes until I could hear her voice. Lost in thought as I dreamed of how the conversation might go, I didn't notice my mother speaking to me.

'Carrie, it's six o'clock. You can call them now.'

I picked up the phone and slowly began to dial the number I had already committed to memory.

A lifetime of questions raced through my mind as the phone began to ring. Had she thought of me as often as I had her? Would her voice sound exactly as I had imagined it? Did I look like her? Could she love me as her own after all these years?

'Hello?' said the voice on the end of the line.

'Hello. Could I speak with Patricia, please?'

'This is she.'

I had waited my whole life for this moment and I was overwhelmed when it actually arrived. We remained silent for what seemed an eternity. Then Patricia spoke.

'So they called you Carrie. That's a nice name.'

I could sense the sadness in her voice. For eighteen years, I had been Jamie to her. I knew calling me by any other name would take some getting used to.

'Yep, that's what they called me. But I always knew you named me Jamie. I actually have a photo of me with that name on the back of it.'

I could hear her crying softly.

'Please don't cry,' I whispered into the phone. 'It's okay. We've got the rest of our lives to get to know each other.'

'I know, baby.'

My heart melted when she said that. She went on to describe my siblings. I had a brother named Travis who was six years younger than me. April, my sister, was born eleven months after me. It didn't take long to do the math and work out that Patricia had become pregnant just two months after giving me up. And although this came as a shock, I still said nothing.

'So tell me, what do you look like? Your hair colour, your eyes, weight and height? I want to know everything.'

'Well, my eyes are hazel and my hair is brown. I'm 5'4" and I weigh about a hundred pounds.'

'God, you're tiny. I thought that you would be much bigger than that. You were quite long when you were born,

28

you know. Is your skin still olive?'

'I guess so. I'm darker than everyone in my family.' Instantly regretting the 'family' bit, I wanted to undo the unintended hurt with an apology but I didn't really know what to say. Instead, the line grew quiet, and I could only wait until she spoke again.

'Carrie, I'm just so sorry. You have to believe me when I tell you that I never wanted to give you up.'

Not wanting to cause her any more pain but needing to know the answer, I eventually asked, 'Well, then, why did you?'

The line grew quiet again and I closed my eyes, waiting for her answer.

'I was only seventeen when I got pregnant with you and things were really difficult for me at home. Life with your father was no picnic either.'

'But you had another baby with the same man shortly after you gave me up.'

'Yeah, I did, but Steve and I had decided to get married by the time I got pregnant with your sister, and that got me away from home.'

I didn't mean to hurt her, but I just couldn't understand why she would get pregnant so soon after giving me up and then decide to keep that baby. Couldn't they have decided to go with the brilliant marriage plan two months earlier?

'You need to know that times were really tough when your father and I were together. He was drunk all the time and into drugs. He would get really violent sometimes and beat me.'

The image of my real dad was shattered before I'd even got the chance to meet him.

'You know, Carrie, in some ways you're probably lucky that you weren't living with us. April and Travis have been through a lot.'

29

My blood was beginning to boil beneath the surface of my skin. Had she just described my life as 'lucky'? Unable to trust what would come out of my mouth next, I settled on, 'Did he hurt your kids?'

'No. But they witnessed it when he used to take things out on me.'

'That must have been hard for them.' I had to fight to control my emotions as I thought about what I'd endured during my childhood.

'Well, enough about me. Tell me about your life. How has it been?' Patricia said.

Suddenly it was my turn to cause the awkward silence. 'It's been fine,' I lied.

For so many years, I had carried in my mind a picture of the perfect family, and it had sustained me when all I wanted to do was give up. In this one phone call, that picture had been destroyed. I could think of nothing more to say.

'When can I meet you?' she asked. 'I need to see you so badly.'

'Oh gosh, I dunno. We are so far apart and I don't have the money to buy a plane ticket.'

'Oh, sweetie, don't worry about that. You leave that up to me. Do you think your mom would let you come stay with us if I can get the funds together for the ticket?'

'She would have to.'

'Well, then, why don't you work on your mom letting you come down to see me and you just leave the rest up to me?'

Three weeks later, I was on a plane back to my home town, the one Mom, Jillian and I had escaped from three years earlier. I was on the way to meet my birth mother. During the trip I tried, with little success, to block out any thoughts of the potential dangers awaiting me there. Nearly four years had passed since I last saw my father. The town was small, but I figured if I stayed mostly at Patricia's house and steered clear of places he was likely to be, I would be safe. Terrified though I was, the yearning to be with my birth mother countered my fear of returning.

My home-town airport was far from international standards, and as my little 'Buddy Holly' plane touched down on the island, I tried to calm my tattered nerves, pinching my arm to remind myself I wasn't dreaming.

Carrying my bag, I began the short walk across the tarmac in the relentless rain, which revived memories of a dreary childhood. As I stepped through the terminal doors, I scanned the waiting crowd and immediately locked eyes with a woman who looked a lot like me. Beside her was a girl about my age and a younger boy in a baseball cap. I realised that they were all staring back at me. Quickening my pace, I moved closer as my body shook uncontrollably.

I gasped as I looked into the woman's eyes and saw my own looking back. I stood in front of her, unable to move. I had never experienced anything like it before in my life. The resemblance was uncanny.

'Look at you,' she said. Tears were streaming down her face. 'You're beautiful.'

'I can't believe how much she looks like you, Mom.' My sister's voice was a distant echo. I couldn't take my eyes off my mother.

Opening her arms to me, she said, 'Can I hold you?'

My body was frozen. My mind was screaming yes and trying its best to get my head to nod its approval. When feeling returned to my body, I dropped my bag and fell into her arms. I had been waiting eighteen long years for that embrace.

When I looked over at the rest of my family there was a second surprise in store. I already knew my sister! Because we were so close in age, April and I had started school at the same time, and although we had lived on opposite sides of the town, there were few schools there. For years, I had stayed with my mom and little sister in a trailer park during the week. But every second weekend was spent at my father's in the same neighbourhood that April grew up in. Her best friend lived across the street from my father. We had often seen each other and I had envied her blonde hair, blue eyes and place in the desirable crowd.

April and I squealed as teenage girls do and hugged each other in excitement. As we walked to the car, we reminisced about the encounters we'd had all those years before and were blown away that we were full sisters, as we looked nothing alike.

The drive back to their house was incredibly familiar, and I struggled for breath as we passed the park directly in front of my father's house. I sat frozen, trying to combat my nerves and the butterflies in my stomach. I thought I might be sick.

Suddenly the adoption agency came into view up on the hillside. As I stared out the passenger window at the blue building, I could sense Patricia looking at me. I turned away, hoping she wouldn't notice the old emotions that were overwhelming me.

'You know, on every single one of your birthdays, I used to take a cupcake to the steps of the adoption agency and light a candle in your honour.'

Of course! It had never occurred to me to show up on the day of my birth.

The car came to a stop outside a dilapidated, white house – two streets behind the agency steps I used to wait upon.

I couldn't believe that my mother had lived just two streets away from the very place where I had daydreamed about her so often.

During my stay at Patricia's, my fear and paranoia grew with each passing day. I saw my father in every grey-haired man that I encountered, and my blood would run cold. I became that scared little girl in the basement once again.

As hard as I tried to suppress it, my anxiety was becoming more evident, and Patricia began commenting on the changes in my mood and conduct. Sometimes I knew what she was referring to, at other times, as often happened to me when asked about my odd behaviour, I had no memory of it. I would simply apologise to her and hope that my horrified expression and the tears burning in my eyes would be mistaken for remorse at causing any upset or embarrassment.

My flashbacks and nightmares had begun at some point in my early teens. Their intensity and severity was overwhelming. I had no idea what was happening to me, and for a long time I told no one. I'd never heard of anyone else having this happen to them and I felt like enough of a freak as it was. I was certain I'd be locked up if anyone knew the truth.

Even with everything I was trying to keep hidden, Patricia seemed to be growing more depressed by the day. There were times when she would slip up and call me Jamie; I would assure her that it was okay, but she would burst into tears and run to her bedroom. Then one day, out of the blue, she told me I was to call her 'Mom'. I told her that I felt uncomfortable saying that and asked if there was some other term we could use that we would both be happy with. She just stared at me blankly and replied, 'Well, then, don't call me anything at all.'

So whenever I had something to share or discuss, I would just sit and wait until she looked at me. Much of the time, I said nothing at all.

'Shit,' Paula said after I finished my little stroll down memory lane. 'I knew I didn't want to meet mine for a reason.'

I continued to stare out over the river.

'So how'd it end?'

'You don't wanna know.'

We got back to the hostel just before nightfall. There was a message for me to ring another backpacker hostel in the city. Worried that my finances would dry up, I had decided the day before to get my résumé out there. I wasn't expecting to hear back so fast.

I rang the number and before I knew it, I was packing my bags to head off to Brisbane's largest hostel – free accommodation plus ten bucks an hour.

Paula walked into the room as I was throwing the last of my life into my backpack.

'What's happening?' she asked.

'Movin' on, baby. I landed me a job in the city at another hostel.'

'Cool,' she said. 'Hope everything works out for you.'

'Thanks.' I swore under my breath at the uncooperative zipper on my bag. 'How many more days before you head to Melbourne, Paula?'

'Five.'

'Well, hopefully we can catch up before you go.'

'I'd like that.'

I arrived at the new hostel and was greeted by a tall, thin man. He appeared to be in his mid-forties and not at all happy with his career choice. He was British and had a gruff demeanour. As he explained what my role would be, I wasn't altogether sure I could keep from laughing.

I was apparently 'laundry girl' by day, and 'entertainment manager' by night. The latter was my formal title, and I still don't know how my new boss was able to tell me this with a straight face. Did I mention he was British? He didn't run an obscene operation, as my title implied; I was simply expected to hop on a bus with other backpackers and organise drinking games and other mundane activities that were only entertaining to drunk people.

'Do I get a company car and business cards with this role?' I joked.

I don't think he appreciated my humour. I thought it best to shut up in case I got fired before my first shift had even begun.

Five long days passed. Paula and I maintained contact, and I was growing quite fond of her abrupt and cranky manner. She certainly had a big mouth, but everything that came out of it was honest. I was discovering that to be a rare trait in people.

On the day Paula was scheduled to leave, I had been working in the laundry since seven o'clock that morning. It was a hotter-than-hell environment that helped me partially relate to anyone working in a sweatshop.

'Carrie,' I heard one of my fellow 'entertainment managers' call out. 'Telephone.'

I put down one of the three million towels I had folded that day – tearing myself away from such stimulating work was difficult. I picked up the receiver, and there was Paula on the other end of the line.

'Hey, girl. What's happening?' I asked.

'I'm leaving for Melbourne tonight, and I was wondering

if you wanted to make your way to the bus terminal later to see me off.'

'Well, if I can get away from this soul-sucking job, I'll definitely be there.'

Sneaking past my grumpy boss, I headed out into the rainy Brisbane weather. To borrow a term from my mom, it was 'coming down in absolute buckets'. I thought the east coast of Canada saw its fair share of rain, but that storm was like nothing I had ever seen before.

I arrived at the terminal looking like a drowned rat with my crazy curls plastered to my head and dripping water down my back. Paula laughed when she spotted me. Catching a glimpse of my reflection in the window, I forgave her. I looked like a scrawny cat that had been dunked in a tub.

'You better appreciate this farewell, girlfriend,' I said. 'On my way back, I just might enter myself in that wet t-shirt competition I walked past to get here.' Looking down at the fabric clinging to my chest, I grabbed my shirt and pulled it away from my body. It made the funniest sucking noise. We both laughed.

'How's the job going?'

'You mean the managerial position? I can't think of anything that would be worse than that place, except maybe the wet t-shirt thing.'

'Why don't you come down to Melbourne with me? I've got to stop off in Sydney for two days but I'm staying with friends. I'm sure they wouldn't mind if you crashed there too.'

'Me?' I showed my surprise.

'Why not? It's not like you're having the time of your life here, are you?'

Well, no, I most certainly was not, but I'd had no intention of visiting Melbourne. I wasn't sure if it was a trip I wanted to make but I figured it would be nice travelling with someone

I knew. And I did have an entire year to spare so six weeks out of my journey was hardly too much to ask. Given my easygoing nature and 'fly-by-the-seat-of-my-pants' lifestyle, a last-minute change of plans was not out of the question.

'How much time have I got to quit and throw my life back into that damn bag?'

With a smirk and a glance at her watch, she said, 'How fast can you run?'

The bus was due to leave in thirty minutes, so with the decision made, we rushed back to the hostel in the rain. Paula followed me up to my room, we grabbed my things and flew downstairs again.

Dashing across the lobby, I ran into my boss on the way out. 'I quit,' I yelled over my shoulder as I dodged past him. 'Gotta go, bye!'

Perhaps I wouldn't have been so rude if I wasn't in such a hurry and he wasn't such a pompous moron.

Racing back through the rain, our raucous laughter filled the late-evening air. Once we were sitting inside the dry bus, I lost myself in the rain outside my window; the same way I had done as a child who had seen one too many miserable days. I began to dream of the incredible adventures awaiting me. With so much to learn in this new, unrestricted world, the sky really was the limit and possibilities laced my imagination. As I looked back on my achievements in those first few weeks, I experienced a range of emotions. The most significant and foreign of them all began to expand like a balloon inside of my chest. I almost found it difficult to catch my breath. At first I couldn't place such a strange emotion, and then it hit me: pride.

3

OUR BUS TRAVELLED through the night. After several stops we arrived in a sweltering Sydney, shortly before noon. Outside the terminal the combination of fumes and humidity blanketed the air like molasses. It was actually hard to breathe. Looking at the bus's massive black tyres baking in the midday sun, I was amazed they hadn't melted in this makeshift baker's oven.

We caught another two trains and eventually arrived at Paula's friends' house. After setting our bags down and getting the introductions out of the way, we were told that a few other Australian friends would be coming over that night for dinner. I was excited about the opportunity to finally just sit down and chill with some real live Aussies. At that point I hadn't run into many on the backpacking circuit. Mostly just Brits and Kiwis. I understood why the British wanted to escape their horrendous weather, but I'd met that many New Zealanders who were permanently based in Australia, I was beginning to wonder what was wrong with their country.

Paula and I volunteered to go to the supermarket to get dessert. When dinnertime arrived, more of Paula's friends began piling through the door. I was quiet for most of the evening and spent my time observing people's interactions and listening to the jovial accents. One of the men was a chef on a navy ship scheduled to sail around Sydney Harbour in the morning. He invited both Paula and me to come along.

In the short time I had known her, I'd not seen Paula so excited about anything. I only wished I could say the same for myself. Spending a day surrounded by chauvinistic sailors hadn't even made it onto the bottom of my 'bucket list'.

In the morning, Paula woke me. It was quite refreshing to see her in such a chirpy mood.

'Will you be ready in the next half hour?' she asked me.

'Oh, I wasn't really planning on coming.'

'Really?' She sounded surprised. 'This is like the chance of a lifetime. I can't believe you don't want to do it. Come on, Carrie, it'll be fun.'

Not wanting to spoil things for her, I decided it wouldn't kill me to go. Paula waited impatiently for me while I quickly showered and scraped my unruly curls into a ponytail.

We arrived at the boat just as they were getting people on board.

'Perfect timing,' I said, and leaned over to pinch Paula for the panic she had been in thinking we'd be late.

She smiled. 'Yeah, you're brilliant. Now shut up.'

The cruise around the harbour was actually quite good. I even challenged myself by climbing to the top of the mast. The waves were choppy, but somehow it didn't seem to bother me. Paula, on the other hand, spent most of the time acquainting herself with the toilet bowl.

When the cruise ended, everyone hung out below deck. Paula was drinking beer with the navy boys. My nose couldn't tell the difference between beer and the inside of a urinal so I stuck with juice. A few of the crew decided to take Paula and me to a pub across the road. Feeling a little apprehensive, I somehow managed to maintain false optimism and look at the situation for what it was: an event I would thankfully never have to experience again.

It was close to four o'clock by the time we left the boat and went to the pub across from the dock. As the night wore on, I noticed for the first time the blatantly obvious: I was the only one still sober. James, one of the sailors from the ship, spent a good deal of time speaking to both Paula and me about Melbourne. He told us he was born there and had lived in that city for most of his life. He named a few places worth visiting and the best areas to stay. Grateful for his tips, I began to relax and even accepted a couple of drinks bought for me by one of the boys. I needed to do something to make the night go faster.

Shortly before it was time to go, I realised that I'd left my bag on the ship and told Paula that I was going back to get it. James said he would walk me down to the ship and that Paula could meet us at the coffee stand opposite where the ship was docked after she finished her drink.

Not entirely comfortable with heading back to the boat with a man I'd only just met, I wanted to speak up but instead just looked meaningfully at Paula. She, as it turned out, was far too busy singing 'Waltzing Matilda'.

I ended up leaving the pub alone with James, despite everything inside me screaming not to. I pretended to be interested as he filled the silence between us with what he obviously considered fascinating facts about sailing.

As soon as we were on the ship, I realised that he was incredibly drunk, and an immense terror crept over me. Immobilised by my fear, I was unable to move when he came up behind me, slipped his arms around my waist, turned me to face him and whispered in my ear.

'You're thousands of miles away from home. Doesn't it feel good to have somebody holding you?'

Actually, no, I thought, it doesn't. I began to feel ill. Just as I told myself it could be worse – at least he wasn't kissing me – he made some dumb comment about how beautiful my eyes were and planted one on my lips.

Oh, Paula, I prayed. *Please hurry up and get to the coffee stand.*

'Where's your bag?' he asked.

I felt totally trapped in the situation. 'It's below deck.'

'Well, come on then. It will be much warmer down below.'

'I am only getting my bag,' I warned him. 'I am not interested in doing anything with you, okay?'

Grabbing my hand, he didn't seem to hear a word I had said. All I wanted was my bag and to get the hell out and return to the pub to see Paula.

Getting the hell out was a lot more difficult than I had imagined. Below deck, I was immersed in darkness. I couldn't see my hand in front of me, let alone that damn bag.

'You know what?' I finally said in an absolute panic. 'Forget the bag, James, I just wanna go back to meet Paula.'

By this point, I had been dragged through the dark in so many directions I couldn't even guess the way out. I searched desperately, straining my eyes every which way, to find my bag. When a porthole window came into view, allowing just enough light through for me to see shapes, my terror ebbed momentarily. Keeping a tight grasp on my arm, James continued to drag me further in.

'Look,' I said, unable to hide my fear. 'I only want to get my bag and leave. I want to go now.'

He still was not responding. Oh God, I thought. What have I got myself into?

When we finally stopped moving, I felt something press against the small of my back. I was unable to go further. At first I didn't know what it was. Placing my hand behind to see if I could make sense of my surroundings, I let out a gasp when I felt the pillow. Shit, this was his bed.

'I want to leave right now.' My voice was the strongest it had been all evening, and despite the tears running down my cheeks, there was no way I wasn't putting up a fight.

Pushing me down onto the mattress, he ripped at my underwear. Of all the days to wear a fucking skirt, I thought angrily.

'Please stop. I don't want to do this.'

For the first time in my life, if only fleetingly, my body didn't seize up. I pushed hard on his pelvis and locked my elbows, trying to make myself as strong as I possibly could. I only weighed half of what he did yet still couldn't believe the rush of power coursing through me. As if from nowhere, my strength seemed to have tripled.

I was going to be fine. There's no way this fucker was going to hurt me like that.

'Get off me!' I screamed. 'I don't want to do this.'

He snapped my wrist back and lowered his lips to my ear. 'You know you want this,' he hissed. 'You wanted to get fucked all night.'

My strength vanished as he forced himself into me. Like so many times before, I froze with terror. My only movements after that were the tears rushing down my cheeks and spilling onto his pillow. From that point on, I remembered nothing else of the act.

'God, I'm sorry.' He pulled his pants back on. 'I was so turned on I couldn't help myself.'

I looked at him, stunned by the words coming out of his mouth.

'I need my bag,' I whispered. 'I want to go home.'

Making our way through the ship back into the dining area where they had been drinking earlier, James spotted my bag and handed it to me. My vision had adjusted to the darkness by then. Grabbing my bag, I turned and ran through the ship. I found the ladder to leave by.

Crying uncontrollably, I passed the coffee stand where Paula was supposed to have met me. Looking over my shoulder to make sure James wasn't following, I fought for air and tried to calm myself.

Finally making it to the pub, I found Paula in the same place I had left her.

'Oh my God, Carrie. What happened to you?'

'Can we just get out of here, Paula?' I cried. 'I just want to get out of here.'

Paula saw James through the pub window and shoved her way outside, screaming at the top of her lungs. 'What the fuck did you do to her? You fucking bastard. What did you do?'

If the evening hadn't been bizarre enough, she proceeded to physically assault the man who only minutes before had raped me.

I remained on the kerb, rocking back and forth.

'Where the fuck are you going?' I heard her scream. 'You stay the fuck away from her.'

In a panic, I jumped up as he raced toward me.

'Get the hell away from me,' I managed to say. I felt my mind start to slip away. In a matter of seconds, I knew I would no longer be present. I didn't know how and I didn't know why, but anytime I was confronted with more stress than I could handle, I became the woman my mother used to be, taking 'time out' in some faraway place.

The events of the evening had overwhelmed me. I heard

myself scream for Paula, who was with a few of the navy guys who had pulled her off James. Shaking violently, I felt a deep pain in my bones. I noticed myself drifting in and out and knew I would continue to do so until I felt safe.

Walking back to the station, Paula kept hitting me.

'Would you stop wrapping your arms so tightly around yourself and get a grip on the situation,' I heard her say. 'You're okay now. Just calm the fuck down.'

Everything was occurring in such slow motion that I thought I must have been dreaming. I was not trying to draw attention to myself; in fact, quite the opposite. All I wanted to do was somehow disappear. This would be my last recollection of the trip back to Paula's friends' place. I don't remember the train ride, nor the walk that ultimately took me to the house and, once there, into the shower.

After showering, I sat down on the mattress in the dining room and curled myself into a ball with my sleeping bag tucked firmly under my chin. I stared into the darkness and began to cry soundlessly as the full magnitude of what had happened dawned on me. In that moment more than any other, I wished that I was fifteen again and being rescued for the first time in my life.

Alone, in the silence of night, my mind took me back to my childhood after we had finally fled the east coast and the chain of events that led to me being taken in by Tami.

During my sessions with Sheila, I filled the hour talking about everything except my horrible secret. Looking back, I suspect Sheila actually knew what I was hiding from her. During one of our sessions she pulled out a sheet of paper that was divided down the middle. On the left-hand side, in bold black lettering was *VICTIMS OF RAPE*. On the right, *VICTIMS OF INCEST*. Listed underneath each heading was the aftermath experienced by the victim of such abuse. Scanning the lists with no ability to keep my eyes jumping from one side to the other, I was unable to take in the content. My heart was pounding hard and familiar fears began resurfacing. Before panic gripped me entirely, I excused myself from the session and started to run. Sheila followed me down the hall to the washrooms. Sitting on the floor beside me, she held my hair and rubbed my back. The realisation that I fit under both columns sickened me. That there was a term for what I was enduring and that it wasn't uniquely my experience. Every new thought I had made me violently ill and the one recurring thought causing the greatest disturbance was this: the same man was responsible for placing me in both categories. It was then that I broke down and told Sheila the truth.

'It was the first time in years that he had hurt me like that,' I began. 'School was starting soon, I was just back from holidays and had to stay with him for the weekend.'

As I got older, my father rarely hurt me in the way he used to when I was little. I remember one particular weekend visit when I was excited about going to his place because I had been invited to a party at a neighbour's. It was a cool autumn day and for the first time, perhaps ever, at my father's house, I felt normal and that I was engaged in an activity that others my age were probably doing as well: getting ready to go out and have a good time like any other regular fourteen-year-old girl.

For some reason, my father's houses never had locks on

the bathroom doors, which was rare in Canada. I always chose my times to shower carefully and did so as quickly as possible. That day, my father was in the kitchen drinking and preparing dinner, and I decided to risk a shower. Having finished, I wrapped a towel around my body and stuck my head out the bathroom door to listen for movement.

When I felt safe, I made my way to my bedroom, closing the door quietly behind me. In my excitement and eagerness to go out, I made the mistake of staying in my towel while I dried my hair. Unfortunately for me it was the early 1990s and big hairstyles were the fashion. I plugged in my curling iron and dried off my hair. With the dryer going, I didn't hear my father come into the room.

He was enraged, drunk and yelling disgusting names at me, all the while accusing me of terrible things he expected I would be doing with boys at the party. I clung to my towel and stared broken-heartedly at my clothes laid out on the bed.

'Please don't do this,' I said.

'*Please don't do this*,' he mimicked in a high-pitched, whiny voice. 'Girl, I am doing nothing to you that hasn't been done a million times before.'

He threw me onto the bed, pulled the curling iron out of the wall, and as with all the times before, I was powerless to stop him. He derived so much pleasure from my fear. I felt the heat of the iron as he brought it close to my face. My body trembled as I stared up at the ceiling. Before my body even experienced the impact, my mind had already begun its journey to that faraway place. The blackouts were my only means of protection, and nothing could take that away from me. It was the only control I had.

He held the iron against the underside of my left breast. The pain jolted me back for a second. But after burning

46

me and before doing what he did next, in my mind, I was
already gone.

'I still made it to the party that night, Sheila,' I said, smiling
through my tears. 'Nothing was going to keep me from that.
Not even him.'

'Carrie, does your mother know?'

'No one does,' I said. 'And no one ever can. He will kill
me if he finds out I told.'

When you have never been taught something is wrong
but you just know it is, that's one thing. But something
happened to me the day I discovered there was a name for
what my father was doing to me and how very wrong it was.
I stopped going to visit him after that and started sharing my
darkest secrets one year into therapy. Sheila gently pushed
me to talk about things, but at the same time mentioned she
was six months pregnant and finishing up in several weeks.
It hadn't occurred to me that she could be pregnant. I know
I struggled to look at her in therapy, but I must have been in
bad shape to not notice her expanding belly heading into her
final trimester of pregnancy. She also began encouraging me
to tell my mother and mentioned that, by law, she needed
to report what I had shared with her. I freaked out so badly
that she promised she would give me time to adjust to her
having to tell my mom and the police. I can't actually recall
how or when, but during this time I did experience my first
emotional breakdown, chased down with a side order of my
mother's anxiety pills.

I spent several days locked up in a psychiatric ward with
very disturbed adults before being released into my mother's
care. On reflection, I believe my time in that hospital only

added to my already traumatised state. Once released, I was kept sedated at home in my bedroom for some time. My mother would sit at the foot of my bed for hours on end. She looked so helpless and terrified.

'Carrie, what can I do to help you?' she whispered.

I stared at her blankly, as I didn't have a clue myself. After disclosing some of the abuse to Sheila, a fear had begun to resonate and burn in the core of my being. Voices were screaming in my head, warning of a very real danger. I had no idea what was happening to me, but the answer I hadn't been able to give my mother before, became suddenly clear.

I sat up and replied, 'I know what you can do to help me.'

'Anything, sweetie. You name it.'

And I did.

'We need to move.'

She sold everything we had, which wasn't much, and within a month we left all we'd ever known and moved across the country to live with my mother's sister. I was fifteen years old and hopeful my life could still turn out okay.

One night, several weeks into my new life and thousands of miles from my old one, my mother came into the bathroom where I had been washing my face before bed.

'Can we talk now or should I come back later?' she asked.

'What do you want?'

In that moment she dropped the bombshell that would rock my world.

'I know your father molested you.'

Betrayal ripped through my soul like a ravenous beast, destroying the few benefits the freedom of being so distant from my father had bought me. Shame and fear prevented either of us from looking at the other. I pushed past my mother and locked myself in my bedroom. Curled up in a ball in the corner of my room, I tried to rock away this ultimate treachery. My mother's pleas and hollow knocks landed upon deaf ears. None of her explanations were resonating. Staring into the darkness, while part of me went deep inside my head, the functioning part of my mind began to plan my escape. The next morning I ran away from home.

I ended up staying at a shelter in the city centre that was set up specifically for young runaways. It was called Avenue 15 and it would end up being the only place I called home in the weeks to come – and the beginning of a whole new lesson into the workings of evil.

I remember that the girls in the shelter slept in a large space in the attic. The boys were on the floor below. As there were no locks on the bedroom doors, both rooms were equally accessible to either gender. Depending on the diligence of the night-shift worker, which ranged anywhere from minimal to absolutely pathetic, I could almost always bet on one or more of the boys sneaking up into our room to get it on with the willing and the not-so-willing participants. Meanwhile, grown men circled the premises for their pick of young, vulnerable girls with a history of abuse that would make them easy prey. Safety was non-existent there.

During the day, Avenue 15 would be off limits to us as we were all expected to go to school. Many of the kids would skip school and hang out downtown. As winter was fast approaching, hanging out in the bitter cold was not an experience I cared to repeat often. I can't actually recall what I did with my days, but I can say that during the nights, more often than not, I slept with one eye open.

I can remember one night when I actually did have both eyes shut. A boy, who had been kicked out of the shelter that day for hitting a worker and threatening the life of one of the girls, was at the window trying to get in. My bed was next to the window, and I reckon I jumped straight out of bed at the first knock. Adrenaline and fear were pumping through my veins.

'Let me in,' he said.

I didn't move.

He began to yell and bang on the window. 'Let me in, you fucking bitch. Let me the fuck in.'

He ducked down briefly and came up with what appeared to be a bat in his hands. That's the last thing I remember.

The next day, I learned that the police had been called, and they took him away before he could get into our room.

While I was at the shelter, I stayed in close contact with a family friend. Her name was Beverly. She worked with troubled teens in a secure treatment ward, and I suppose I was a walk in the park for her in comparison. She was trying her hardest to find someone who would agree to take me in. Placing a teenager anywhere is never easy. It was a cold October evening when Beverly picked me up from the shelter and took me to a cafe in the city to talk about my limited options.

We spent the first few minutes discussing my mental state and practical things such as how safe I was.

'Your mom is really worried about you,' she said. 'And we are all worried about both of you. Jillian told me that your mom went through all the photo albums last night and cut your father out of every single picture.'

I felt my guilt build and rise, but then my anger and sense of betrayal countered the emotion, making it possible to harden myself again.

'I don't care, Bev. I'm not going back. She told me that she knew what he was doing to me.'

'No, sweetie. The social worker from your home town told her what you had disclosed when you were in the psychiatric hospital. She also told your mom not to confront you on it as it would freak you out and you would run. Which you did.'

My head was spinning. I was so tired of everything, nothing made sense to me. My anger toward my mother was so strong it made me shake every time I relived the moment she confronted me.

'The main thing is keeping you safe, kiddo, and if you're set on not going back home, I have found a safe place you can stay.'

Tami was a thirty-four-year-old, recently separated, single mother with a three-month-old baby girl. And she was Beverly's sister-in-law. Why she wanted to take in a troubled runaway, I'll never know, but in doing so she undoubtedly saved me from a much crueller fate. I had spent just under three weeks at the shelter and was already at breaking point. Secretly relieved but too proud to say, I couldn't wait to get out of there. Beverly organised to pick me up the following night.

Tami's house was so cosy it would have been hard not to feel at home. It wasn't messy but appeared lived in. She had paperwork piled in a corner of the kitchen, and what didn't fit there was spread across her dining table.

My anxieties almost got the better of me that first night as I struggled through our awkward conversation.

'How did you find living at Avenue 15, Carrie?'

'It wasn't so bad,' I lied.

'I bet there were times that were pretty scary. I'm glad you're here now.'

She looked at me with a welcoming openness in her eyes. In all my life I had never experienced such intense positivity from someone. I was terrified she was going to discover the shameful secrets of my past. I looked away, praying my secrets would not betray me.

Like Beverly, Tami worked with troubled teens, many of whom were street kids. I sat there for what seemed a lifetime, staring at the floor, as she described a world of drugs, prostitution and the eventual death of young girls at the hands of men who called themselves pimps.

The whole conversation was making me very anxious. I was already frightened of the gaps in my memory, and I worried what I'd forgotten about my time in the shelter. I reassured myself that there was no way I'd ever choose to get mixed up in a life like that. Feeling a headache coming on, I politely asked if she would show me to my room.

After Tami resettled her baby, she came into my bedroom where I was wrestling with the bedsheets. Grabbing one end, she helped me finish the job while she sang. I listened to her beautiful voice. When my bed was made, the two of us sat on the edge of it in silence.

She looked at me for the longest time, then with the back of her hand, she reached out and gently stroked my cheek. I jumped up as if she'd shocked me with a cattle prod. No one had ever done that to me before. Instinctively, everything inside of me screamed to pull away.

'I'm sorry, Carrie. I didn't mean to scare you.'

'Yeah, uh, that's okay.' I tried to play it cool and hide the fact that I was a freak. 'Guess I'm just really tired.'

The way I had shuddered at Tami's touch did nothing to dissuade her. She stood up, leaned toward me, kissed me on the forehead and told me that she was only across the hallway if I needed anything.

I closed the door behind her and turned off the bedroom light. Staring into the night, I feared that moving in with her could be the most challenging thing I had ever done – then again, it might also be the most healing.

As the days turned to weeks and the weeks to months,

Tami continued her affection. She was so free with her love and seemed to give it unconditionally. This was different from the way I had grown up. My mother was never openly affectionate with us and she always busied herself with cleaning instead. She loved us, and Jillian and I were her world, but affection was a luxury my mother never willingly displayed. The absence of cuddles and substantial presence of cleaning products in our house might have explained why I was so uncomfortable with human touch and also why dust never had the opportunity to settle on any stationary objects.

Even in a supermarket, if someone brushed past me, I'd get an indescribable feeling of disgust that began in the pit of my stomach and would resonate throughout my entire body, causing my flesh to feel as though it might crawl from the bone. It would always make me shudder involuntarily.

Tami touched me all of the time. She probably wasn't even aware of the number of times throughout the course of a day her hand would come into contact with my back, or the way she would stand behind me when I was sitting down and stroke my hair. She didn't even seem the least bit worried when I would recoil and flinch the moment she made contact. Thankfully, she never took it as rejection, but viewed it for what it was: the actions of a young girl who had endured a lifetime of hurt, and had struggled for years with immense shame and worthlessness. She was very aware of the emotions that physical contact brought up for me – and still she continued to touch me. For she also knew that, more than anything else, I desperately needed to be loved.

Tami and I had many conversations during the five years I would float in and out of her life. She would always go to great lengths to assure me that she loved me unconditionally and, no matter what I told her, the love would never change. I hoped she was right.

We were sitting in the warmth of her lounge room one winter's evening when my secret came out. Tami waited patiently while I found the courage and the words to tell her what had been haunting me for so long. I remember fearing she'd judge me for what I was about to say. I also knew that if I didn't tell someone, I would probably go mad.

'His name was Toby,' I finally said. 'And he was the dog my father bought when I was eight years old.'

The first time I spotted Toby I was standing on the front porch beside my little sister. My parents had divorced the previous year, and my father had access every second weekend. I was waiting for him to find the right key to open the door when something in the lounge-room window caught my eye. He was absolutely the cutest thing I had ever seen, and once I noticed him I can honestly say that it was the first time I couldn't wait to get into my father's house.

'Daddy, there's a dog in your house,' my sister said, squealing with anticipation.

Greeting us at the door with his tail wagging furiously, the puppy jumped all over us.

'What's his name, Dad?' I asked.

'Toby,' he said. 'I got him from the pound.'

'So we own him?' There was a mixture of excitement and suspicion in my tone.

Jillian continued to jump up and down. 'A dog! We have a dog!'

As much as it pleased me to have something so precious to love and care for, I couldn't help but wonder why on earth my father wanted an animal. He could barely look after himself and, as for his family, well, the track record on that one spoke volumes.

Having Toby there to play with made the access weekends go by more quickly. He was the most loving dog, and with my sister rarely at my dad's with me due to the mysterious 'ailments' she would suddenly develop before we were meant to go over, it was Toby that kept me company. It wasn't long before he became my closest friend.

As the months passed, I noticed Toby had become a lot more skittish than when he first arrived. His behaviour changed considerably, and he would jump at the smallest noise. Whenever my father raised his voice or came near him, Toby would run and hide under the table in the hallway – which really was the perfect hiding spot. A brown fuzzy blanket was thrown over its surface and hung down to the floor. I remember pretending it was a cave high on a mountaintop. There were plenty of times that both Toby and I fled there to escape my father's many moods.

One rainy afternoon Toby went missing. It wasn't unusual for him to head off and explore the great outdoors, but with the weather as bad as it was, I was worried.

I paused the movie I had been watching, stuck my head out the front door and called Toby's name. No response. Then I grabbed his box of treats, took them with me to the porch and shook them. If all else failed, this proved time and again to be a foolproof way of getting my dog's attention. There was still no sign.

Before panicking, I decided to take one last look through the house, and if absolutely necessary, I'd approach my father and tell him the dog was missing.

After searching the entire place, I came to my father's bedroom door. It was closed and did not look at all inviting, but I was past caring about my father's foul mood. He needed to know Toby was missing before my poor little dog was lost forever. I reached for the doorknob and walked in on a situation that still sickens me.

'I said get in here and close the goddamn door!'

I jumped at my father's voice and shut the door behind me.

Leaning against the wall, I found myself unable to move as my mind slowly began to take in what I was seeing. Although it was happening right in front of me, it seemed too awful to comprehend. I kept thinking there must be some other explanation for the disgusting act going on in front of me. At the very least, a horrible misunderstanding. How could my father be doing this with my dog?

I always knew my father was an evil man, but it was then that I became fully aware of his sickness. I finally understood that there was nothing my father was incapable of – and all I wanted to do as a result of this was die.

Without a doubt, the longest moment of my life occurred when my father grabbed my hands and pulled them toward Toby's snout. Completely hysterical, I shook my head and started screaming at my father, begging him to stop the madness. With his free hand, he slapped me hard across the face.

'Don't you dare raise your voice to me, girl,' he hissed. 'Do as I say.'

'No, Daddy, please! Don't hurt him.'

It was no use. Kneeling on the bed, in absolute hysterics, I had become the accomplice my father needed to brutally hurt the one thing I truly loved.

After the assault, my poor little dog fled to our secret hiding place. My father went off to shower while I was still kneeling in the middle of the bed. I knew I had to comfort my dog. Lifting the brown fuzzy blanket high enough to crawl under, I approached poor Toby.

At first, he was lying so still I thought for sure my father had killed him. However, as I got closer, I could see his body trembling as he huddled in a protective ball. Biting my lip and trying not to cry, I slowly put my hand out to pat my closest friend.

I stayed with my dog for the rest of that day. As he shook and tried to lick the pain away, I stroked his fur, told him he was a good boy and that I loved him very much. I told him all the things I longed to hear during the times I needed comforting. The guilt I felt was overwhelming. It bore down on my shoulders and created a nausea in the pit of my stomach that I carry to this day. More than anything, I needed to know that Toby didn't blame me for what had happened to him. At the very least, I needed to know he hated me far less than I already hated myself.

During the ride back to my mother's house, my father spent the journey hissing at me every horrific thing he would do to me if I ever told.

But my mind carried me elsewhere. His threats were unnecessary. I already knew that no person on earth would understand what I was living with. That's why upon my return to my mother's, like so many times before, the thought of mentioning my father's deplorable conduct did not even occur to me.

I came back from that weekend in a state of shock that made everything around me seem dreamlike. What my father had done to my dog I had never imagined possible. As the witness to a crime of such appalling horror, I knew there was nothing he could not and would not do to me. With this realisation, not only did my sense of helplessness grow, but so too did my anger. It was deep and so full of venom that it permeated every cell in my being.

The unjust world I found myself in was unfathomable.

Tami listened as I recounted how my father had forced me to hold my dog's snout while he raped him from behind.

'I didn't want to, Tam. He grabbed my hands and forced them around Toby's mouth and wouldn't let them go. Toby searched my eyes for help. It was me who made him even more vulnerable than he already was.'

Sobbing, I reluctantly looked up at her for the first time since sharing what happened and watched in amazement as a steady stream of tears ran down her cheeks. She came over and wrapped her arms around me. Holding me tightly, we both cried as I recounted what it was like for me to witness such a brutal attack on the only friend I had at my father's house.

4

EARLY THE NEXT MORNING at Paula's friends' house I was still in the same position I had placed myself in the night before – upright, and hugging my knees to my chest. All these memories had flooded through my head as I'd tried to sleep on the mattress on the dining-room floor. I listened to hear if Paula was awake yet. Hearing nothing, I lay down to stretch my back. I knew it must be early – the first birds welcoming the day with their song had yet to appear. Closing my eyes, I finally drifted off to sleep.

Later, I ran into Paula on the way to the shower. I could tell by her mood that she wasn't happy with me. Too tired to be bothered, I walked past with my head down.

We got a lift from one of her friends to Sydney's central train station. Two hours had passed and Paula still hadn't spoken to me. Once the tickets were purchased we sat on one of the station benches, and the silence between us continued.

I turned to her. 'Paula, are you angry with me, by any chance?' I asked as our train pulled up. I could feel the blood rushing to my cheeks.

'Now why would you think that?' Her demeanour was cold.

Shame began to well deep inside of me, eroding any sense of dignity I'd managed to hold on to. Although I knew what happened to me was not my fault, as Paula sat there in judgement, self-doubt became an enemy I was left to battle on my own.

'I told him no, Paula. He didn't listen. I fought back and I screamed. What more could I have done?'

She remained silent. Following her onto the train, I dropped my bag and reluctantly took my seat next to her.

'Could you at least say something?'

She continued to stare out the window. I got up and moved to another seat. The last thing I needed was her punishment. I'd been doing enough of that all on my own.

Hours passed with the two of us not speaking to one another. Just when I had reached the point of no longer caring what her problem even was, I felt a presence beside me. Turning to look, I discovered Paula.

'Listen, I'm sorry,' she said. 'It's not you I'm upset with. It's me.'

I sat quietly as she described to me her interpretation of the previous night's events.

'I'm really ashamed of my behaviour, Carrie. I was drunk and totally out of control. I attacked him and if he wants to press charges, he has every right to.'

'Paula,' I interrupted. 'He wouldn't dare. If I wanted to press charges ...'

'Carrie, when I saw you looking as messed up as you were, I knew what had happened. You wouldn't tell me, but I knew. And, yeah, I'll be honest with you, there is a part of me that resents you for putting yourself in that situation, but mostly I'm ashamed of how I handled it.'

Paula's hand brushed my arm and she continued.

'I'm sorry I didn't handle things well. It wasn't your fault and I should have been there for you. There's a part of me that feels responsible for letting you go by yourself. I never should have allowed you to.'

'Paula, I never expected your protection. I'm big enough to look after myself. I take full responsibility for the mistake I made going back with him alone. I made the wrong choice, but I don't want to beat myself up for the rest of my life for making it. I need to put it behind me and move on.'

Paula laughed nervously. 'You say that as if you're talking about an everyday occurrence. My God, Carrie, you were raped.'

Looking out the window, I noticed kangaroos jumping in the distance. I watched them until they were no longer in view. Yes, I was assaulted, and Paula's observation showed me just how different I was from most. I continued staring out the window at this foreign landscape while the memories of my incarcerated childhood filled my mind.

The train pulled into Melbourne's Flinders Street Station. It was dusk. Paula and I walked through the city and checked ourselves into the cheapest and closest hostel we could find. The hostel we chose was as seedy-looking as the one I'd stayed at during those first nights in Sydney. Too weary to care, all I wanted to do was sleep.

When morning arrived, I was shocked to discover I hadn't woken in the night. And more surprised to learn that for the first time in my life, I had slept in. I sat up to see Paula standing before me, showered and ready to start her day.

'Wow,' I said. 'I slept so well I damn near forgot where I was.'

Paula smiled. 'You were having nightmares again last night.'

She had mentioned this to me a few times already over the course of our travels together. I said nothing and headed to the door with my toiletry bag in hand and towel over my shoulder.

'Are you going to see about finding someone you could talk to regarding what happened in Sydney?'

I could feel her staring at my back. My hand remained glued to the doorknob. 'I haven't given it any thought,' I said and continued to the shower without looking back.

I returned to the room to find Paula sitting on her bed flipping through a city map.

'Carrie, do you really think not talking to someone is such a good idea?'

'What do you mean?' I asked, failing miserably to mask my agitation.

'Do you just plan on pretending that things are fine and not addressing any of the issues I know must be coming up for you?'

Was it possible she had the ability to read my mind? She walked over to sit beside me.

'You were crying in your sleep last night. I tried to wake you, but every time I touched you, you only seemed to freak out more.'

I knew she was probably right, but if I opened myself up and allowed emotions I had blocked to resurface, I wasn't certain I would be alright. My confidence and independence had already been dented by the rape, but if I admitted that to be the case, what did I have left? In a foreign country on my own, I couldn't afford to fall apart without anybody there to help me pick up the pieces.

Even though some part of me resented the fact Paula doubted my coping abilities, I did realise that I was in denial. After much discussion, Paula convinced me to go to the hospital to find out if there was anywhere I could go to talk to someone.

She had already put her efficiency skills to work and located the closest city hospital to us on the map. Before I could change my mind, we were out the door and on our way. After a short tram ride and a beautiful walk in the sunshine, we reached the Royal Women's Hospital. With a name like that, I was hopeful no male doctors would be allowed on site.

Once in the lobby, I began to panic at the thought of telling a complete stranger the details of my life. Paula took one look at me and realised all I wanted to do was run.

Grabbing my arm, she said, 'You wait here and I'll ask the receptionist if she can help us.'

Sitting me down on one of the chairs not far from the main desk, Paula again gave me a look that said, *If you take off, I will hunt you down, chop you up and sprinkle you on my cereal.* I decided it was best to stay exactly where I was, as history had shown she was more than capable of acting on her rage.

Paula and the woman behind the desk spoke for no more than a couple of minutes. When Paula returned, she looked concerned. She sat down beside me and told me what little information she'd learned.

'It's going to be tricky because you have no Medicare card or health insurance. The hospital can't treat you but the receptionist has given us the name of an organisation able to help.'

I continued to listen as she spoke of a place called CASA House, which was only across the road from where we were. CASA stood for Centre Against Sexual Assault, and there was a female social worker expecting us.

I was pleased to see the building was an inconspicuous white terrace house on the corner of the street opposite the hospital. No flashing signs to draw attention to what had happened to me and why I was going in there.

I went through the door with Paula following. I couldn't help but feel she was only behind me so I wouldn't turn and run. I looked over my shoulder at her as we walked into reception. Her eyes told me to keep moving forward.

Once the woman at reception took me through to the waiting room, Paula seemed to relax a bit and asked if I wanted her to wait for me.

'No, thanks. You go off and explore the city. I'll see you back at the hostel at some point.'

While I sat anxiously in the waiting room, I was overwhelmed by the number of pamphlets and posters condemning violence against women and children. I stared at slogans and pictures of battered kids. One poster with a little girl huddled in a corner clutching her teddy bear caught my eye. I was unable to look away. Each poster seemed to portray some aspect of the life I had escaped. In time, a woman entered the room.

'Hello, you must be Carrie.' She had a strong European accent but spoke to me in a gentle manner. 'My name is Yvonne. Would you like to come through?'

I followed her up a flight of stairs to a door located on the left.

'Come in, Carrie, and have a seat.'

Looking around the room, I took the seat as close to the door as possible. I smiled as I thought about my habit of always choosing the chair closest to the exit and with my back against the wall. No matter where I was, I always had to face what was coming toward me. One never knows when a speedy exit is required.

'So, Carrie, I understand you were assaulted in Sydney two nights ago.'

I stared at the floor and nodded. I was so nervous I began to feel sick.

Waiting for a response that was not forthcoming, she continued to gently push me to talk. 'Can you tell me what happened?'

I began to recount in a very matter-of-fact manner what took place that night and how, in my stupidity, I failed to exercise better judgement. I could sense she was looking at me, and for a while neither one of us said a thing. I wondered if perhaps she too blamed me for what happened.

Finally, Yvonne spoke. 'So tell me this, Carrie,' she said. 'You fought back, yes?'

I nodded.

'You said no and told him to stop?'

Again, I nodded.

'Now tell me this. When the two of you were struggling and you were crying and begging him to stop, only he didn't, how did that make you feel?'

My mind took me back to that night. Before I realised where my emotions were headed, I discovered anger devouring me whole. Yvonne gave me enough time to think about the unjust manner in which I had been treated. She allowed me the space to recall the overwhelming feelings I had experienced when I said no, and like so many other times in my life, I was ignored. Before I had the chance to honestly answer her question, she leaned forward, her grey-blue eyes filled with immense passion and intensity.

'Carrie, do you want to charge him?'

Immediately following her question, I became consumed by not only the recent events, but also by every trauma that had occurred throughout the course of my life. The brutality I had been forced to live with for years hit me with such intensity, I had to hold back the tears I'd spent years convincing myself I hadn't the right to cry.

'What the hell is wrong with me?' I blurted out.

'Absolutely nothing. What happened to you is not your fault.'

I said nothing, silenced by years of shame. My mind continued to drift between what had once been and what had remained the same. As my thoughts shifted back to the present moment, I looked at Yvonne who was waiting patiently.

'Did you just ask me if I want to get the cops involved?' A rush of adrenaline charged through me.

She assured me that was what she had asked.

Looking at Yvonne with an intensity to match her own gaze, I surprised myself with my response. 'Yeah, I think I do want to press charges.'

Yvonne went to call the police, and while waiting for their arrival, a barrage of questions went through my head. Did I deserve to defend myself in such a bold manner and, if so, where on earth would I get the strength to do such a thing? Would the police want to know about my father? And if they found out about my history, would they then think I should have seen this coming? Whatever the answers were, when Yvonne re-entered the room, I had to excuse myself and run directly to the toilet to throw up.

Yvonne and I continued to talk about the rape. Our conversation was stirring up many emotions I had tried to leave back in Canada. I looked at Yvonne and tried to imagine what she would think if she knew what I was withholding.

Yvonne's phone rang. 'Okay, thank you. Send them up.'

Oh God, the police had arrived.

'Are you ready?' she asked.

I could only shrug my shoulders. Was anyone ever ready for something like this?

There was a knock at the door, and I was sure I would throw up again. Sensing this, Yvonne told me she would stay if that would make things easier. Anytime I needed a break or couldn't continue, all I had to do was let her know. I wondered if I should let her know that right then the only thing that could have made life easier would have been several quick shots of vodka.

Two female officers entered the room. They appeared to be in their thirties, and one definitely looked much nicer than the other. They were in civilian clothes, which I appreciated as it was less confronting for me.

'It's Carrie, is it?' one of them said, glancing up from her notes. She was the less friendly of the two, and the one who would be doing most of the interviewing. Her name was Senior Constable Debbie Schultz – and I was sure her red hair would match her fiery personality.

I swallowed hard and nodded, hoping not to pass out. She asked me a series of questions, but I did not respond. I could tell my silence was driving her mad, but I was unable to speak.

Yvonne sat with me as promised, but said nothing either – that was apparently my job, only I couldn't find the words. I was still grateful for her presence, as I was convinced if she left me alone with the cop holding the clipboard, I would be vaporised by her stare alone.

Constable Schultz continued to ask me the most intimate questions that required graphic detail in response. Instead of hearing answers, we all could have heard a pin drop in the next room. I knew I was only making her hate me more, but I just couldn't seem to find the words to describe what had happened to me. So I sat silently enraged at my own stupidity.

'You know I can't help but draw parallels between interviewing you and extracting teeth,' she muttered.

When I finally lifted my head to look in her direction, her blue eyes softened slightly when she saw the tears spilling down my face.

'Carrie, I can't help you if you don't tell me what happened.'

Trying to keep hold of my emotions, I struggled to find my voice. All I could do was shrug my shoulders and apologise. A gesture I would instantly regret.

'What do you mean, you don't know? You were there, weren't you?'

'Yes. I was there.' A huge lump formed in my throat. Maybe that was her gloved fist going after my back molars.

Unable to even think the word 'rape' let alone utter it, I was once again rendered mute. Constable Schultz's already diminished patience was wearing thin. Before she completely lost her temper, I summoned every last bit of courage I possessed and found a way to speak. I knew I had to tell my story; it was just that I would rather have died than do it. It was then that I experienced an eerily familiar out-of-body experience. As I listened to my own words, they seemed to come from far away and from somebody else. Unsure of what was going on, I gave into the exhaustion and somehow found a way to convey what had happened to me two nights before in Sydney. Though I wasn't sure what I said or how I managed to relay the events of that night, I knew I had because the grumpy officer was now happily scribbling down notes, her frown lines far less visible.

'The following morning,' I added, 'Paula and I caught the train to Melbourne.'

With the interview nearing an end, Constable Schultz even commented on the discovery of a personality buried under my mountains of thick, curly hair. I smiled, because that was the first time she'd smiled too. Up until that point, I wasn't entirely sure the woman even had teeth.

The police offered me a ride back to the hostel where I was staying. Constable Schultz also mentioned that she wouldn't mind interviewing Paula to get her side of the story. I swallowed hard at the thought of two strong-willed, like-minded women getting together. I was almost certain Paula would have met her match in Constable Schultz.

Before leaving CASA, Yvonne took me aside.

'That was a very brave thing you did in there, Carrie. You should be proud of yourself.'

'Thank you for your support, Yvonne.' I breathed a sigh of relief, just glad it was finally over.

'I will be away until next week, but give me a ring after that and I will be happy to see you again. Something tells me you have much more to share.'

How was that for the understatement of the century? Unable to believe her intuition, I thanked Yvonne again and left her office, wondering if she was some kind of gypsy fortune teller. Whatever the case, I was certain she would be more than able to handle my secrets if I did choose to open up to her.

Walking with the two officers up the dirty, run-down staircase of the hostel, I was embarrassed by the state of the building, as if I had something to do with it. I wanted to explain that we did in fact plan to leave the following day but was too tired to bother.

As I stood at the door to our room, I realised that I was worried about Paula's reaction to getting the police involved.

I turned to face Constable Schultz. 'I can't go in there.'

She looked at me with confusion and impatience. 'Why not?'

'I'm afraid Paula will be angry when she finds out I spoke to you. With the guy being a friend of her friends and all, it just makes it, well, you know, messy.'

'Listen, why don't you wait downstairs and we'll talk to Paula?'

I agreed and sped away from the room, leaving the two officers alone to do the dirty work for me. My day had already been as action-packed as I was willing to allow. I just wanted everything to be over and hoped what I had done didn't put any unnecessary strain on Paula.

While I waited outside the hostel, I watched the congested buzz of downtown Melbourne swirl around me. Although I'd been assaulted not even thirty-six hours before, the fear that had always followed me in Canada was still absent here in Australia. What happened to me was unfortunate but would not take my freedom away. It would, understandably, take me a while to get my confidence and independence back, but I was still far from the condition I'd been in before coming to this country. And besides, I told myself, I was now a person with power and choice and courage. Not even two seconds after finishing that last thought, an impatient taxi driver landed on his horn and yelled out of his window at some incompetent driver. I jumped a mile into the air.

Some courage, I thought.

I heard the hostel door swing open, and Constable Schultz emerged by herself. Holding her clipboard to her chest, she placed her sunglasses back on and came over to where I was standing.

'Paula is fine with you reporting it.'

'Really?' I breathed a sigh of relief. 'Thank you for telling her for me.'

'Carrie, why didn't you tell me about your father?'

'What?' I couldn't hide my shock and felt numb with

devastation and shame. I hated Paula in that moment for telling them what little she thought she knew about my life. Did she think she could possibly have me figured out through piecing together my nightmares? My past was the last thing I expected to be sharing with this tough cop. Not knowing what else to do, I prepared myself for whatever lecture was bound to follow.

'She told us that you lived through some pretty horrific stuff at some point in your life. I was just curious as to why you wouldn't think that might have been significant information for me to have.'

'Well, I suppose I didn't think it had anything to do with what happened to me in Sydney.' I felt so small and insignificant around her. I tried to hide my shame but I knew the expression painted on my face betrayed me. 'So does this mean that because this has happened to me before, now it's no big deal?'

'Of course not,' she replied. 'It just would have given me the background I needed to understand you a bit better.'

I looked at her, not knowing where she was headed.

'How old were you when it all began?' she asked.

'Four.'

'And how old were you when it stopped?'

All I could do was stare at the ground and try my best not to throw up. She said nothing. For ages we just stood there in silence. I was so over the events of the day, I too had finally reached the point of no longer caring.

'I'm sorry I was so hard on you earlier,' she said finally. 'If only you had given me this information in the beginning ...'

Her voice trailed off, and I looked up to see what was happening. She was offering me her card.

'Here's my mobile number. I want you to ring me in the morning if you decide to go through with this.'

I looked at her card and nodded unconvincingly.

She patted me on the arm. 'You better ring me, Carrie. I'll be waiting for your call.'

I half smiled at her attempt to make me feel better. 'I'll speak to you in the morning then,' I said.

The following morning I picked up the phone to ring Constable Schultz. I had decided to complete the statement. Down at the police station, reliving what happened in Sydney proved no easy task, though I managed to do a much better job the second time around. We spent a gruelling three and a half hours documenting the night I was raped. Knowing what she did about my past certainly brought out her softer side. Well, as much as I'm sure anything ever did. But what surprised me was the respect I noticed I had for her. I felt able to draw on her unwavering strength to get me through the interview. It was either that, or my fear of crying in front of her. Whatever the reason, it was working for me.

I was amazed that we could even share some funny moments. I hadn't had all that much experience in dealing with Australians at that point and wasn't used to the strange way in which they shortened and pronounced words. There were times during the interview when I was completely lost.

'So tell me,' she said, 'approximately how old was this black?'

'I'm sorry?' I was confused and shocked by the racist remark.

'The black,' she repeated. 'How old was he?'

I looked at her and wondered how on earth she'd come to the conclusion that the white guy who had assaulted me was black. 'He wasn't black. He was white.'

She stared at me as if I was the one making no sense.

'How old was the black?' She slowed her enunciation down and spoke to me as if I was wearing a nappy and had my finger halfway up my nose.

'I guess he was in his forties,' I said. 'But he wasn't black, he was white.'

Looking perplexed and slightly cross, she then burst out laughing. I waited, hoping she'd eventually let me in on the joke.

'No. Not black.' She laughed again. 'Bloke.' She pronounced the word as slowly as she could.

'Bloke?' I repeated. 'What the hell is that?'

'It's a word we use to describe a man.'

'Oh, so is that your fancy cop lingo?'

Again she was hit with fits of laughter. 'No. It's just something Aussies say.'

It was good to see her having such a good time at my expense. 'You people are bizarre,' I said.

'Hey, when in Rome.'

I laughed. 'Hang out with blokes who drink wine and eat pasta?'

When the time finally came to pack up and leave, I was so glad it was over. As I sat in the car on the way back to the hostel, I realised how important my actions were. In standing up for myself, I'd finally broken the silence. No longer was I going to allow myself to be the victim. For the first time ever, I respected myself enough to fight for my rights – as a human being and as a woman.

'You did really well today, Carrie,' Constable Schultz said. 'I'm very proud of you.'

Hearing that, I nearly fainted. The tough cop, who seemed to hate me in the beginning, was now proud of my accomplishments? I smiled, remembering how much I disliked her at first too.

'Listen, if there is anything you need, I've written my home number on the back of this card.' She handed it to me and told me to put it somewhere safe.

I was so shocked I didn't know what to say.

'Whether it be a place to stay, someone to talk to or whatever – just pick up the phone and ring me.'

Shaking her hand, I thanked Senior Constable Schultz for her generosity and the help she had given me in more ways than she would ever know.

'No worries, anytime,' she said. 'But, please, call me Deb.'

5

THROUGHOUT MY TEENAGE years, both Tami and my mother spent their time taking me to numerous therapists. I was as fussy with them as I was about food. But whenever I was asked by any of the potential shrinks to pinpoint the beginning of my father's abuse, my memory always took me back to when I was four and my mother was diagnosed with breast cancer. It had spread into her lymph nodes, and her chance of survival was very slim. The day she left for the hospital I was given two different outcomes by my parents. My mother took me aside and told me she was going away to work really hard at getting better so she could return to my little sister and me. My father told me she was going away to die; that she would die because I was bad and that my mother blamed me for making her sick.

'If you ever breathe a word of our secret to anybody or they find out about all the bad things you've done, your mother is going to die.'

His words did two things to me that day. They disconnected me from my mother and they kept me silent for years while he tortured me. For a long time I believed I was the cause of my mother's illness. And even though she somehow managed to 'survive me', I knew deep down she must have hated me. Perhaps the main reason I kept my father's abuse to myself was because I believed that was the punishment I deserved for nearly killing my mother with cancer.

While she explained to me she was going to a place that was going to make her better, I had already been told differently. My father convinced me that she was going away to die. For whatever reason, I believed this to be the truth and I hated my mother for leaving us. Mostly, though, I couldn't bear the thought of my life without her in it.

Peace never existed in our household – only conflict, and the understanding that no matter what any one of us said or did, we were all held prisoner to my father's violent rampages. From the moment my father got up, there was tension. In his presence, we walked on eggshells. Landmines planted throughout that three-bedroom bungalow of ours wouldn't have made any of us bat an eye. Relief only came when he headed off to work. Everything would immediately feel safer in his absence. My mom wouldn't seem so anxious, and my little sister would be able to smile again. I was still nervous. My father terrified me whether he was under the same roof or in a completely different area code.

Every day, the cycle of fear, tension and then brief relief continued. It seemed that those short eight hours when he was at work recharged us. But just below the surface, panic was always building. We all felt it, knew it consumed our lives, and the closer it came to five o'clock, the further away from relieved we all grew.

What was worse than the tangible yet unspoken tension and the frequent arguments was the terror that developed at night. In our home, evil seemed to thrive in darkness. For years, I went to sleep every night with my pillow over my head. I'd lie there in the dark and listen as my father yelled and struck my mother. And no sooner would I pray for peace and contemplate whether to breathe than I would hear the sound of a horrifying crash on the other side of my wall, as my father flung my mother against it.

'You are the most pathetic piece of shit,' he would scream at her. 'I don't know why I just don't kill you now and put us both out of our misery.'

As disturbing as it was for a four-year-old to hear her own mother taking a beating at the hands of her father, it was certainly better than the alternative. With her unanswered cries for help filling the air, I knew that he was too busy to start in on me.

My mother came back from hospital around Christmas time. Even though she had somehow managed to cheat death, she looked terribly frail and was a shadow of her former self. During that time, my father took over their bedroom and made my mother sleep on the couch. Too weak to argue, she held hatred in her eyes for him when he entered the room. When he tried to pick a fight with her, she maintained a level of calm in her voice. She had returned a different person from the broken woman who I had been told was leaving us to die. Despite her weakened body, her mind was now stronger. Too young to understand it at the time, later on I worked out the cause of her change. She had made a decision. All that was left for her to do was pick the appropriate time to leave the source of our hell.

I was halfway through grade one when my parents divorced. Mrs Adams was the teacher who taught me both before and after the visitation weekends began. Looking back, I find it infuriating that throughout all of my thirteen years of schooling, of all my teachers, only she and my junior high-school counsellor ever questioned whether there was something about me that was cause for great concern. It's truly astonishing to me how I managed to make it through school as far as I did without anybody ever picking up on the fact I wasn't exactly the same as the other kids. Did teachers not notice me walking strangely at times? I know that other children, in their pointing and snickering certainly did. Each Monday after a visitation weekend, I endured laughs and taunts as I gingerly made my way around the playground during recess and lunch.

One day in class, Mrs Adams went around and asked all of the children what it was their fathers did for a living. The answers ranged from doctor to lawyer to Indian chief.

'And how about your dad, Carrie?' she asked. The eyes of the class were boring holes through my head. 'What is it your daddy does?'

I sat there for ages, pulling out my eyelashes, without the slightest idea of what I was going to say. Very aware of the children in the class and the laughter that was born in my silence, I simply stated, 'I don't have one.'

Mrs Adams seemed quite perplexed by my response. 'What do you mean you don't have one?'

Picking up the pencil that had been resting on my desk, I began to tap it nervously as I shrugged my shoulders and cleared my throat. I could feel my face growing red with a combination of anger and embarrassment.

'I don't have one,' I repeated, this time much louder.

'Carrie,' she said. 'Everyone has a father. Perhaps he's no longer living. Is he dead?'

'No.'

'Well, are your parents divorced?' she asked.

'No, it's not that,' I said, unable to hide my frustrations. 'I just don't have one.'

Sensing she would not get anywhere else with her line of questioning, she moved on to interrogate the next kid.

That afternoon, my teacher rang my mother and asked if she would be willing to come down to the school for a chat. While the rest of the kids collected school bags and made their way out to their buses, I sat in the room with the teacher and waited nervously for my mother's arrival. Mrs Adams placed herself behind the small desk in front of mine and began grilling me on my life outside of school.

'So tell me, Carrie,' she began. 'How are things at home?'

'Fine,' I lied. I was distracted by the way she was able to squeeze into the chair and rest her massive boobs on the desk.

'Are you happy there?'

I nodded and shifted my gaze to my mother, now at the door. I was grateful to see her as her presence brought an end to these unwelcome questions.

My teacher got up out of that tiny wooden desk to greet my mother at the door, and I was surprised the desk actually let her escape. She shook my mom's hand. Mom looked just as nervous as I was.

Mrs Adams spoke to my mother so quietly that I was unable to pick up what was being said. I was, however, able to discern the worry on their faces, which fell directly onto my shoulders – and I was already carrying a load too heavy to bear.

My mother's disappointment was apparent as we walked toward the car in silence.

'Why would you tell your teacher that you don't have a father?' she asked, seeming not so much angry as curious.

I switched from apprehensive to agitated. 'I guess because I don't,' I replied as I climbed into the passenger seat. There was no way I was going to get into trouble for lying. I had to show her from the beginning that, in my mind, her ex-husband was no longer relevant.

'Your teacher tells me you are quite an angry little girl in class.'

She might as well have been talking to herself at that point in time. I hated the world – her included.

'She also said that maybe you might find talking to somebody helpful.'

My breathing became heavy, and my fists sat in tight little balls on my lap. I wondered why everyone couldn't just mind their own business and leave me alone. I had enough going on in my life. Sworn to secrecy, and with the threat of death hanging over my head, was how life had been for me those past three years. I felt I was doing rather admirably just pretending to function in the world.

After spending several weeks in Melbourne with Paula, the time soon came when we would go our separate ways. She had found a more permanent place to live, and I didn't have the money to follow her. Although I was anticipating working my way around the country, the whole Sydney incident had set me back a bit.

'You sure you can't come with me?' she asked.

'No, girl,' I said. 'We'll keep in touch though.'

Our hostel location was ideal for me. It was a close walk into the city, and also to the University of Melbourne where I'd started playing pick-up basketball. I had met a great group of friends, which gave some normalcy to the day. The university was also only a few minutes' walk to Yvonne at CASA House. I had been desperately looking forward to seeing her again.

I sat on my bed with my journal watching Paula rush around throwing last-minute things into her bag. I knew it would be weird not having her there. Although we'd only known each other a short while, it felt as though we had crammed a million experiences into that time frame. I was certain I wouldn't hear from her again. To tell you the truth, I probably preferred it that way. Not that the Sydney incident could even compare to my childhood, but I often felt immense guilt when I thought about how those events must have affected poor Paula with her Brady Bunch background.

After shoving her final item into her bag, she looked at me.

'I'll call you,' she said.

'Bye, Paula.'

Turning to leave, she suddenly stopped. 'You never did tell me if it ended badly with your birth mother.'

'It did,' I said.

'Can I ask why?'

Setting my journal down on my bed, I turned to her and said, 'Because she found out about my father.'

My birth mother's life came crashing down the day she walked in on me dressing in my bedroom before school one morning; I'd been going to my old school in my home town while I was staying with them. As I stood there naked from the waist up, she took one look at me and gasped. For it was the sight of me standing before her without my clothes that painted for her the horrific picture of the life I'd lived.

'What on earth happened to you?' she asked, staring in disbelief at the scar under my left breast.

I quickly turned away, grabbing my shirt and throwing it over my body. My first feelings were of shame and embarrassment, but these were tinged with relief. I no longer had to hide. Then I saw the look of terror in her eyes, and I felt more ashamed.

'I don't know what to say,' I replied, casting my eyes toward the ground. 'I guess my life hasn't always been fantastic.'

How was that for downplaying my life experiences?

'Who did that to you?' Her shock was palpable.

I remained silent, staring at the floor. With my arms folded across my chest, I hoped the earth would open up and swallow me whole.

'Who did that to you?' This time her voice was shrill, and I trembled at the intensity.

'It was my father,' I replied flatly, finally making eye contact with her.

I could no longer protect her from the truth. The time had come for me to share some of what I had endured since the day she had given me up. Though I knew the news would not be well received, I couldn't have predicted how badly she would react to the few facts I was willing to share.

'How old were you when he did that to you?' she asked, pointing at my chest. She looked as though she was going to be sick.

'Fourteen.'

She was quiet for a long time and then she erupted with a fury much like that of my father.

'Where was your mother when all this was happening?'

Where was my mother? I thought angrily. *Where the hell were you?* I knew I couldn't say what my mind was screaming. With the situation already well out of my control, all that was left for me to do was defuse her anger as best I could.

'My mother was very sick when things began,' I said, fighting back the burning tears in my eyes. 'I was only four years old. My father threatened me so badly, after a while I didn't know how to tell anyone what was happening to me.'

I'd spent years being angry with my mother for what my father had done, but God help anyone – birth mother included – who criticised the only mother I'd known.

'You were four?' she shrieked in absolute disgust. 'Well, he didn't rape you, did he?'

I was feeling completely overwhelmed. Panicking, my mind began to cloud over as a recognisable feeling passed through me.

'Oh God, Carrie. Did he rape you?'

'Not when I was four,' I said calmly.

Her voice was a million miles from where I was headed.

'What do you mean, "Not when you were four"?' she screamed. 'So are you telling me that your father raped you? What the fuck? How old were you when he did it?'

My body floated above the situation in front of me. I needed to get the hell out of there.

'How old were you, Carrie?' She was repeating the question, but it was already too late. Memories were filling my shattered brain. With everything closing in around me, I knew I was slipping away.

I led my birth mother over to the bed, tears flowing freely down her cheeks. I will never forget the look on her face. It was a look of guilt no words could ever do justice.

'I was eight years old,' I began.

My father was sitting in the front room watching pornography and drinking his unique concoction of milk and Scotch. Twisted, right down to his drink of choice, I always thought. Perhaps it appealed to alcoholics concerned with maintaining strong bones to compensate for deteriorating livers.

I was in the kitchen, quietly mesmerised by the rain as it fell heavily upon the pavement underneath the open window. The boredom had been building in me from the second I had woken up to the sound of rain. The sky was grey and overcast. The air thick, smelling of the sea.

Taking two kitchen chairs, I set them six feet apart facing each other. I made a rectangle with my red skipping rope with the yellow handles and began jumping in and out of it. Caught up in the fun I was finally having, I didn't notice my father standing directly behind me.

'Jesus, Mary and Joseph,' he said. Anytime he mentioned the three of them at once, I knew I was in trouble. 'Do you think this is a fucking playground? Take that shit off my chairs and quit being such an idiot!'

While I untied my only chance of entertainment for that weekend, he dug the Scotch out of the freezer and poured himself another drink. I got more nervous with every drink he consumed, because with each one he lost more of what little humanity he possessed. I never understood why alcohol made him so crazy, but I just knew it did. And mercy, if present in the slightest, was drowned in the sorrows brought on by that whisky bottle.

When my parents were together, my father had never been a huge drinker. He only began drinking excessively in my mother's absence. I suppose it's funny, because despite his behaviour and the massive consumption of his favoured beverage, I never thought of him as an alcoholic until many years later, when someone described him as such.

84

Quite some time after my father squashed my fun, I made the bold and regrettable decision to get the skipping rope back into action. Creeping up the hall, I went to where my father had been watching television. I almost laughed out loud when I found him passed out and snoring in his chair.

As the rain continued to fall, and my father snored, I defiantly practised my skipping games in his kitchen. That is, until he woke up and caught me doing exactly what he'd told me not to. And for this, I was severely punished.

'You're sorry alright,' he screamed at me. 'The sorriest thing I've ever seen in my life. I'm sick to death of you fucking little bitches! You and your sister come over here, thinking you can do whatever you want. I don't know what shit your mother lets you get up to in that fucking trailer of hers, but you're in my house now and this isn't a fucking playground.'

Wrestling with the skipping rope caught up in one of the chairs only added fuel to my father's already raging fire. He was the angriest I had ever seen him. The chair crashed against the cupboards at the other end of the kitchen. With the skipping rope still in his hand, he grabbed my arm and dragged me out of the kitchen and into his bedroom.

Slamming the door behind us, my father grabbed me by the shoulders and looked at my face for the first time since he'd woken up. He shook his head violently and threw me on top of his bed. Before I knew what was happening, he had my skipping rope around the headboard and had tightly tied it around my wrists.

The punishment I received that day changed my life forever. Unable to move, I remained where he left me – on his bed, lying in my own blood. I can't say for certain what happened during and after. My only crystal-clear recollection remains the ferocity of the pain ripping through my body upon impact. I don't even know if I passed out, but something tells me I must have. I remember my father swearing at me loudly and telling me to get up. Focusing on what was being said was near impossible for me. I was no longer in my body. All I could do was pretend that I understood what he was saying and lie still as he carried me off to the bathroom to clean me up.

For the rest of the weekend, I stayed in his bed, wearing his blue pyjama top while being forced to lie still and allow him to tend to my wounds. Having no other choice, I waited for the replacement of the cool washcloths with both apprehension and anticipation. Beyond the anger in my father's demeanour, I saw fear in his eyes.

At some point, I vaguely remember a man with a bag coming to stitch the wound my father had left me with. I remember being given medicine but not much else is clear. My body and the place in which I lay were saturated with sweat after my fever broke. The violent chills made me convulse and sent severe pain into my back, which I suppose was a welcome distraction.

After the rape, the part of me that believed there was good in the world had been almost destroyed. At eight years old, I had experienced evil in its purest form, and from then on, shame began to grow deep inside of me. The pain my body had endured as a result of the assault created a fear that would isolate me from the rest of the world. Yet, at the same time, it also instilled a wisdom that allowed me the opportunity to acknowledge my spirit's impressive ability to survive anything.

Even then, I knew what that man did to me was surely the most heinous crime anyone could commit against another. The evils done to humanity by humanity were extraordinary to me. Animals wouldn't even act as viciously toward their own kind. Yet we maliciously demoralised one another at will? This was the lesson I learned at eight years of age, barely out of grade two.

My birth mother was silent for what seemed an eternity and then erupted in a fit of rage.

'I can't do this anymore,' she screamed, storming out of my bedroom.

'Can't do what?' I asked, both terrified and confused by her comment.

She was talking to herself as she ran down the stairs to the front door.

'Patricia?' I called from the top of the dimly lit stairway. 'Where are you going?'

'To kill him,' she muttered under her breath.

The door slammed shut, and she was gone.

Two hours passed before she walked back through the door in what appeared to be a trance. I ran toward her to see if she was alright. Her common sense seemed to have returned, but I could tell the last thing she wanted to do was speak.

I knew she hadn't killed him. I don't know how, but I just did. She brushed past me and went up to her bedroom, slamming the door behind her. I realised then that the time had come for me to return home.

Patricia spent the next few days locked up in her room. I had to tell her I was going back home, but I just didn't know how. The odd occasions when I did see her, she wouldn't even look at me. I understood that what she was dealing with must be causing her terrible grief, but I told her many times that none of it was her fault, that I didn't blame her for what happened to me. She would only stare blankly and nod before returning to her room. I was unsure what else I could do.

Three days before the date on which I had arranged to return to my mother and sister, I decided to inform Patricia of my decision. Trembling with fear, I slowly made my way up the stairs to her bedroom. Knocking on her closed door, I entered with caution. She was sitting up in bed reading.

'I just want to tell you that I've decided to go back home.'

'That's fine,' she muttered, her face devoid of emotion.

I left the room, closing the door gently behind me, but I wasn't even halfway down the stairs when she threw open her door and began screaming at me in a fit of uncontrolled rage.

'You go back. That's fine,' she yelled. 'I wish I'd never met you. My life was so much better without you in it.'

My sister April ran up the stairs, in an attempt to save me from her words, but it was already too late. What she said wounded me so badly that my heart dropped and my spirit broke. Packing my belongings, I phoned a school friend to come get me and said goodbye to my brother and sister.

Three days after the fight and minutes before my plane was to leave, Patricia showed up at the airport. I had been standing with my friend saying my goodbyes when April came over to ask if I would go and give Patricia a hug. I turned in her direction – a hug looked like the last thing she wanted. Going against my better judgement, I placed my backpack beside my friend and told her I'd return in a minute. I feared another crazy scene as I approached this woman who had become a complete stranger once again.

As I walked toward her, I recalled the feelings I'd had exactly three months, one week and two days before when we'd met in virtually the same spot. Only this time, I was about to walk away from the arms I had waited eighteen years to fall into.

I stood in front of her and waited for her to speak. All she seemed able to do was cry. Our roles had shifted. It became my turn to wrap my arms around the woman who had given me life and attempt to ease the pain I had caused.

When my final boarding call was made, I pulled away, wiped a tear from her cheek and told her I had to go. I quickly hugged my brother and sister and told them one day we would see each other again.

Pulling my hood up over my head, I walked into the rain toward the plane and away from the life I had spent my childhood searching for. I did this without once looking back.

6

SITTING ALONE AT a local pub in North Melbourne, I was daydreaming, looking out the window while awaiting Deb's arrival. My relationship with the police officer had come a long way from our rocky start over that police statement. My twenty-first birthday had just passed, and she wanted to 'shout' me a drink – apparently it was the Aussie way. She arrived minutes later and ordered me a vodka to go with her glass of red.

'Have you ever thought about charging your father?' Deb asked.

'I'm sorry?' I said, choking on the generous sip of vodka I had just taken.

'I was just curious if you'd ever considered charging your father.'

'I don't know,' I said. 'I honestly never gave it much thought.'

'You see, I was thinking: what if it were possible for me to take the police statement from you, and when we're finished we just send it off to the blokes in Canada.' She threw that word in for old times' sake. I forced a contrived laugh.

'Well, I don't see how it would even work. Is that even a possibility?'

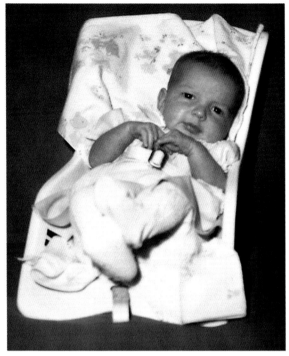

At the adoption agency on 8 December 1975.
This is the first photo ever taken of me and it has the
name my birth mother gave me handwritten on the back.

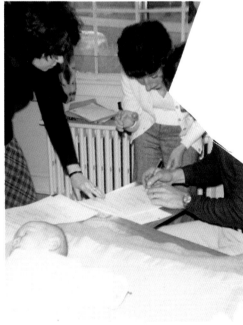

My parents signing the adoption papers. My mother cut my father out of all of our family
photos when I ran away at fifteen and she learned of the abuse I'd experienced.

I was a happy one-year-old.

With my mother at sixteen months old.

*I often climbed into Jillian's playpen to
be with her. I was three in this photo.*

Christmas 1979, when I was three.

Two photos of my fourth birthday, clearly not a particularly happy day –
note where my hands are placed in both shots.

Standing between a family friend and Jillian. I was six and Jillian was four.

With Mom in Florida after the divorce in 1983, when I was seven.

My mother at my cousin's wedding where Jillian and I were flower girls.

A collage of images that I made for Tami before I left for Australia. You can see that I started out as a happy child, but once the abuse started there was a significant shift in my demeanour.

In a distinctly '90s dress for my Grade 9 graduation. I was fifteen years old. A couple of weeks later my social worker, Sheila, had me placed in hospital.

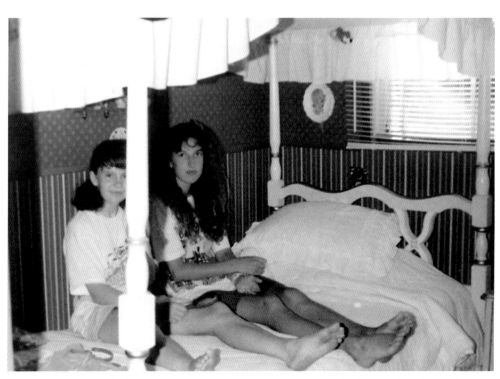

Sitting on my bed with Jillian just a few weeks after I was discharged from hospital, and shortly before we fled the east coast of Canada for Calgary.

In Calgary at sixteen on the high school basketball team. The only time when I felt truly happy during that period of my life was playing basketball.

At the airport meeting my birth mother, Patricia, and my siblings for the very first time.

I'd waited eighteen years to receive this hug from my birth mother.

Patricia on her thirty-sixth birthday
with my siblings April and Travis to her right.

With Mom at my high school graduation.

'Dunno. It wouldn't hurt to look into it though.'

I couldn't disagree with that. 'Okay,' I said, believing there was no way it would ever come to anything.

She raised her glass and I did the same.

Over the next few days, I began thinking more and more about charging my father. I wasn't naive enough to believe that justice would be swift and forthcoming, but there was a side of me that believed at some point everyone has to answer for the damage they've caused to the life of another. Perhaps the distance from Canada and my father would enable me to bring my dark past into the light. Then again, maybe by doing so I would jeopardise the peace I was slowly discovering in Australia and drown myself in a familiar hell. Only time would tell.

A few weeks after Paula left, I'd found a cheap place to live. I had moved in with the older brother of a girl I met playing basketball. Strange didn't begin to describe him, which wasn't altogether surprising given his sister didn't seem to be operating with a full deck either. At least I had my own space and didn't have to share a room with others as I had been doing in the hostels. My new flatmate preferred the company of men, which suited me just fine. Sticking with women looked pretty good to me. In fact, finding a vacancy in a convent where I could pretend sexuality had no relevance was of even more appeal.

One evening I was sitting in front of the television and trying to work out how Australians survived with only four stations. If I missed anything about Canada, it was the sports channel where I religiously followed the Chicago Bulls. With the season underway and me unable to follow my team, the withdrawals, at times, made me cranky. Basketball had saved me as a teenager. Though my recollection of much of my life is sketchy, I believe I can recall each and every basketball game I watched on television in which Michael Jordan played.

While I pondered over the oddness of my memory gaps, the phone rang. It was Deb.

'Oh, hey, Deb, how are you?'

'Wonderfully well, thank you,' she replied. This was her standard answer no matter what, regardless of her emotional state. Hearing it always made me smile. Then she said four fateful words. 'We can do it.'

'Do what?' I asked.

'The statement against your father.' Beating around the bush had never been Deb's style.

'Holy shit. When?'

'We can start Saturday morning.'

It was Thursday evening – two days before the day she was referring to – and suddenly the silence on both ends of the line became very uncomfortable. Attempting to form words in my brain and somehow drag them out of my mouth proved futile.

'You still want to go through with it, don't you, Carrie?'

'Yeah, just a little shocked right now.'

'Listen. Whether we go through with it or not is totally your call, but I reckon you have absolutely nothing to lose if you give it a go.'

Again, I couldn't really disagree with her.

'I'll swing past and pick you up Saturday morning on my way to work.'

'See you then,' I whispered. She had already hung up.

Sitting in the dark with the muted television casting its coloured glow against the walls, I wondered if the large rocks resting in the pit of my stomach would ever leave. Just before I panicked, I remembered the appointment I had booked at CASA House with Yvonne the following morning.

I could feel my anxiety building throughout the night. If I did decide to go through with making the statement against my father, I was going to need all the support I could get. Given I knew almost no one in Australia, my options were limited. I recalled the brilliant way in which Yvonne slowly drew me out with her sensitive yet direct questioning. I realised then she wasn't simply my only option, she was my best one.

The next day I sat in Yvonne's office, and memories began to swirl around in my head. As I struggled to find the easiest place to begin my disclosure, I felt Yvonne looking at me, and it made me consider whether her silence was deliberate in order to encourage me to open up. Whatever the case, her tactics worked.

'Yvonne, I need to tell you something.'

She looked at me calmly.

Just tell her, I told myself. It's not like hearing about abuse will be news to her. She's a sexual-assault counsellor for godsake.

'I'm going back to the police station tomorrow morning,' I blurted out.

'Okay, why's that?'

'To make another statement.'

'You are going to make another police statement? Tell me more.'

The walls of her office appeared to be moving. They shifted every time I inhaled, almost as though they were connected to my lungs. When I exhaled they blew back out. A million different scenes were going through my mind. All I needed to do was concentrate on the here and now and not get lost in the past.

'Breathe, Carrie,' I heard her say to me. 'Tell me what's happening.'

I looked down at my hands, convinced they no longer belonged to me. Resting in my lap, my clenched fists seemed like the hands of a stranger. I desperately searched around the room for anything that would help me make sense of the insanity that was resurfacing. Experience had shown me time and again that if I got too worked up, I wouldn't have a hope of keeping my mind away from the places nobody wished to know about. I frantically tried to gain control of the situation.

'It's just a memory,' I said under my breath. I fought for air and brought my knees up in the office chair as my body began to rock back and forth. With my face buried in my hands, I tried as best I could to stay present, hoping that the terror would pass. I wanted to run away, to escape the noise and imagery in my head, but there was nowhere to go.

Just as I thought I would reach the point of absolute madness, my mind grew still.

'Carrie, it's Yvonne. Can you tell me what you are seeing?'

'Yvonne, I'm scared. I just need my head to stop for a minute. I can't catch my breath.'

'It's okay, Carrie. Are you having a flashback?'

I had only enough time to nod before the madness swallowed me whole. A loud buzzing in my head grew closer. It sounded like a crowded theatre before a show starts. I knew I was only working with seconds. Trying my best to stay in control, I looked into the eyes of this kind stranger, tears rolling down my cheeks.

'What happened to me in Sydney had already happened to me when I was a little girl.'

By this point, the memories I had been trying to keep at bay since leaving Canada came rushing back with a vengeance. Images of my childhood flashed before me and

I was unable to stop them from resurfacing. The present moment had slipped away and, like so many times before, I was at the mercy of another flashback.

Playing back as vividly as a movie, a scene from my childhood transported me to another time and place. One minute I was twenty-one years old, sitting in Yvonne's office. The next, the windows behind her desk disappeared and the eucalyptus trees in the distance melted away. The sunshine spilling into the room vanished, and cold cement walls surrounded me. The carpet beneath my feet transformed to a concrete slab. I was nine years old and back in that old, dark basement, fighting for my life.

The air was bitterly cold. I struggled to keep myself calm. My terror was so vivid that I began gasping for air. There were men surrounding me in every direction. Slowly they began to close in. Grabbing me by the back of the neck, one of them dragged me over to an old tub in the middle of the room. Pulling me closer to the water, the smell of it made me sick to my stomach. I could see things floating in the dirty brown water. The tub was being used as a toilet. Seconds later, two men stood alongside the tub and urinated into the water. Struggling as hard as I could to get away, the man behind me became more forceful, pushing me down to the level of the putrid water.

'No, please,' I begged. 'Please don't make me go any closer.'

It wasn't until the man began to laugh that I realised it was my father.

'Come on, you little piece of shit,' he said. 'You're gonna fit right in here.'

Taking me by the back of the hair, he shoved my face into the tub.

Struggling to hold my breath, he eventually let me up, and all eyes were focused on me – and the disgusting mess that remained all over my hair and face. The sight made them all burst into laughter. The smell and the realisation of where my face had just been made me vomit. For this, I had to be punished.

My head was once again shoved under the water. An excruciating pain ripped through me. All I could do was try to hold my breath and not take in any of the dirty water.

Curled up in a small ball in the corner of the room, I remembered where I was and realised Yvonne was sitting on the floor beside me.

'I'm sorry,' I told her, my gaze never leaving the floor.

I knew I had just had a flashback because its hangover still lingered and my body continued to experience a deep ache. Devastated by shame and humiliation, I didn't know where to look. I was hit with a rush of anger. God, I hated myself in that moment. I got up and sank into the chair. Sensing her eyes on me, I feared meeting them and finding judgement there.

'Carrie, please,' Yvonne said. 'Drink this glass of water for me.'

Not knowing what else to do, I took the water with gratitude.

'You're back now,' she said. 'Are you okay?'

I nodded and stared off into the distance.

'How are you feeling?'

I shrugged my shoulders.

'Do you remember what happened?'

Glancing at my watch to see how much time had passed, I shook my head. I knew I'd had a flashback. I'd been in her office nearly two hours. Wanting to know what happened but too terrified to ask, I sat in silence.

'Carrie?'

I raised my eyebrows in acknowledgement but still didn't look up from the floor.

'Who did this to you?'

I felt the tears welling up. I raised my head until my eyes met Yvonne's. It was the first time I'd looked at her since sitting down in her office two hours before.

'Who did it?' I repeated. 'Who did it?' I heard myself laugh inappropriately. I was losing my mind.

'Carrie, you're okay. Do you need to take a break?'

'A break? Do I need a break? You mean like a breakdown?'

The concern on her face was mounting. 'Do you remember my question?'

'Yes, I believe I do.' The voice sounded nothing like my own.

I looked at her face and found calm in the warmth of her expression. I didn't know what was happening to me, but I got the impression that this woman had seen it all before.

'You asked who did this to me,' I stated again. 'It's kind of more complicated than that.'

'I'm listening.'

'I don't know where to begin,' I said, unable to catch my breath.

'So start from the beginning.'

I took myself back to that day on the swing at four years of age. It was my first memory of him hurting me. I decided it was safe to begin with his imaginable sins; the unspeakable I'd leave for another time.

I remember that day as an unusually hot summer's afternoon. My sister and I had been left at home with my father to play in the 'safe enclosures' of the fenced-in backyard. I'd always felt untouchable on that swing of mine. It seemed the higher I swung, the safer I felt. Climbing onto the swing, my mind began its journey. With the breeze rushing through my hair, I envisioned myself higher than the treetops. In midair I could look down upon the life I was leaving behind while soaring into the world of a child's imagination.

The sun was blazing in the summer sky. As I grew hot and tired of the swing, I wandered over to cool down with my sister in our little turtle pool. On the other side of the fence, several neighbourhood boys pulled up on their bikes and motioned for me to come out to them. I did. Once I was with them I remember being told to take off my swimsuit in order to play a game.

As it turned out, just as I had finished undressing and was standing before the boys, my father came around the corner pushing a wheelbarrow full of dirt. Upon seeing me naked, surrounded by four boys, he stopped dead in his tracks. The boys must have noticed him at the same time as I had because they were back on their bikes and out of there before I had time to reach down for my bathing suit.

Swearing loudly as he charged toward me, he snatched my bathing suit from the ground and held my arm in a death grip as he dragged me into the house.

Not one word was spoken between us. I struggled to keep up with his frantic pace as we sped through the kitchen and made our way toward the bathroom. Once there, my father let go of me so that he could fill the tub with water.

I could sense my father's rage, and with every silent passing moment, I grew more terrified.

Unable to look at me, he stared into the bath as it filled with water. His beet-red face showed signs of his high blood pressure.

'Get in the tub!' my father commanded.

His shrill words startled me and sent shivers through my entire body.

'Get in!' he screamed.

Almost as if by reflex, I jumped into the bath. However, the water was boiling hot, causing me to jump back out.

'It's too hot, Daddy,' I pleaded.

My father grabbed me and forced my body to go where my instincts would not allow it to. Upon hitting the scalding water, the shock was too much for me to endure and straight away I tried to stand up. His hands gripped my shoulders and held me down. The pain was excruciating, and yet I somehow managed to block out most of what was being done to me.

There was a lesson to be learned from him scrubbing me with a toothbrush in the places the soap wouldn't reach. However, the gesture that was meant to wash away my filth did nothing but cover me in shame. That was my first memory of the sexual abuse.

'Go to your room,' he muttered after he'd finished. It seemed to be the only thing my father could bring himself to say.

Wrapped in a towel, I walked gingerly to my bedroom. Once there, I changed into my pyjamas and crawled onto my bed, where I sat curled up in a ball, trying to rock away the pain. My mind was racing, but mostly I was terribly confused and desperately wanted my mother. But she was still very sick and regularly had to go away for treatment and to

CARRIE BAILEE

visit specialists. Looking out my bedroom window, I could see that my sister was still playing in the pool. I continued to stare at her through the fog my breath created on the glass. I understood nothing of the punishment I so seemingly deserved. As far as I knew the only crime I had committed was playing a game that was unfamiliar to me.

Not long after, I heard crying and swearing coming from the living room. It was my father. At first I dared not move for fear something more would happen to me. Before I knew what I was doing, I was halfway down the hallway and approaching a situation I did not quite know what to make of.

My father was slumped in the chair next to the front window. With each long, laboured breath that he took, I slowly crept one step closer. I followed the path made on the carpet from the sun spilling in through the window. It wasn't until I stood directly in front of my father's silhouette that I dared to open my mouth.

'Daddy,' I whispered. There was no response. His face remained hidden in his large and powerful hand, while the sun cast a halo around him. I was not old enough to appreciate the irony.

'Daddy?' I asked in another terrified whisper.

His display of emotion was like nothing I had ever seen before. I couldn't say with any degree of certainty what possessed me to do what I did next, but upon doing so, I had immediate regrets.

'Daddy, I'm sorry. Don't cry.' I crawled into his lap in an attempt to comfort him. I somehow felt responsible for his sorrow. Maybe by holding him, he would eventually begin to feel better. Maybe comfort was exactly what he needed. Lord knows I could've used some.

'Get off me, you stupid whore!' he shouted, pushing me

100

with enough force to throw me off his lap and onto the floor.

I didn't think it possible, but walking back to my room I felt worse than I had when leaving it. And although I didn't understand what I had done that was so wrong, I knew that it was. And for that, I felt deeply ashamed.

'This is the first time I can remember hating myself,' I said to Yvonne after my mind shifted back to the present.

'Carrie, what your father did to you was very wrong. He was bad, Carrie, not you.'

I exhaled deeply, somehow trying to relinquish old emotions. Years of shame welled up inside of me, crushing what little progress I had made thus far.

'What are you thinking?' Yvonne asked.

I looked over at her. 'I'm thinking my father would be the perfect mentor for serial killers.' Before she could answer, I quickly added, 'And believe me, Yvonne, what I just shared with you is only the beginning.'

She nodded in understanding. We both sat comfortably in the stillness until Yvonne finally spoke.

'You are angry, yes?'

'I am.' My breathing increased as I sat wringing my hands until the skin nearly peeled off.

'Are you able to get in touch with it?'

'Me?' I laughed. 'In touch with my anger? Um, no.'

'You have every right to feel angry, Carrie.'

'Thank you,' I replied, unable to mask the sarcasm.

I looked the other way and felt the blood rush to my face. I suppose the funny thing about rage for me was that it was an emotion I was too terrified to deal with. I stored so much of it inside myself that I feared even letting a small portion of it out could be catastrophic.

'Carrie, let me tell you something. Children are made to feel responsible for what is being done to them. This is the abuser's most powerful weapon. It prevents them from telling.'

I sat there while she told me all of the things I already believed when it came to other people. For some reason, I was finding it too difficult to relate the blatantly obvious to my experience. Yes, my father was an asshole. Yes, I carried shame for his actions. But when shame and guilt become a part of daily living, what then?

As if reading my mind, she said, 'Shame is a terrible thing, Carrie. Many children have been tricked, manipulated and threatened by their abuser. When someone is told something for long enough, especially a child by a parent, why would they not believe it?'

Again, I shrugged.

'You mentioned something about what you just told me being – how did you put it – only the beginning?'

I began to panic. I was an idiot. Why did I say that? I wanted so much to run. My anger prevailed and before I knew what I was doing, I found myself stupidly defending my right to feel shame.

'Okay, maybe what he did was wrong, and maybe I was scared and threatened, but all that aside, it's the details, Yvonne.' I began to cry. 'What makes me ashamed are the acts committed upon my body. It makes me sick to my fucking stomach and I don't know how in God's name I'm going to be able to make this disgusting statement to the police.'

And there it was. I had left a lifetime of trauma back in Canada, yet the shame was about as curable as diabetes. I would be afflicted for a lifetime.

'I mean,' I blurted out, 'if there isn't something wrong with me, then why the fuck does this shit keep happening?'

The rape in Sydney had validated my deepest fear. I really was worthless. If I wasn't, then why me? I couldn't make a statement against my father. Who the hell was I fooling?

'Carrie,' Yvonne said. 'You have every right to feel angry. But what you don't have a right to do is blame yourself.'

She had spoken my thoughts aloud.

'Carrie, there is nothing you can tell me that would shock me or make me think less of you.'

I stared in Yvonne's direction, clearly unconvinced.

'Carrie, listen to me,' Yvonne said. 'You know of the Holocaust, don't you?'

I nodded, annoyed at her question.

'Well, millions of innocent people experienced the most horrific atrocities. Can you blame them for what happened to them?'

'Of course not,' I snapped. 'It was absolutely disgusting what happened to them. And what's more disgusting is that millions of people stood by and allowed it to go on.'

'Of course,' she said. 'Well?'

'Well, what?'

'Well, can you not draw the parallels between innocent people being harmed by evil individuals?'

There was a great deal of passion in Yvonne's European features. I wondered if she was Jewish and if her family had experienced such atrocities in her homeland. My demeanour softening, I apologised for my anger.

She smiled. 'You do not have to apologise. Carrie, you have every right to feel angry.'

'I'm no Holocaust survivor, Yvonne.'

'No,' she said. 'But you have survived your father.'

My defences melted away. I sat in the chair for a very long time and lost myself in the rocking, rhythmic motion of my body.

'Yvonne,' I cried. 'My father was evil.'

'I know,' she said. 'But you're not.'

7

THE NEWPORT COMMUNITY Policing Squad, where Deb worked, became my second home in the months to come. Walking through its doors for the first time since my initial statement brought a rush of different emotions back. Still unsure I had made the right decision, I reluctantly sat down next to Deb and waited for her cue.

'You ready to get to work?' she said, her eyes searching my expression.

'We'll soon see,' I replied.

Deb explained that what we had to do was start at the beginning with the first abusive incident I could remember and end with the last time my father touched me.

'That's ten years of abuse,' I mumbled. 'Are we planning on writing an epic saga?'

And so we began.

Suddenly, I looked at my watch. I'd been there for over an hour, yet it seemed like only two minutes had passed. Deb seemed unaware of my blackout. She sat in front of the computer quickly typing everything I was saying.

Turning to face me, she said, 'Do you need me to repeat the question?'

'What question?' I asked.

'I asked you if you've ever been abused by anyone other than your father.'

Now what the fuck kind of question is that? I thought.

Searching for the words to answer, I panicked as a familiar feeling began to devour me.

'What age are we up to?' I managed to say.

'Nine.'

I stared at the floor as the room began its transformation. My eyes darted from side to side as I watched a million different images fill my vision. There was a tunnel. Dark and cold – and there I was. Standing at the top of a stairway.

'I don't wanna go down there,' I begged.

'Down where, Carrie?' Deb asked.

'No,' I said. 'I'm not going. You can't make me go.'

'Make you go where, Carrie? I'm not making you go anywhere.'

'No, please,' I screamed, sliding out of my chair and onto the floor. 'Don't you touch me. I'm sorry. Please don't hurt me.'

'Carrie?' a voice in the distance called to me. 'Carrie, what's happening? Please talk to me.'

A shadow began to push me down the steps, leaving me nowhere to run. Help me, please. I can't breathe. Pain was surging through my body. Everywhere I turned, large shadows lurked in the background. Voices yelled loudly as dark figures closed in around me. I tried screaming, until I remembered it was no use. It would only make matters worse.

'Carrie, please.'

That voice again. The room was dark, and I couldn't see what I was supposed to be looking for. I couldn't even remember what it was I had lost – and then her voice.

'Carrie, it's Deb. I can't help you if you don't talk to me.'

I wanted to respond, but I was mute with terror and blinded by the darkness that surrounded me. Too scared to make a noise, I continued the struggle. I knew that once I got to the twelfth step, it would be too late. Then my pants were being forcefully ripped down. I tried my hardest to keep them on. But being nine years old, the battle wasn't mine to win.

In a desperate attempt to save myself, I brought the heels of my palms up to my tightly closed eyes. As I rocked back and forth, I again became the silent witness to the nauseating acts down there in the basement. With nowhere to run and no one to save me, I tried to turn back toward the twelfth step. My body screamed in pain. Blood-curdling screams filled the air. Were they mine? I knew I couldn't lose myself in the basement's corner forever. They would soon remember me and when they did …

'Carrie?' the voice said. 'Carrie, come on. It's okay. You're with Deb.'

'Deb?' I cried, remembering who I needed to fight to get back to. 'Deb, please don't let this happen to me.'

'It's okay, Carrie. No one is going to hurt you.'

But the voices in my head screamed louder. Oh God, please don't make me go back there. The dark shadows fell over my huddled body. Large and powerful hands were gripping me, forcing me onto my hands and knees, and dragging me toward the middle of the room.

'No, please,' I screamed. 'I don't want to. NO! NO! NO! NO! NO!'

There's a breaking point in all of us when our pain threshold is crossed. Mine was shattered repeatedly in that basement. And for each time my mind had forgotten, my body violently jolted as it remembered. Deb was powerless to help me.

Another hour passed. Sweating profusely and shaking in the corner of Deb's office, I brought my knees up to my chest and slowly rocked away the pain.

'Carrie?' said the distant voice. 'Carrie, are you back with me? Can you feel my hand, Carrie? I'm just going to put my hand on your back.'

I moved as far away from the shadow as I could. But suddenly the scene changed, and another shadow was lurking behind me, pushing my back – forcing me down the stairs and off to places I didn't wish to revisit.

'Don't touch me!' I screamed. 'Don't hurt me. Please don't hurt me, Daddy.'

'Carrie, breathe,' the voice told me.

I looked up to see Deb kneeling on the floor in front of me.

'Carrie, can you hear me?' she asked.

I nodded cautiously, still confused as to whether I was back in the present or still lost in the past.

'Do you know where you are?'

I nodded again. My senses were finally returning to me. 'Are you okay?' I asked her, wiping tears from my face that I didn't remember crying.

'I'm fine,' she said. 'But are you okay? You smashed your head hard against the door a little while ago. I tried to stop it but you're strong when you want to be.'

Pain began to rush to all the places on my body that I'd inadvertently hurt while trying to get away from the images of my past.

'Can you tell me what just happened to you?' Deb asked.

I looked at her only to discover she was just a blur beyond the edge of my tears. Too ashamed to look her in the eye, I lost myself in the lines on my palms. I prepared myself as best I could for what I was about to disclose. It felt as though

I wasn't in control of my own movements. It was an internal struggle for me to summon the courage needed to speak of the unspeakable. Knowing there was no easy way around it, I used one simple sentence to sum up the most horrific time in my childhood.

'When I was nine years old,' I began, 'my father started selling me to other men.'

Deb just sat in front of the computer and said nothing for some time. I could feel her eyes upon me, but mine remained on the floor. I startled when she got out of her seat and made her way toward me. Placing her hand in mine, she squeezed it and guided me back to my seat. My legs were like lead. She sat and quickly patted the chair beside her. I somehow managed to slide onto it and finally our eyes met. The concern on Deb's face only heightened my already tattered nerves.

'The second your head drops,' she said, 'we stop this.'

I managed to offer her a nervous smile. She waited for me to speak. Looking into the distance, I could see the vastness of my past as I began to retell the trauma. The memories that flooded my consciousness were the very reason I left Canada. The sound of Deb's fingertips as they hit the keyboard was receding, but acted as a catalyst for the trance I could feel myself slipping into.

'The two longest walks of my life took place that first day,' I said. 'One was the stroll from my father's old blue car to the house. It couldn't have been more than twenty feet yet seemed to go on forever. The second was my descent of the creaky wooden stairs that led into the basement.

'That day in the basement and each one following, I always counted the stairs as I took them. There were twelve steps to the bottom of that basement and I will remember that walk for the rest of my life.'

Counting the stairs seemed to have a hypnotic effect on me, as if my mind was preparing itself for what was going to happen once I passed that twelfth step.

'At the bottom of the stairs, there were two closed doors. One leading right, the other left. On that particular day, we went right.'

Once again, in the retelling, the basement started to close in around me. The warm air blowing in from Deb's office window turned cold, and suddenly smelled stagnant. It was repugnant, reeking strongly of sweat and urine. The only sounds I heard were my breathing and a constant dripping of water into a hollow container. The concrete walls confined me.

'Polaroid photos of naked children covered the back of the door and once I discovered them, I was unable to turn away. Looking at those photographs and into the eyes of those children, I could see their tormented souls. I could sense their terror and feel their shame.'

Deb continued typing as I relived the events.

'I could only wonder what it was that had been done to them to take away the life in their eyes and replace their innocence with such worthlessness.'

'Did you actually see other children there, Carrie?' she asked.

'Yup.' I was starting to feel sick.

'Can you give me more detail, please?' she asked. 'For instance, could you tell me how many children, how old they were and what they were doing?'

My whole body shuddered involuntarily. The horrific details of that day came back with terrifying clarity. So much so that my body remembered the pain that was inflicted upon it by the men in the basement, while my mind took me back to the experience.

'Each of the children had a script they had to act out,' I whispered. 'All of us were told what to do. There were more men than children. Maybe four or five of us. We were roughly the same age. Some were bigger than me, some were smaller. I only remember one boy.'

'Were you being recorded, Carrie?'

Her voice was miles away from where my mind was headed. Vivid pictures flashed into my memory and suddenly I was transported back to a time and place I wanted so desperately to forget. I was slipping. I could feel myself slipping.

'Carrie, keep your head up.'

Feeling pressure under my chin, I began swatting at whatever was trying to force my head in the direction of light. I didn't want to see what was going on before me.

'"Fuck this up and I'll kill you," my father used to say,' I blurted out. 'Each time before I left his house with any of the men that would pick me up and take me God knows where, my father would lower himself to my level and hiss this into my ear.'

I started laughing and crying at the same time. 'Can you believe that? I don't know why Hallmark never hired him to write those warm and fuzzy verses in their encouragement cards.'

'Carrie, slow down. How about we take a break?' The worry on Deb's face was mounting.

'A break? I don't need a break, Deb. Do you need a break? Because if you need a break we should stop now before I let you know what those sick fucks did to us, with their big, clunky polaroid cameras and video recorders on tripods capturing everything from the corner of the room.'

I paused.

'You know, to this day, I refuse to have my photograph

taken with a polaroid camera. They would stand there and fan the images in their hands and wait for them to dry and then they'd gather around and watch as the picture appeared. My God, I can still smell it.

'They had books, Deb. Books and magazines that we actually had to study.' I found myself laughing. 'I mean, really, can you believe that shit? Where do these assholes find each other?'

Deb stayed quiet and stared at her screen. I took a few minutes to calm myself down. I always tried not to get angry. Probably because whenever I did, it struck with such force that I feared it would destroy me.

'Carrie, where was your sister when this was happening? Did she ever go to these places with you?'

'Never.' I surprised myself in a loud voice. 'She was never there.'

Protecting Jillian had become my full-time job, and I prided myself on my ability to shield her. Also, her strong personality and 'stand-up-for-herself' manner were no doubt deterrents.

'My sister was smarter than me, Deb,' I replied flatly. 'She was clever enough to lie and say she was too sick to go over there. Mom would always take her to the doctor because of her "stomach problems". They never found anything wrong with her.'

'Did he hurt you when she was there?'

'Of course. It's not like it never happened when she was there. He was just more careful about it.'

I found it difficult when Jillian wasn't there, but my emotions were a mixture of fear and relief. Fear because my father had free rein over me, but relief knowing she was safe and he wasn't able to use his threats of hurting her to manipulate me.

'Sometimes he would wake me up in the middle of the night and place me in someone's car. I suppose with my sister there, his window of opportunity grew smaller.'

'So what would that mean for you?' Deb asked.

I was growing more agitated, and my anxiety made it difficult to breathe. Deb waited for my response.

'That usually meant I didn't end up down in any basements. Just mostly the back seats of cars in empty parking lots. But sometimes there was a campervan. Whatever the case, I was always back in bed before she woke up.'

I must have been wringing my hands again because Deb's hands came down over mine. She separated my hands and held them in hers, as the tears streamed down my face.

'I think that's enough for today.'

After my disclosure to Deb, the increase in my flashbacks became a concern to both her and Yvonne. Deb felt well out of her depth dealing with both the severity of the abuse I'd endured and the toll my flashbacks were taking on all of us – mostly me. Given what I had recently revealed, and the embarrassing way in which my mind and body were reliving the events, Yvonne took one look at me and rang around the city until she found a safe place for me to spend some quiet time. Shortly thereafter, I was picked up and taken to a secure location. This would be the beginning of my life in a refuge. I was relieved to get away from the man I had been renting with in the previous weeks. The combination of his creepiness and my fragile state did not mix well.

There was a worker on each night at the refuge and several on during the day. I found it comforting, as my nightmares were becoming too intense for me to deal with on my own. Not that I wanted support when I woke, sometimes naked and curled up in the corner of the room. But at least I knew I couldn't sleepwalk too far outside in the same condition. The staff were nice to me – mostly they left me to go about my business and respected my wish to stay independent. Although as time wore on, it became more difficult to try to hang on to whatever scrap of dignity I had left.

As the weeks passed, my mental state grew worse and I was unable to leave the refuge. There were times when I would shake violently in the corner of the room after having lost a significant amount of time. On other occasions, I 'came to' in the middle of the night to discover a worker sitting on the floor with me. I looked around the room to find pillows all over the place. Although I'd quickly tell them that I was fine, my humiliation at what the workers must have witnessed became the driving force behind my seclusion. They didn't have to say a word. The horror in their eyes spoke volumes.

In between the nightmares and the flashbacks at the refuge, I continued with my police statement. Once a week, Deb would pick me up from the refuge on her way to work. On one of these mornings, the temperature was predicted to reach forty-two degrees Celsius. It was already thirty-three degrees by the time she collected me at nine o'clock.

The heat was baking through the passenger window and being absorbed into my already flushed skin. Even the air conditioning didn't seem to be helping much. Yvonne would be meeting us at the police station as Deb was no longer able to take my statement unless someone was in the room with us to support me. I was quiet for the duration of the trip, preparing myself for the hell I knew awaited me after I tore open old seeping wounds.

Deb went off into her office to prepare for the day while

I sat in the lobby and waited for Yvonne to arrive. My legs were bouncing up and down like Mexican jumping beans. They seemed to have taken on a life of their own. Directing all of my energy into presenting as normal as possible, I didn't notice Yvonne sit down beside me.

She leaned toward me to check in. 'How are you going?'

'I'm okay,' I said. 'Thanks for being here.'

Her face held so much concern. My shame caused me to look away.

We were told that Deb was held up by another case. I felt the knots in my stomach tighten. Staring down at these unfamiliar hands dancing around on my trampoline lap, I could feel Yvonne staring at me. Too scared to meet her eyes, I got up from my seat and went toward the window. There wasn't much of a view but at least standing up stopped my legs from shaking. Yvonne followed me to the window. My eyes never left the eucalyptus trees, blowing in the hot northern breeze.

'Carrie, tell me something,' she began. 'Is your father the only one you are running from in Canada?'

Her question shocked me. Unable to hide my discomfort, I didn't know what to do. Her question shook me to the core and made my mind flash back to the brutal encounter I'd had eight months before I left Canada. The room spun around me, and it felt as though I was being sucked into a black hole, transported to another existence.

'Carrie?' she said. 'What's happening?'

Panic struck, all I wanted to do was run. I was having a hard enough time coping with the shame of my father's abuse. I hadn't the words nor the inclination to ever revisit what happened to me as a teenager.

I don't remember walking into Deb's office to make the statement. Nor do I remember how I got into the back of the police car heading to the emergency department. My head was throbbing badly, and I tasted blood in my mouth. Reaching for my lip, I felt the warmth under my fingers. I watched, dazed, at the burgundy trickle running down my finger. I felt my mind drifting off again.

I had nothing to say to the two women in the car during the drive. The lady driving looked scary, and I didn't want to be her friend.

'Carrie,' she said. 'Keep your head up.'

It is up, I thought to myself. Why does she keep saying that? The lady sitting next to me had brown hair and seemed a lot nicer. Not as bossy anyway. I liked that. Bossy people were mean.

'Have you ever been to the hospital before, Carrie?'

It was the nice lady beside me. She had a funny accent. I shook my head.

'You hit your head pretty hard back at the police station,' she told me. 'We just want to make sure you haven't badly injured yourself.'

Pulling my knees up to my chest I turned to look out the window and didn't speak for the rest of the journey. The next time I spoke was in a small hospital cubicle. A lady in a white coat stood in front of me.

'I want to go home now,' I told her.

The doctor gave the two ladies from the car a worried look. I couldn't remember their names. I continued on pretending to be brave, but really I was scared and wanted my mom.

'Can you tell me your name?' the doctor asked.

She had a funny accent. What was it with all the accents? I nodded. I didn't feel like being the one person who sounded different from everyone else.

'What's your name?' she asked again.

I liked her. She was nice to me.

'Do you know where you are?' she asked.

Again, I nodded.

'Can you tell me?'

I looked at her and felt my eyes become really big. I then leaned forward and whispered, 'I'm in the hops–ital.' I never could say that word correctly.

'That's right,' she told me. 'Can you tell me your name yet?'

'It's Carrie.'

'And how old are you, Carrie?'

'Nine.' I liked how my legs felt hanging freely down from the high bed. I closed my eyes, moved my legs back and forth, and pretended I was on my swing.

'You're nine?' she said, looking over to the ladies.

Why were they so worried?

The bossy lady with the red hair whispered something to the doctor. The two of them left me behind the curtain with the other lady with the brown hair and the nice smile. I smiled back.

'Hello, Carrie,' she said. 'Do you know my name?'

I shook my head and looked back down at my feet dangling from the bed.

'My name is Yvonne,' she told me.

Her accent was different from the doctor's and the other lady's. I couldn't help myself. I had to ask. 'Why do you talk funny too, but different funny?'

She laughed. 'Funny, huh?'

I nodded as my face turned red.

'My accent is different from yours, yes?' she said.

'Uh-huh,' I replied. 'And different from the doctor lady and the mean one who drove us here.'

'Ah, that is because I am from Poland.' She smiled. 'You

sound different to the doctor as well, don't you?'

'Yeah, cos I'm from Canada.'

She looked at me for a while. Her face seemed worried. 'Carrie, do you know what year it is?'

'Uh-huh.'

'What year is it, Carrie?'

'It's 1985.'

'Ah, right, 1985. I see,' she said.

I didn't think she was very smart, because usually adults know the year we're in. Maybe you could forget the day of the week sometimes, but the year? I smiled at her because I figured she needed all the help she could get.

'Well, what if I told you it was actually 1996,' the lady said.

'I would say you were silly,' I replied.

The doctor came back into the cubicle. I could see through the gap in the curtain that the other lady was on the phone. The doctor took a little stick light out of her pocket and shone it into my eyes. She told me to stare at it and follow her finger with just my eyes. I did – but I didn't much like doing it.

I woke later to find myself in my bed at the refuge. I had no idea what day it was, let alone what time.

One of the workers stuck her head in. 'Hi, Carrie,' she said. 'How are you feeling?'

'Okay,' I said cautiously.

'You must be starving. Can I fix you something to eat?'

I told her no thanks and asked her how long I'd been sleeping. She told me probably only thirty minutes but said I had been curled up in the corner for hours.

'For hours?' I repeated. 'How many?'

'Thirteen.'

I didn't know what to say.

'Carrie, one more thing before I go. I've been told to ask you what year it is.'

She looked embarrassed asking me that but no more embarrassed than I felt answering.

'It's 1996.'

8

OVER THE COMING weeks, I continued trying to proceed with the epic drama of the police statement. Each attempt seemed less successful than the last. I had given myself a concussion, bitten through my bottom lip, bruised the hell out of my knees and shoulders, as well as increased the frequency of my blackouts. Yvonne was always there with me, but eventually Deb pulled the pin on the whole exercise, as there had been a few occasions where the three of us had spent the better part of a day in the hospital's emergency room.

At first, I begged Deb to give me another chance. We were so close to finishing. She said we'd just take a break and reassess at a later date. What could I do? She wasn't the flexible type. Deb had also informed me of a number of times where she was certain I had lost my mind. It wasn't as though I could disagree either, as I couldn't recall the instances to which she was referring.

From what I was told, I would become so traumatised by trying to describe the details that it was as if I would get stuck in the time I was speaking about. I needed to find the balance between providing Deb with enough information while distancing myself from what was being said, so I didn't get overwhelmed by the emotions attached to the memories.

Imagining myself at twenty-one and being told I presented as a child was terribly humiliating.

The mind is an amazing thing. My body may have been severely traumatised but, as a child, I somehow managed to remove myself from the incidents – no doubt to protect my mind from the trauma my body was forced to endure. I suppose it's the mind's brilliant way of keeping its sanity in an utterly insane situation. And it worked for a while. The only problem being, what my memory had forgotten of the trauma, my mind and body had no choice but to store. And over time, what I had managed to bury of my childhood began resurfacing in nightmares and flashbacks. They were so real that I would lose all touch with reality. So vivid, that it appeared as though I was reliving those episodes right then and there all over again.

I could never remember my past with much clarity, and I recalled nothing from the ages of nine to eleven. Those years simply did not exist. I would later learn that the flashbacks were like pieces of a puzzle my mind was rebuilding. I would only ever get snippets in the beginning, entering into a world of absolute darkness. It was only in time that the jigsaw began to fall into place, but as the pieces began fitting together, my life began falling apart.

Christmas and New Year came and went, not that I paid either of them much attention. Deb had invited me to spend Christmas with her family, but we still hadn't returned to the statement. As my life seemed to be getting back on track without the stress of having to recall and re-experience my past, I spent less time focusing on the fact I was failing to bring my father to justice and more time putting my energy into moving forward. It was now well and truly into 1997, and I only had seven months left on my visa. I had spent nearly three months living in various women's refuges. It was time for me to pack my things and try my luck back in the real world.

I spent close to two weeks searching through ads in the paper for shared rentals and hopping on Melbourne's trams to meet my prospective roommates. I had all but given up, convinced I'd met every perverted weirdo in the city, when I spotted a listing for a flat in North Melbourne – close to where Paula and I had first stayed. Getting this place would be ideal as it was near to the only things I had in Melbourne: Yvonne and basketball.

It was late on a Saturday evening, but feeling lucky, I picked up the phone and dialled.

'Hello?' answered a woman with a strong Aussie accent.

'Oh, hi. My name is Carrie and I'm enquiring about your ad in the paper.'

'Oh, sorry, I think I've found someone.'

I was unable to hide the disappointment in my voice. 'Well, it sucks to be me then, doesn't it?'

She laughed. 'Why didn't you ring earlier?'

I told her of a place I thought I had secured and how I found out I had been 'screwed over' by the guy at the last minute.

'Screwed over, huh?'

'Yep.' I sighed. 'You'd be surprised at the number of freak shows out there.'

'Tell me about it. Listen, why don't you come by tomorrow morning and we'll have a chat.'

'Really? Thank you so much. What was your name?'

'Deanne.'

The next morning I arrived on her doorstep. The rental was an old terrace house that seemed a prime candidate for demolition, but times were desperate and fussiness was a luxury I couldn't afford. Ringing the bell, I held my breath and hoped for the best.

It was a while before anyone came to the door, and when a woman did, she looked as though I had dragged her out of bed. I decided I'd better be funny if I was to win over this unhappy, hung-over household.

'Hi,' said the red-headed girl. 'You must be Carrie. Come on in. I'll go wake Dee.'

Walking through the lounge room, I stepped over a passed-out body. The redhead was hollering up the stairs to wake Deanne. I smiled to myself, as things were definitely not going the way I had imagined. A tall blonde eventually emerged and made her way down the stairs. She was laughing and apologising for the chaos I had walked in on.

'Sorry, Carrie,' she said. 'I was hoping to get up early and clean the place up. But we had a big night last night.'

'I can see that,' I said, carefully stepping through the minefield of mess to get to her.

'Tracey,' she said to the redhead. 'Why don't you show Carrie the nicest part of the house while I go find my pants.'

Tracey laughed. 'Follow me. I think she could only be referring to the back garden, because as you can see, there's not much good about this place.'

'Except the cheap rent and gorgeous flatmates,' Deanne yelled from the top of the stairs.

Tracey and I chatted in the garden while waiting for Deanne to join us. After several minutes, she came out and the conversation was off and running.

All of us got along incredibly well, as if we'd known each other for years.

'So a Canadian, huh?' Dee said.

'Unless you hate them,' I replied. 'Then I'm American.'

They laughed.

At some point, the girl who had been passed out in the lounge room poked her head out of an upstairs window and yelled, 'Hey, Dee, have you seen my other shoe?'

Deanne yelled back. 'Hey, Suzie, why don't you hang out a bit further and look down?'

'And why would I wanna do that?'

'Just do it and you'll see,' said Deanne.

'Oh, Deanne,' she said. 'That's disgusting.'

Deanne burst into fits of laughter.

Tracey yelled up, 'Why? What is it?'

'Deanne puked out of her window last night.'

'What colour is it?' I called up.

They all looked at me and roared with laughter. I was pretty sure they knew I would fit in perfectly. I was right. I moved in the following Friday.

Deanne was a journalist working for the Department of Education. We had a similar sense of humour; both known for our quick wit, our sarcastic barrages as well as a shared talent for shocking others with crude remarks. Deanne was great. I loved her genuine nature, and it wasn't long before she became my closest friend in Australia. She knew nothing of my past or the refuges I'd stayed at before moving in with her. I hated hiding things from her, but I was afraid she might not want me living there if she thought I was, well, crazy. Besides, living there with Deanne helped me feel normal again. Maybe even normal enough to function properly, find a job and get on with my life.

Six weeks after moving in with Dee, I received a phone call from Deb.

'Looks like we're going to trial,' she told me.

'Who is?' I asked.

'Nazi war criminals. Who do you think?' she said. 'The rape trial in Sydney, remember?'

'God,' I said. 'That was months ago.'

'Indeed. However, the solicitor in charge of your case seems to have had a change of heart. While he was reading through your file, he told me he believed that we did in fact have a case against the navy officer.' She stopped for a moment then continued. 'He asked me if you would be a credible witness. I assured him that you would, and now he wants to fly you up to see for himself.'

I couldn't believe it. She'd taken my statement back in October of the previous year. It was now mid-March, and I'd assumed nothing would ever come of it.

'So when will this be happening?' I asked, both nervous and excited.

'Monday,' she said.

'Far out. As in this Monday?'

'That's the one.'

'But it's Friday already,' I said under my breath.

Monday came, and I woke early as I had a plane to catch. Deb had offered to drive me to the airport and would arrive at any minute. Deanne was getting ready for work.

'You're up early, darl,' Dee said when she saw me. 'You got big plans today, do you?'

'You could say that,' I said.

Sensing my nerves, she stopped what she was doing. 'What's wrong?' she asked.

'I'm flying to Sydney this morning.'

'Sydney? What are you doing there?'

'Meeting up with a solicitor.'

'What on earth for?'

I took a deep breath. 'I am going to be a witness in a trial.'

'What did you witness?'

My heart seemed to be thumping out of my chest. I was certain she could see it beating.

'Carrie, what was the crime?'

Staring down at the ground, I feared losing everything if I told her the truth, but being the world's worst liar wasn't going to get me far either.

'It was a rape.'

'Oh my God,' she said. 'Who was raped?'

I could feel the tears burning steadily in the back of my eyes. 'I was.' I thought it best to go the matter-of-fact route. 'I've charged him and it looks like they're going ahead with it. My lift will be here any minute, Dee, and you have to get to work.'

Deanne's usual cheery expression was replaced by a sickening, pained look.

'Oh my God,' she repeated several times as she comforted me.

'I'm okay now, Dee,' I said. 'And it looks like I have the opportunity to get him.'

'Well, you'll be back tonight, won't you?'

'I will indeed.' I smiled.

She gave me a hug just as I heard Deb pull up in front of the house.

We drove to the airport in silence. It wasn't until we were walking toward my departure gate that Deb said, 'Now I told him you'd be terrific and that I have full confidence in your abilities. Don't let me down. I believe in you and I know you'll be fine.'

No pressure there, I thought. Perhaps I should have asked

to borrow her gun to play Russian roulette on the plane ride in order to calm my nerves.

When I was safely buckled into my cosy economy seat, I gazed out the window while trying to recall how Deb had described the man I would be searching for on my arrival at the airport in Sydney. I was so nervous. It was a short flight, which was both a good and a bad thing. An hour didn't give me much time to totally freak out. But it also didn't provide me with enough time to pull it together.

Once the plane landed and I was in the terminal, I searched for a tall, balding man with a sign stating his last name: *YOUNG*.

It took no more than a minute for me to find the poor guy. I could tell he felt silly having to hold some stupid sign up with his surname on it, and I smiled at the way he had the sign dangling at his side, nearly falling out of his hand. I was just glad I didn't have to carry one too. Once I spotted him, my nerves lessened. He had a kind face that actually reminded me of the balding DA from the hit TV series *Law and Order*.

'Hi,' I said, extending my hand. 'I'm Carrie.'

He smiled and offered his own. 'Hello, Carrie. David Young. I'm pleased to meet you.'

When we arrived at his firm, the two of us went over my statement and he began quizzing me about the night in question, putting my memory of events to the test.

He told me he was extremely impressed and had no doubts that I would make a credible witness on the stand. He did warn me that my past would probably come out, as Paula had told the accused about my father while she was assaulting him.

When we finished, he drove me back to the airport and thanked me for my help.

'Thank you for taking my case,' I said. 'I guess the next time I see you, you'll be in the snazzy robe with a full head of curly white hair.'

He laughed.

Deb met me at Melbourne airport. She said David had rung her to let her know how well I had done.

'I told him that I only dealt with star witnesses and to expect nothing less,' she said.

I laughed at her boldness. 'Deb?'

'What?'

'Well, if I'm such a star witness, don't you think I would have been able to finish the statement against my father?'

She glanced at me, saying absolutely nothing, and continued to drive me back home.

Just as we pulled up in front of Dee's place, Deb turned to me and said, 'Do you think you can finish it?'

I shrugged my shoulders. A huge part of me didn't ever want to go back there: to the past or to the police station. But then, there was another part of me that just wanted to push myself to the absolute limit and put that bastard and all of his fucked-up friends behind bars. The only way to get to them was through him. I had no idea who any of them were. My father was a coward, of this I was certain. He would not take the blame on his own. If he was to answer for the crimes he'd committed, he was the type who would take everyone else down with him. It was this character flaw that I would be relying on to ensure that they'd all be brought to justice.

'Does Deanne know anything about the statement?' Deb asked.

I shook my head and turned away. Once I was back with Deanne, I knew she would want a more detailed explanation.

I owed her that much at least. And I had reached a point where I needed to have a friend to confide in. Living with Dee had become my stability in those passing months. She'd provided me with the best fun I'd had in ages. We'd shared many laughs at the expense of many others. Times like those were invaluable.

After thanking Deb and saying goodbye, I went inside my house and looked around for Deanne. I walked through the kitchen and found her out in the laundry washing her clothes. We were the only ones home, so I knew that it was as good a time as any to have the chat I'd been putting off for weeks.

I stuck my head into the laundry. 'Hey, Dee.'

'Hello, darl,' she replied. 'How did you go?'

'Yeah, good. It looks like they'll be flying me back into the country for the trial. It's scheduled for some time at the end of this year.'

'That's great. Not that you have to go to trial, but you know what I mean.'

I nodded.

'Besides, now you get a free trip to Australia and you better bring *yer ass* back this way.'

Her butchered impression of my accent made me laugh. I watched her load her clothes into the washing machine and suddenly felt ill. My vision began to blur, and I reached blindly for the doorframe, trying to anchor myself.

'Carrie, you don't look so good. Come, let's go sit in the lounge.'

Grabbing my arm, she guided me through the kitchen and onto the couch.

'What's up?' she asked.

I didn't speak for some time, trying to calm down and allow the nausea to pass. It suddenly hit me that in order for me to attend the trial without staying in Australia illegally I would have to go back to Canada first. What about this beautiful life I'd created for myself? How was I expected to leave my freedom behind and once again go back to fearing for my safety?

'I need to tell you something,' I said to Dee.

'Okay,' she said. 'Talk.'

'When I left Canada, I never intended to go back.'

She waited for me to continue.

A shiver travelled up my spine. My hands began to quickly rub back and forth on the velvet of the couch on either side of me. I always did strange things I couldn't control when I was upset, and for some reason, it always involved my hands. I gave her the shortened version of my life – leaving out, of course, the really nasty details.

I ended by telling her about the statement I was doing with Deb. Managing to reveal to her how incredibly traumatic it was for me, I could not find the words to explain the toll it had taken.

When I finished, I smiled at her in an attempt to soften the anxiety on her face.

'You poor thing,' she said. She must have sensed there was more. 'So is there anything else?'

I wondered how I was going to explain my blackouts and flashbacks without her throwing me out or putting padlocks on my bedroom door. I managed to say, 'I have nightmares.'

'Well, that doesn't surprise me given everything you've been through.'

I knew how my flashbacks affected others and I didn't ever want her to witness me experiencing one. Deciding to do everything possible to control my bizarre mind, I left my disclosures to a bare minimum and hoped that I was able to keep things under control.

The months passed quickly as I continued to build my life in Melbourne. I managed to find a job working in a laundry at a hotel in the city. As mundane as the work was, my sense of freedom and newfound confidence soared, and I realised I had never felt more alive. I could feel happiness and peace becoming a fixture in my life. The only downside was that my visa was only good for a year and that time was nearly up. Because I was going to be flown back down to Australia as a witness in the Sydney rape trial, I couldn't exactly disappear into the outback, never to be seen again, appealing as it was.

A couple of months after I'd told Deanne about my nightmares, my housemates and I were staying in on a Friday night to watch *Top Gun* on the television. I had had a particularly tough session with Yvonne that day, so a night in was exactly what I needed. Halfway through the movie, a well-known panic began to build. I'm not sure what triggered it, but given the stress I had been under and the amount of time and energy I was spending 'facing fears' in an attempt to rebuild my life, the flashback was inevitable. In no time at all, I was fighting to catch my breath as scenes from my past invaded all of my senses. Before I was able to explain what was happening, I completely lost touch with where I was and who I was with. Deanne disappeared into nothingness as pictures of naked children filled my vision, and the concrete walls closed in around me.

On the cold cement floor lying beside the far wall was a filthy, blood-stained mattress. On that mattress lay an old frayed rope with knotted loops. I had never seen anything like it before in my life.

Preoccupied with my findings and the terror that grows when one's imagination has the opportunity to run wild, I didn't notice a man speaking to me.

'You're a deaf bitch, ain't cha?' he said and sneered. 'I told you to take off your clothes!'

My mind started to transport me a million miles away. The time had come for me to float to the safety of the room's corner. There wasn't a thing I could do to protect my body from the pain it was seconds away from receiving, but I had control over my mind, and by that point in my life, I had become a master of dissociation.

With his hand hot against my back, he began pushing me further into the freezing room. The rancid smell hanging in the air turned my stomach. I began furiously scanning my surroundings. I needed to find a window so I could focus on trees or grass or sky – anything familiar.

The man saw me staring at the rope. Slowly he bent over to pick it up. There were three simple loops in an otherwise normal rope. The first loop was much larger than the other two. He placed that one over my head, making adjustments so it fit loosely around my neck. From that loop there hung a single piece of rope, which fell down my back. Grabbing me by the wrists, he forced them together and slid them into the second loop. The third and final loop hung just below my knees. He was able to slip that loop around my ankles.

Once tied up, my movements then determined how easily I was able to breathe. Every time I struggled, the loop around my neck grew tighter, restricting the airflow. Trying not to move, I still had to fight for air. Grabbing hold of the ropes, the man dragged me onto the middle of the soiled mattress.

As I lay on my stomach with my face pushed into the mattress, all I could smell was urine. The man stood directly behind me. The only sound I heard was that of his zipper going down. I shook with terror and tried to prepare myself for the pain I was about to receive. As with the children I saw in the pictures on the back of the room's door, their terror and mine would be remembered for years to come.

With the rope restricting my movements, and my arms and legs bound behind me, I was unable to put up a fight. Struggling didn't make it less easy for him either. I had to remain motionless, find a way to breathe and concentrate on something beyond the excruciating pain being inflicted upon me.

A dog barked continuously the entire time I was in the basement. Loud and deep, it certainly didn't belong to the miniature poodle or Jack Russell family.

At one point, the man left and ran up the stairs. Unable to turn my head to see, my ears took over to compensate. I heard him walk across the floor above. The floorboards creaked with each of his steps. When I heard a screen door open, I wondered if he was leaving me to rot. As long as I never had to see him again, I didn't much care. I wanted to escape, but struggling to wriggle my way out of the ropes hurt so badly. I realised my efforts were futile. I wasn't going anywhere. And so I remained still.

It felt as if my insides were hanging out. Pain burned through to the pit of my stomach, leaving agonising stabbing flashes where he had damaged me. Like an electric current, the pain travelled down my legs to the soles of my feet. Surrendering to my fate, I realised it was easier to look down at my broken body from the safety of the corner of the room.

From the basement, I heard him re-enter through the screen door and listened as he came back down the twelve steps. A snarling German shepherd, bound by a muzzle and chain, suddenly jumped toward me as the man grew closer. He tied the dog up to the green metal post in the middle of the room, but I couldn't take my eyes off the vicious beast. Freeing me from the ropes, the man dragged me to my feet and walked me toward the dog. The terror I experienced each time the snarling beast lunged toward me minimised every horrific encounter I had had up until that moment.

For the first time in months I returned to Deb's office. Scheduled to go back to Canada in a couple of weeks, I knew this was the last chance I would get at trying to finish the statement. The most necessary years to document were the most painful to talk about. It seemed no matter what I did to prepare myself for the sessions, I could never share what was done to me without having horrific flashbacks and blackouts. Regardless of how anyone tried to reassure me, I was nine years old again and back in Canada.

For days, Deb listened to me recount the abuse I suffered at the hands of my adoptive father. The statement to date had documented everything leading up to age nine and only a few instances thereafter. One evening with Deanne beside me, I tried to fill in the gaps.

I told Deb about the previous flashback I'd had at Deanne's house. She typed furiously as I recounted the first time I was in the man's basement. I cried as I remembered the pain and the terror. Struggling to breathe, I sobbed as my body recalled the torture and immense pressure placed upon it. Deb continually tried to stop me from placing my fingers frantically around my wrists and neck. I was trying to remove the ropes I believed had come back to restrict me.

'Carrie, you're okay,' she would say. 'There's nothing around your neck.'

'I know that,' I said, but my hands moved up toward my

neck anyway.

Putting her hand on mine, Deb repeated, 'Carrie, calm down. There is nothing around your neck and you are fine. You are sitting here with Deanne and me and we're just having a chat, okay?'

Deanne's face radiated concern. Fighting for air, I removed my hands from Deb's and brought them back up to my collar. Tugging frantically at my shirt, I began to cry. 'I can't breathe.'

Deb told me to stand up and take a break, so Deanne and I walked out to the lobby and got a drink of water. It was after nine at night, and things were pretty quiet.

'How you doing, darl?' she asked.

'I don't think I can do this, Dee.'

She smiled and gave me a hug. 'If you don't finish it,' she said, 'then you don't finish it.'

Set on giving it one more go, I quickly drank my water and walked back to Deb's office.

'You ready?' she asked.

I nodded. My thoughts jumped in every direction, and my focus was as watered down as the alcohol in a cheap hotel bar.

I told her what had happened next when the man returned with the German shepherd.

'That's all I can remember about that day,' I told Deb when I'd finished.

'Is that the only experience you had with the German shepherd?' she asked, moving away from the keyboard.

I stared into the distance, remembering.

'Carrie?' she said.

'Sorry, could you repeat the question?'

'Did your father ever send you back to that basement?'

My mind was suddenly bombarded with flashing images.

I heard voices screaming and I didn't know which way to turn. As the present moment began to melt into the past, I gasped for air. I thought I was going to pass out.

'Carrie, calm down,' Deb said sternly. 'You're okay. Nobody is going to hurt you.'

'I know, but I think I'm going to be sick.' As I got up to walk toward the door, everything around me vanished. I dropped to the floor and darkness surrounded me. Yet again, I was at the mercy of a blackout.

I visited Yvonne one more time before heading back to Canada. I felt sad sitting in her office, wondering if this would be the last time we would see each other.

'You have done good work, Carrie. You are very brave,' she said.

'I don't think I can go back there, Yvonne.' Fighting emotion, I bit my lip and stared at the ceiling.

'Tell me what you are most looking forward to when you return to Canada.'

I thought for a second and smiled. 'Seeing Tami.'

'Tell me about Tami.'

'She saved my life,' I began. 'I was a fifteen-year-old runaway on the streets heading down the wrong path and she took me in and loved me through my heartache.'

'Tell me more about the time you ran away?'

It wasn't really something I spoke about but sitting there talking about Tami made me think about the not-so-great stuff too. I told her about my mom and how her confronting me that night in the bathroom about my father's abuse was the catalyst for me running away. Mostly, I realised in that moment I was running from myself.

'You must have felt such betrayal, Carrie.'

I nodded. 'Yes, but I didn't find out until later that my mom didn't actually mean she always knew and never did anything. She was told by a social worker I'd been seeing when I was fourteen. But Mom didn't have a chance to explain that. I locked her out of my bedroom and left the next morning.'

'Can you tell me what it was like for you in the shelter?' she asked.

I hadn't really thought much about it for years, but it was during that time I met the person who had a drastic impact on my life. Taking a deep breath, I went back six years in time and spoke about my life on the street, and my first encounter with Terrence.

One morning, Danielle, a seventeen-year-old prostitute staying at the shelter, decided to take me out with her for the day. Walking up one of the city's avenues in the bitter October cold, we both stopped in at a bar run by Danielle's pimp.

'Are we allowed in here?' I asked nervously.

Laughing at my naivety, Danielle replied, 'Yeah, girl. Don't even sweat it. You're with me now.'

Happy to be out of the cold, I followed Danielle into the dimly lit room. A stale smell of cigarette smoke was thick in the air and brought a sick feeling to the pit of my stomach. Three men were playing pool at the back of the bar, and as they turned their attention to us, I felt my blood run cold.

'Girl, you stay here. I'll be back in a minute,' Danielle whispered.

And with that, Danielle and one of the men who was staring at us disappeared into another room. Sitting down on one of the bar stools, I tried to blend in as best I could. Lost in thought, I was unaware of a man pulling up a stool beside me.

'Now, I know you don't come here often.'

Startled, I spun around to see who was speaking and if the person was even referring to me.

His name was Terrence, and he was a twenty-five-year-old black man from Trinidad. He smiled at me and offered his hand. I politely shook it as I didn't know what else to do.

'So tell me,' he asked as he leaned in, 'what brings a girl like you to a place like this?'

Blushing, I responded, 'Oh, well, this is actually my first time. I came here with my friend, only she left me to do God knows what with some guy out the back.'

'Yeah, I know Danielle,' he said. 'But what I don't know is why someone like you is hangin' with someone like her.'

I loved his Caribbean accent. He had an amazing ability to make me feel comfortable, and after chatting to him for a while I was just grateful his presence kept the other creeps away.

'Now tell me, girl, what kind of things do you like to do with your time?'

That gave me the perfect opportunity to talk about the one thing I could speak about with total confidence: basketball. I knew the ins and outs of that game and loved it more than anything. No matter if I was playing it, watching it or having a conversation about it, my excitement couldn't be contained.

After a long discussion involving every hotspot in the city to play ball, a dishevelled Danielle finally emerged from the other room. She saw me and turned to leave, gesturing with her finger for me to follow. Before I left, I thanked

Terrence for making me feel welcome. Taking my hand, he promised the next time we saw each other it would be on the basketball courts. I nodded and started to follow Danielle outside. Terrence chased after me and discreetly slipped his number into my hand.

'Anytime you feel like playin' hoops,' he said, 'just give me a call.'

So smooth but still not arrogant, and I found myself surprised I was into him. As I watched the tall, handsome man head back into the bar, I folded the piece of paper and placed it in my jeans pocket.

9

MY LAST NIGHT in Australia arrived, and Deanne and I arranged to meet at a pub with Deb and her husband, Nick – a computer programmer by day who occasionally moonlighted as a rock star. Nick would be putting his fantastic piano skills to work, playing with a band that had a Gary Glitter impersonator. It wasn't really my bag, but I knew it would be fun. Besides, I couldn't think of a better way to end my fabulous stay than among true friends who knew all of my secrets and loved me for and despite them.

The night ended at one in the morning. Once we finished our drinks, the goodbyes began. I walked beside Deb to her car. The time I had dreaded most was right in front of me: saying goodbye to the tough cop whose strength had inspired my own. I knew I was about to start crying, but I continued to fight hard to control my emotions.

Once we got to the car, Deb turned to me and said, 'Carrie, you should feel proud of yourself. Look at how far you've come in such a short time.'

Upon hearing this, my tears began to flow. 'I let you down, Deb.'

Grabbing my arms, she made me face her. 'Fuck off and listen to me.' She had such a lovely way with words. 'You did not let me down at all. Look at how you've turned out.'

'I wasn't able to complete the statement.'

'That's okay. I have sent it to the Canadian authorities already. You think they won't be able to work from the forty pages we've got?'

I looked up at her through my tears and smiled. 'Thank you for everything you've done for me in these past nine months. Your support has meant the world to me.'

'It's been a pleasure, Carrie. You're an amazing young woman.'

'I'm going to miss you,' I said, fighting back more tears.

'Oh, you'll see me before you know it.' She gave me a hug. 'And besides, we have a date in Sydney in a few months, remember?'

'Do you mean you're going to be there for the trial?' I couldn't contain my surprise.

'I wouldn't miss it for the world. Promise me something though. No matter what happens, I want you to continue with your writing.'

Throughout my travels, I had kept a journal documenting my adventures Down Under. I reserved sections of the diary to write about some of the more horrific experiences I was unable to voice, and I had allowed Deb to read them.

'Oh, and Carrie, one more thing. You best not forget about us when you have written that book of yours.'

I laughed and turned to head back home with Dee.

Going through passport control at Sydney airport was an incredibly emotional experience for me. I handed the official my documents and cringed as the loud metal stamp came down hard on my passport. I looked at the wet ink pressed on my passport. The departure date in bold black letters was stamped right next to my arrival date. The officer smiled as he handed back my passport.

'Just like that, huh?' I said, more to myself than to him.

'Just like that,' he replied. 'Have a nice flight home.'

Home? Why did it feel as though it was actually home I was leaving? As I took my window seat, my heart filled with sorrow and dread. I was leaving behind the first real life I had known. Closing my eyes in an attempt to gain composure, I saw the faces of those back in Melbourne who had started as friends and quickly grown to become family. If home is where the heart is, my heart had done most of its healing in Melbourne, and Australia definitely felt like home. The plane took off, and I stared out the window at the Sydney skyline until it was no longer in view.

For the first month I was back in Canada, I dreamed nearly every night of my father's imminent death. For as long as I could remember, I'd often lie in bed at night speculating as to whether the death penalty would apply to my father in the eyes of the law; wondering if I would ever live to see the day he was strapped into an electric chair and executed for the sins he'd committed against me. Disturbing, yes, but that thought had gotten me to sleep faster than counting sheep ever had. However, during that first month that idea seemed to have pervaded my subconscious, and what I was left with was the vivid reality of my father's demise.

My dreams revealed his electrocution down to the very last detail. I saw the uniformed guard standing by to hit the switch. I watched from behind the glass as the guard took a dripping wet sponge out of a wooden bucket and placed it on top of my father's head. Another guard positioned the metal helmet so it rested neatly on the sponge, and when the leather chinstrap was secure, the water slowly began dripping down my father's face. It was at that moment he slowly turned to me and mouthed the words: *forgive me.*

The clock directly behind my father read three minutes to midnight. Everything occurred in slow motion, and while the guards went systematically about organising his fate, I continued to stare into the eyes of my tormentor.

His peaceful face was nearly unrecognisable. And for the first time in my life, I witnessed a hint of compassion in my father's eyes, which sent a shiver running down my spine. The same cold blue eyes I'd looked into as a child for signs of mercy – only to discover later that mercy did not exist.

With just seconds remaining before the sentence was carried out, the guards would clear the room, leaving him alone in there. Pressing my forehead to the thick glass separating us, I surprised myself with the compassion I felt for the monster in front of me. Just as the switch was thrown and the lights grew dim, I mouthed back the words: *I forgive you.*

What I was unable to comprehend – and still find disturbingly baffling – was the way in which my subconscious birthed compassion for the one person who had not once shown mercy to anyone – least of all me. The last thing that man deserved was forgiveness.

I never did stay asleep long enough to see him fry in that chair, though I suppose that was for the best. To be honest, I don't know if I was more disappointed at missing out on his execution or at my ability to forgive him the unforgivable in my dream.

Back in Canada, I found the struggle to maintain my sanity grew harder with every passing day. When I initially returned, no one could believe the dramatic change in me.

Having left as a scared, insecure teenager, I had come back as a confident, assertive young woman. Tami was blown away by the turnaround. She, more than anyone, knew of my prior struggles. I made the decision to live with her while I waited for the prosecution to request my return to Sydney.

As the days turned to weeks, I began to slip back into a familiar hell. Sadly, the freedom and inner calm I'd been carrying since my return was diminishing by the hour. Once again, I found myself looking over my shoulder whenever I went out, jumping every time the phone rang and terrified of becoming a victim. I had hoped that living with Tami would help me feel safe.

Over dinner one evening when I was pushing my food around the plate, Tami started the conversation I had been dreading.

'Has Terrence tried to contact you, Carrie?' she asked.

I shook my head and closed my eyes, attempting to block out the memories. But my mind immediately focused on the very last encounter I'd had with Terrence – eight months before I'd left Canada for Australia. The room started to spin, and I could feel myself drifting off to another place. Tami and I had never really spoken about what had happened. I cringed remembering what the sight of my brutalised body had done to her.

Tami had always suspected that Terrence was bad news right from the very beginning. It was in her kitchen six years earlier that she'd first grilled me for information about him. By that stage I had been living with her for about six months.

144

'So who's Terrence?' Tami asked and tried to smile.

'Oh, he's just a guy I met when I was staying at the shelter.'

The smile she had painted on her face disappeared. Worry took its place.

'How old is he, Carrie?'

My new friendship with Terrence was one of the few things I could recall from that particular time in my life. He was the only person who seemed truly concerned for my welfare, though I know now that the search for mentors is less successful when done on the streets. I was sure he was not the kind of person Tami assumed he was.

'He's twenty-one,' I lied. 'But before you say anything, Tam, just hear me out. He treats me so well and he understands me better than any other guy I have ever known before.'

Not that I knew many, but this line seemed to fit nicely with my persuasive argument. I could feel my shame growing, though I was uncertain why. The guilt of not telling her about him sooner began to consume me. We sat down at the kitchen table and I told her every detail to prove to her that he was nowhere near the monster she suspected him to be. How he played basketball and how we had a lot in common. Her face held a mixture of worry, disappointment and sadness. Worry, I suppose for who she feared this man to be. Perhaps her disappointment was in me for not telling her of the relationship sooner. I can only assume the sadness was for my naivety. Somehow, despite my childhood, I had remained oblivious to the dangers in the world.

After listening to my account of all of Terrence's good qualities, Tami said, 'Has he made you have sex with him yet?'

The question shocked me completely, but I realised I could finally convince Tami she was wrong about my friend.

'No, Tam, I swear. He has never even brought the subject up.' And that was the truth. He had asked me if I'd ever had sex before, but I didn't mention that, as it seemed more a passing comment than anything else.

'Carrie, promise me you'll be careful.' She reached for my hand and held it in her own. I looked into her eyes and nodded. The worry on her face troubled me. I loved her so much and the last thing I wanted to do was cause her unnecessary grief. I again felt compelled to assure her that she couldn't be more wrong about this guy. No matter what I said, though, her anxiety could not be hidden.

I met up with Terrence many more times after that conversation with Tami. The more time I spent with him, the more convinced I became that he was the last person in the world I needed to be scared of.

After school one day, Terrence was waiting for me outside. He asked me to go to his house with him. My initial reaction was to say no because I wasn't ready for whatever it was that he might want me to do. But back then, I found that 'saying no' wasn't one of my greatest strengths. My self-esteem around that time was probably the lowest it had ever been. The shame of my past, in combination with recently turning the awkward age of sixteen, explained my inability to speak up. My self-loathing only added to that. Consequently, I went to his place that afternoon.

Sitting in his room, he told me, 'Baby, you are so beautiful. All I want for you is to realise how special you are.'

I thought of all the time spent with my father when I had longed for him to say I was special and lovable. Terrence's words brought up mixed emotions: I was happy knowing somebody cared enough to tell me I was beautiful, but I felt guilt for wishing my father felt the same way despite everything he had put me through.

'Baby, I want you to undress for me,' Terrence said, holding me in his arms.

'No. I don't think I'm ready to have sex.'

He laughed kindly at my outburst. 'Who said anything about sex? I just wanna see that beautiful body of yours.'

The thought of anyone seeing me naked brought back horrible memories of the times my father would laugh at my small frame. I shook my head furiously.

'Come on, baby, you're beautiful. You got nothing to be ashamed of, girl. I just wanna look at you.'

I stood up and walked toward the corner of the room. My ears were ringing and all I wanted to do was scream. He followed me and, wrapping his arms around me, he told me that it would be okay. I didn't know why, but every time he held me, I felt safe. He was so much bigger than I was, and I felt protected.

Not wanting to offend him, I eventually did take off my clothes. My mind was almost able to feel removed from the situation and, in a way, it felt as if the experience was happening to someone else.

I stood in front of him in nothing but my bra and underwear. He looked at me and smiled.

'Damn, baby, look at that bad-ass six pack of yours.' He came toward me, rubbing his hand down the muscles on my stomach. As he began to unhook my bra, I stood there with my eyes squeezed shut. I wanted so badly to tell him to stop – that I wanted to go home. But at the same time, there was a part of me that just wanted to please him.

As I stood there in that alien moment – more tender than any I had experienced with a man – I felt as if I were being loved in the way a woman was meant to be loved. I knew if I had told him no, not only would I be rejecting him, but his love as well.

Not wanting to disappoint, I let him remove my bra. My entire body trembled with fear. As I drifted to a safer place inside my head, he touched my breast.

'Who did this to you?' He was referring to the scar my father had left with the curling iron. At that time in my life, no one had seen it before. Ashamed, I stood there, head down.

He lifted my chin and brought my watery eyes up to meet his. He then knelt down and softly kissed the hideous scar. Overwhelmed by what he had just done, I covered my face and began to cry. Placing a finger over my lips, he stood up and kissed my forehead. Never before had I been treated with such kindness when naked. It was the most vulnerable I had allowed myself to be. He promised me that not one horrible thing would ever happen to me again – at least not while he was around – and I believed him. I left Terrence's house that night with a little of the dignity my father had stolen from me during all of those years of my childhood. I felt, for the first time in my life, as if I were possibly falling in love.

While Tami and I were washing up after dinner one night, the phone rang. Yet again, it was the detectives from the east coast who were investigating the incomplete statement against my father that Deb had sent them. Since I had been back from Australia, the Canadian authorities had been calling me weekly and pressuring me to talk to them. They needed to interview me themselves and wanted to fly me back to my old home town. Back to my father's domain. That night, Tami passed me the phone reluctantly, unable to mask her concern.

'We really want to get your father,' the detective said. 'Carrie, we can't put him away without you.'

'I know that. But I've got a trial I'm being flown back

to Australia for. My stress levels couldn't be any higher, and the last thing I need right now is my father coming after me. I just can't handle anything else at the moment. I'm sorry.'

'We can protect you.'

I stayed on the line but was silent.

'What if he's still abusing children?' the detective continued. 'Do you feel comfortable sitting there and doing nothing while other little girls are being hurt?'

'Of course I don't.' I began to cry, cracking under the pressure. 'Please, just let me get through the rape trial and I promise I will ring you after that.'

Not at all pleased, the detective demanded I contact him as soon as I returned from Sydney. He told me that the case was on hold until I would agree to be interviewed.

After I hung up the phone, Tami came over to sit beside the inconsolable heap I had become on the floor. I sobbed in her arms.

'I can't take this anymore, Tami.'

She stroked my hair and rocked me back and forth. 'Baby, you just focus all of your energy on getting through each day. Don't worry about other people and the pressures they are putting on you. You just look after yourself and stay safe so that you can get on that plane when the time comes.'

'I can't handle any more stress, Tam. It's bad enough I'm scared of running into dangerous people here, but now I'm terrified my father will have me killed for telling.'

Tami held me in her arms and carried on reassuring me.

Three months after returning to Canada, the phone call I had been waiting for finally came. I was at my mother's house.

'Hello, Carrie?' It was a male voice with an Australian accent. 'It's David Young here. How are you going?'

'I'm okay,' I managed to say. 'Please tell me this is still happening.'

He laughed. 'Yes, it's certainly still going ahead. Trial is set for Monday the eighth of December.'

'That's three weeks away.' I was more thrilled to be getting out of the country than I was concerned about what awaited me when I did.

'So when am I flying out?'

'Well, I assumed you would want a few days to recover from the journey,' he said. 'I've made a tentative booking that has you arriving on the fourth of December, giving you four days to adjust to the time difference. Does that suit you?'

Did that suit me? God, I couldn't wait to leave. I was having such severe flashbacks that I hadn't really left the house in over two weeks. I was so desperate to return to Australia that I was willing to float over in a beer cooler.

'That sounds great,' I confirmed.

Moments after hanging up the phone, my whole body shook violently. I was not surprised given the range of different emotions I was experiencing. Although I was terrified about the court appearance I would have to make, I knew it was my only chance at freedom. In these few months back in Canada, my mental health was worse than ever. I was blacking out almost daily, and as scary as that might sound, I almost welcomed it as a break from my hellish reality. The blackouts broke up the terror of my days. I wasn't sure how I was going to achieve it, but I knew with absolute certainty that once I landed in Australia, I would never be returning to Canada to live.

10

IN EARLY DECEMBER 1997, I stood at Calgary airport in the same spot I'd stood fifteen months before, when I'd left for Australia that first time. The people I had with me were the same three. The most obvious difference this time was the hope they all shared. It replaced the fear that had been on their faces before the previous trip. My rapid deterioration since coming back had shown all those who loved me that remaining in Canada would likely be the end of me. If I were to find peace and happiness in my life, it would not be in my native country. I told them I would not be returning.

Mom came toward me, her hands resting on my shoulders. 'I only ever wanted you to be happy, Carrie,' she told me.

'I know that, Mom. And I will be.'

'You do whatever it takes to get that peace back, you hear me?'

'I will. Mom, are you okay?'

'I'm fine, sweetie. You just do what you need to do.'

'It's my time now, Mom,' I said, tears running down my cheeks.

'I know it is, baby. And you will find what you are looking

for. Good things come to those who wait, remember?' She kissed me on the forehead, and I fell into her arms.

As I approached my sister, I smiled at the predictable state she had worked herself into.

'Girl, you gotta do something about these airport breakdowns,' I told her as I held her in my arms.

'I'm going to miss you, Carrie.' That was all she was able to say before grief overwhelmed her.

'You'll see me again. Only when you do, we'll be on a beach a million miles from here.'

Handing her over to my mom, I turned to Tami, who had taken a step back while I said goodbye to my family. Walking toward her, I noticed she had been crying. Placing my hands on her cheeks, I gently brushed away her tears as my own spilled down my face.

'I need to do this, Tami.'

'I know you do. You look after yourself, my Carrie-kid.'

She reached into her bag, pulled out a thick yellow envelope and passed it to me. 'Now each card inside is dated as to when you can open it. There is one for the plane ride to Sydney, one for your arrival, and the others are for before, during and after the days of your trial.'

Taking the package, I thanked her for her support. She held me in her arms and told me how much she wished she could be there. I cried, wishing the same thing myself.

As I headed through the departure gate, I took one last look back at the life I was leaving behind me forever. I choked up seeing the image of my mom comforting Jillian, and of Tami comforting my mom. The time had come to put the past behind me. Canada was a place I would never again call home.

I had been flying for several hours when I remembered the package Tami had given me. I reached into my carry-on bag and fished out the yellow envelope. Searching through the cards, I found the one marked 'for the plane'. There was a scribbled drawing of two girls on the envelope. One of them was wild with crazy curly hair and much skinnier than the other. Her depiction of me made me laugh.

I opened the note and read.

> My sweet Carrie-kid,
>
> I love you so much and my only wish for you is that you find peace and happiness. Life is a strange thing, baby girl, and sometimes in order to improve a situation, we must walk the hard path to come out the other side of it. I love you like you are my own, and only want what's best for you.
>
> Take care, sweet girl. Love, Tami.
>
> PS Don't cheat and open the other cards. My spies are everywhere. Mwah ha ha!

Placing the card back in my bag, I rested my head against the window, and eventually drifted off to sleep.

I awoke with a sharp pain in my ears due to the change in cabin pressure as the plane began its descent. I had never liked this part of any trip. As the Sydney skyline came into view, I prepared for the initial struggles I was going to face in court, as well as the opportunity to find my freedom again in Melbourne. Whatever the verdict would be, I just wanted to get through the trial and move on with my life.

I suppose what calmed me more than anything was knowing that I would eventually meet up with the others who were flying to Sydney for the trial. Paula was coming in from Canada as a witness for my side, and Deb would be making her way up from Melbourne to act as my support. I couldn't wait to see her again, because I knew her tough love would pull me through.

I stood patiently in line at Sydney customs, staring down at my passport and birth certificate and thinking these were the last two legal documents tying me to Canada. Once I cleared customs, I thought to myself, what was stopping me from ditching them?

Deep in thought, I was oblivious to the cranky passport official motioning me to come through. I rushed forward, smiled apologetically and handed him my documents.

'How long is your intended stay, miss?'

I didn't respond.

'Miss?' His insistence snapped me back to reality.

'Sorry?'

'Your intended stay,' the officer repeated. 'How long will you be in Australia?'

I was terrible at last-minute lies, certain that 'forever' wasn't the response he was expecting.

'Just a month,' I said, avoiding eye contact.

When the metal stamp crashed down on my passport, I remembered the desperation I had felt leaving Sydney three months prior. And now there I was on the other side, coming back in.

He handed back my passport. 'Have a nice stay.'

'Thank you, I will.'

Unlike my first trip from Canada to Australia, this time I had someone there to meet me at the airport. David Young had told me that a police officer would be waiting for me somewhere around the baggage area. After retrieving my bag I spotted a man staring in my direction.

Walking toward him, I hoped I had guessed right.

'Carrie?' he asked.

I was relieved that I had picked correctly and not accosted some stranger. He was one of the officers who had investigated the offence in Sydney. I shuddered as I realised that in only a few days I would be facing the man who had raped me fourteen months earlier.

Paula's flight came in early the following morning. Deb wouldn't get to Sydney until the day before the trial. Sitting in the hotel lobby, my stomach churned as I anticipated my reunion with Paula. I hadn't spoken to her since she'd left Melbourne and had no idea how she felt about coming all the way back for such a short trip. I sat and half-heartedly people-watched, but Paula somehow slipped under my radar. Suddenly she was before me and smiling at the look of surprise on my face.

'Betcha never thought I'd be the one getting you a free trip to Sydney, did ya?' I said, in my Canadian twang.

She laughed and came closer to give me a hug. I could feel myself breathe a huge sigh of relief.

'You holding up alright?' she asked.

I shrugged and asked if she wanted to take a walk.

'Like the good ol' days?' she said.

'Yeah, girl. Something like that. Hey, was it hard for you to get the time off work?'

'No, it's all good.' She smiled. 'I got me an all-expenses-paid holiday.'

We walked outside for a while without saying a word. My emotions began to get the better of me. Seeing Paula again brought back memories. When the reality of what we were there to accomplish finally hit me, it was my nervous voice that broke the silence.

'I hope this doesn't turn out to be one of those nightmare rape trials like in the movies. You know. Like that movie Jodie Foster starred in?

'*The Accused.*'

'Exactly! I haven't actually seen it but I heard about the court scene where the defence lawyer is a complete pig of a man and the victim practically gets raped a second time on the witness stand.'

'Have you spoken with your lawyer yet? Has he prepped you or done any run-through?'

'I think he's sending a car over this afternoon so he can meet with both of us,' I said.

Paula acknowledged my reply with a silent nod, and we turned around to walk back toward the hotel.

Deb arrived at the hotel lobby late the following day. At first I was taken aback by her aloofness. She offered me a cold and brief hello, then headed off with the same detective who had picked me up from the airport days earlier. I cringed, remembering how intimidating she could be. After sorting out whatever business she had with the Sydney cop, she came back over.

'Are you ready for the big day?' she said in her matter-of-fact way.

'Are you ever ready for these things?'

'You will be,' she said, tapping me on the shoulder and walking back toward the check-in desk.

The morning of the trial arrived, and I was having serious doubts as to whether I would be able to testify. I was completely unnerved by the thought of all the people in the jury box looking my way, and the way the defence lawyer would try to discredit me. I knew I had to be strong and do whatever it took to get through the tough three days ahead. I began my preparation by reaching under my pillow and pulling out one of Tami's cards. After I finished reading her inspirational words, there was a knock at my door. Slipping

Tami's card back under my pillow, I got up to see who it was.

'You ready?' Deb asked when I opened the door.

'I feel like throwing up.'

She came into my room and straightened the collar of the shirt she had ironed for me the night before. 'You will be fine,' she said. 'You just get up there and tell the truth; that is all that is expected of you.'

I breathed deeply trying to calm myself. I didn't want to hyperventilate. 'I'm worried about the cross-examination, Deb. What happens when the stuff with my father comes out?'

Deb took me over to the bed and motioned for me to sit. I reluctantly did.

'Carrie,' she said, as she dragged over a heavy chair from the corner of the room. She placed it in front of me and took a seat. Her face had softened, although her rigid posture prepared me for the pep talk. 'You will do this. You have no choice but to do this, and you are strong enough to handle whatever comes your way.'

'And what if I can't do this?'

'You can,' she snapped. 'I believe in you and I know you wouldn't want to let me down.'

I could only nod. There was no room to feel sorry for myself when she was around. I walked to the elevators, grateful to have Deb but wishing Tami was there instead.

At the courthouse, Paula and I spotted her friends who we'd stayed with in Sydney during our stopover on the way to Melbourne that fateful night. They looked over at us, giving a brief nod of recognition. It felt hollow and cold and seemed sides were already taken. I felt ill again.

We walked into the hearing, and before I took my seat next to my two lawyers, Deb stopped me and said, 'Remember, I believe in you.'

Feeling slightly better, I walked to the table, not once looking toward the defence team. The last person I wanted to acknowledge was the defendant. Standing next to David, my legs locked and I was unable to bend my knees and sit. I fleetingly entertained the idea of getting the hell out of there, running hard and fast and never looking back. But I did look back, as David had pulled my chair out and was motioning for me to sit down. I wondered if he read minds or had actually had other clients before me flee?

I don't know where my mind drifted when the proceedings began, but eventually the better part of the morning had passed and a recess was called. Still feeling unwell, I sat off to the side and tried to prepare myself to take the stand. David came over with a glass of water and told me that Paula would be called first.

I had to wait outside the courtroom while she was examined by my lawyers and then cross-examined by the defence. Deb waited outside with me, but neither of us was much in the mood for small talk.

Some time passed before the doors reopened. Deb and I stood at the same time as my lawyers approached. The judge had adjourned the session for a lunchbreak, and my party decided to meet at a local cafe and discuss how the trial was going so far. I learned over lunch that Paula had stood her ground under tough cross-examination. The defendant's lawyer tried to destroy Paula's credibility by bringing up the amount of alcohol she had consumed prior to 'brutally attacking' his client. As much as they tried to shake her, my very tough friend stayed strong.

'So overall how's it going?' someone in the group asked.

'It's hard to say right now,' David answered. 'We'll have to wait and see what happens when you are called to testify, Carrie.'

Everyone turned to look at me and due to the fact I had spent most of lunch holding my breath, I felt as though I was about to pass out.

Deb leaned toward me and said, 'Don't worry, you'll be fine. Just tell the truth and that's all you can do. And remember, I believe in you.'

It wasn't long before the break was over, and we had to go back to the courthouse.

Approaching my seat, I again entertained the thought of fleeing. Ignoring the urge, I took my place in the courtroom.

As soon as my name was called to approach the witness stand, I mumbled under my breath, 'Well, it's too late now to roll on out, isn't it?'

I managed another of my habitual deep breaths as I walked to the stand. After swearing to tell the truth, the whole truth and nothing but the truth, my attorney asked me to recount the events of the evening in question. I remember describing every detail as best as I could while waiting for the hell I expected to face when the defence lawyer went for my exposed jugular.

'So tell me,' the defence lawyer began. 'When you went down to the bottom of the ship with my client, what did you expect to happen?'

'All I wanted was to get my bag. That's all,' I answered.

'So you had not been flirting with my client throughout the evening?' He directed his look to the jurors.

'No,' I said, completely disgusted. The guy was probably twenty-five years older than me. The last thing I had been was interested.

'Why did you wear a skirt on the day?'

I couldn't believe he was taking it there. This cross-examination was playing out just like in the movies. After pulling myself together I managed to reply, 'It was hot outside and I thought I would be coolest in a skirt.'

'Are you a man-hater, Ms Bailee?'

I thought carefully before answering. 'I'm not a man-hater, but if you are wondering if I pursue them, then the answer is no.'

'And why is that?'

I knew where this was headed, but I felt trapped and unsure. He was trying to portray me as an abused basket case and I was not about to let that happen.

'I suppose because I don't trust men, that's why,' I said, biting my bottom lip and preparing for the barrage.

'Is there any reason you would hate men?'

Before I even had a chance to think of a response, he began bombarding me with questions related to my past.

'Well,' he said, his tone dripping with cynicism, 'I have your statement here in front of me and you said, and I quote, "For a lot of reasons, I hate men." Can you tell me what that means, Ms Bailee?'

'You know what it means,' I said. My skin was crawling as he continued his line of questioning.

'Yes, I do,' he said. 'Isn't it true that you've had a very traumatic childhood?'

I wanted to slap the smirk off his face. I could feel a lump forming in my throat, but there was no way I was going to let that sleazy defence lawyer break me.

'I believe it was your father, was it not?' he asked, almost flippantly.

'Yes. But I still don't see what that has to do with what your client did to me last year.' My cynicism began to match his.

He quickly jumped to my behaviour after the 'alleged' rape occurred.

'Now it has been stated by your own friend that you

began acting rather strangely when you went back to get her. Similar to how she had seen you act before.'

I knew the jurors were lost, and I also knew he would bring up my flashbacks and nightmares to cast doubt on my credibility.

'I suppose the way I was acting when Paula saw me afterward was because of the traumatic experience your client inflicted upon me,' I explained. 'She may have seen me distressed at another time when I was recalling past abuse.'

'Yes,' he exclaimed. 'Flashbacks, I believe they are called, are they not?'

I said yes. He went on to question whether or not I was just confused, recalling past events and mixing up my father's abuse with what had happened to me on that night. My lawyer objected to the line of questioning. I can't remember what the ruling was.

It continued to go from bad to worse as he tried to make me speak about my father and what he had done to me as a child. My lawyer objected again as to the relevance, and the defence was forced to move on.

'Ms Bailee, what did you think would happen if you went below deck into a private area with a man you had been flirting with all evening?'

'I wasn't flirting with him.' I fought back tears of frustration.

'Did you think that you would just go downstairs and hold hands?' he asked sarcastically, looking over at the jurors with a smug look on his face.

'No, but I also knew that if he tried anything I would just say no,' I replied. 'Whatever I was thinking at that moment, him raping me wasn't something I had envisioned. I suppose you feel as though the punishment I received for failing to exercise better judgement was sufficient, do you?'

By that point I was past caring what people thought of me. While the defence lawyer pleaded with the judge to have my remark struck from the record, I looked up at the ceiling and held my breath, hoping that by doing so I would prevent the tears from falling. I couldn't bring myself to glance at Deb, as I was sure I'd get a stern look of disappointment for losing my composure.

Walking into my hotel room that night, the jet lag and the stress of the case had me surrender to utter exhaustion. Crawling into bed with all my clothes on, I curled into a ball and closed my eyes. With my heart racing the way that it was, I knew sleep was unlikely. Turning the light back on, I walked over to my luggage, reached into my pack and pulled out another one of Tami's cards. It was just a silly one that was meant to do nothing but place a smile on my face. It worked.

'Hey, four eyes. You have little wrists. Girls can't shoot baskets. You're not slender, you're emaciated! Mad yet? Huh? Did it work? So get pissed off, and let the truth fly in their faces. I love you; I'm on your team. You make me so proud.'

The following day the defendant took the stand while his wife looked on. It was finally his turn to sweat under the cross-examination from my side. His version of events was that sex never took place. He said he'd only kissed me, I'd said no, and that was the end of it.

Working alongside David Young was a tall, attractive, softly spoken woman. The plan was to use her to lull James into a false sense of security. Hopefully, he would open up to a friendly woman, and when he least expected it, she'd go in hard for the kill and run him into the ground.

Before he knew what hit him, she had already made him contradict himself a number of times. He left the witness stand with a huge sweat patch on his backside, perspiration dripping from his face. We all thought that was a rather odd reaction for an 'innocent' man.

The jury was sent out to deliberate. It took them only forty minutes to come back with their decision. My lawyer told me that such a short deliberation didn't look good for our side and to prepare myself for the verdict to go in his favour.

When we were called back in, I walked through the door, focusing on the ground.

Before I took my seat beside Deb, she put her hand underneath my chin and said sternly, 'Don't let me ever catch you with your head down. Whatever happens, you be proud of yourself for what you have done.'

I looked at her. Tears were blurring my vision and the prospect of defeat was weighing on me.

The judge received the envelope and asked the defendant to rise.

'Has the jury reached their verdict?' the judge asked.

The jury foreman stood up. 'We have, Your Honour.' Taking a long breath, he adjusted his glasses and read from the paper. 'We, the jury, find the defendant not guilty.'

I could only sit back and stare at the defendant as he looked upward and mouthed the words *thank you*. I wondered would he also be thanking the Academy for its recognition of his astounding performance? He turned to his wife. She held her hand over her mouth and ran out of the courtroom crying.

The defeat and the stress of the trial struck like lightning, swift and without warning, on my already broken spirit. Preparing for a loss was one thing, but actually losing destroyed even the smallest bit of hope I had managed to hold on to. Drowning in my own insignificance, I remember nothing further of the courtroom.

I do remember that when I got back to the hotel, I took out a final note from Tami.

> To Carrie,
>
> I don't know how the trial went (or is going). I only know I'm so proud of you for making the right moves, even when they're hard ones; for pushing your own limits all the time; for loving yourself enough to move out of the victim role, forever; for being one of the funniest friends I've ever had (and most beautiful) and for the non-stop growth I've seen in you since we first met. I mean it when I say 'You Go Girl' because I know you can, and you will. After the trial is over – win or lose – you emerge victorious in my books! Never look back. Something wonderful is waiting for you. Just being finished with this whole trial – and finding yourself in Australia – will be a wonderful start. You're awesome and so is your future.
>
> Your forever friend, pseudo-mother, ally, fan,
> Tami xx

My lawyer later told me that he felt sure that many in the courtroom suspected that James was guilty because of the way in which he had conducted his defence and because his version of events often sounded preposterous. But as the jury was obliged to abide by the 'beyond reasonable doubt' instruction, there was not enough evidence to convict. It came down to a 'he said, she said' battle. And this time it was 'she' who lost.

11

TWO DAYS AFTER losing the case, I hopped on a train bound for Melbourne. I took comfort in the company of friends. Deanne had offered me the laundry room at the back of her house. Having arranged for a mattress to be set up, she told me it was my home for as long as I needed. I assured her it was only until I could find a job and make some money. After the trial I was paid nine hundred dollars for appearing as a witness. It was compensation for the pay I lost in Canada by appearing before the court. I didn't know how long I could make that stretch, but my focus was on setting up a life in Melbourne. My visitor's visa only allowed me three months in the country. How I would manage to find a way to stay permanently in Australia during that short time period, I hadn't a clue, but the alternative was motivation enough. And although losing the trial was a devastating blow, I didn't allocate much time to wallowing in self-pity.

'What are your plans for Christmas, darl?' Dee asked before heading off to work one day.

'Christmas? To be honest, it hasn't even crossed my mind. What's the date, anyway?'

'It's the twenty-third of December today, love,' she said

wryly. 'I am heading up to the farm tomorrow and you are more than welcome to come.'

Deanne was one of eight kids. Her parents had raised them in a small town, smack bang in the middle of the Australian bush. Dee was now leading a double life. If you were to run into this tall, beautiful blonde in the city, you would assume she was just another incredibly driven, hardworking professional woman. It wasn't until she jumped into her little red hatchback, crammed full of horse blankets, dust, junk and riding gear that you realised there was more to this girl than met the eye.

Christmas Eve arrived, and I found myself stuffed into the passenger seat of the red hatchback, surrounded by all of Deanne's belongings and heading toward a family celebration where I hoped I was welcome.

'Are you sure your family doesn't mind me joining you guys for Christmas?'

'You idiot,' she said affectionately. 'Of course they don't mind.'

After driving for a little over two hours, Dee and I pulled into the long driveway of her parents' farm. Darkness had fallen, and there were a million stars in a black sky that seemed to curve down and meet the earth in the distance. The view was magnificent and drew me out of the car and into the empty field. Deanne was oblivious to the beauty of her surroundings. She was far too busy attempting to dig Christmas gifts out from the back seat without everything else falling on top of her. I stopped sky watching to help my friend with the presents before she was lost under the deluge.

While walking toward the house, I noticed the property was full of fairy lights and countless little gnome statues.

I spotted two gnomes in an old toy truck that was parked in front of a broken-down television set.

'What the hell is all this?' I asked.

Deanne laughed. 'What you are looking at now is two gnomes at a drive-in.'

'Are you serious?'

'Sure am.'

I was in awe of these scenes and the hours of work that must have gone into creating them. There was the gnome at the local pub with an empty beer can on a rock beside him, gnomes gathering at the post office mailing letters, and gnomes going to church. But nothing beat the nativity-scene gnomes.

'Really?' I said. 'Jesus, Mary and Joseph gnomes?'

She could only roll her eyes and sigh. She had no words and none were necessary. I loved everything about the gnomes and knew these would be good memories to draw upon during the difficult months ahead.

'It must take forever to clear this shit away when Christmas is over.'

'Who said anything about putting it away?' she said. 'It's been like this for years.'

'So who the hell set all this up?'

'My mother,' Dee replied, and rolled her eyes once more.

I awoke on Christmas morning to what was heating up to be a forty-degree day. Tiptoeing out of the shed that Dee and I had slept in that night, along with about seven others, I walked over to the house. Deanne's mother and I were the only ones up.

'Good morning, Carrie,' she said. 'How did you sleep?'

'Really well, thank you.' I'd met some of Dee's family before and liked them, her mother in particular. 'Can I help you with anything?'

'I'm glad you asked.' She had a kind smile that reminded me of Deanne's.

She handed me a bag of unshelled peanuts and asked if I would go out and put a peanut in each of the gnome's stockings! My eyes widened as I remembered the scores of gnomes spread out all over the property.

'Are you serious?' I said, not sure whether to laugh or not.

'Of course, Carrie,' she said. 'After all, it is Christmas, you know.'

So there I was, out in the scorching heat, batting flies from my face and filling miniature stockings with peanuts. I glanced up to see Deanne and her sisters laughing at me. I smiled and had to laugh myself. Never in my wildest dreams could I have imagined this was how I would be spending Christmas morning.

In the weeks and months following Christmas I continued to explore every conceivable angle that may have helped me to remain in Australia. I managed to land a volunteer job in the inner city in late January, helping out with African youth at a community centre near Deanne's place. I loved it. I would wake up in the morning, head down to the centre and play basketball with the kids all day. The manager even offered me a full-time position if I was able to get a working visa. All I needed was a plan that would make that happen, and time was certainly not in my favour.

Every passing month, in order to extend my visa, I had to visit the Department of Immigration and Multicultural Affairs to prove I had enough funds in my account to support myself in the country. I'd already let my return ticket to Canada expire because I had no money to change it again. Jobless, flat broke, no apparent way of staying in the country and not a chance in hell that I was returning to Canada willingly, my options were becoming slimmer by the day. Deanne was increasingly concerned about my state of mind. I had begun to rapidly withdraw and was refusing to face the fact that there was no way I would be allowed to remain in the country. And with the end of another month quickly approaching, I couldn't prove to the Department of Immigration that I was able to support myself. My visa would certainly be declined.

I'd seen Yvonne several times upon my return. Sitting alone in the house one morning, I picked up the phone to ring her. Yvonne was one of the few people I had told about my circumstances, and she could hear the panic in my voice. She knew about my growing depression and my fears of returning to Canada. I decided it was time to tell her my secret.

As I walked to my appointment, I reminisced over the hundreds of times I had freely made this journey, and thought of the many other opportunities Australia had given me. The experiences I had, as well as the friends I had made, enabled me to gain a new outlook on life. How could I willingly relinquish all this?

When I entered Yvonne's office I wanted to burst into tears. She allowed me the space and time to settle, knowing that I would speak when I was ready.

'Yvonne,' I finally said. 'I have spent over a year building the life for myself that, as a child, I could only dream of. I've achieved more in this short time than in my entire life. At last I have found a place where I feel safe. Where I can leave my house and not wonder if today is the day I won't make it back alive.'

For most of the session I managed to avoid the subject I had gone there to discuss. She seemed to know I had something big to share. I just didn't know how.

'I can't go back to Canada, Yvonne. My father knows I have told authorities about the abuse and I know he will want me dead. Or worse.'

She listened as I told her about every obstacle I was encountering trying to find a way to stay in the country. I was so desperate I seriously contemplated marrying somebody. She let me vent for nearly an hour, allowing me the time to voice my fear and frustration. And then, bang! She cut right to the chase, and I had nowhere else to hide.

'Carrie, remember last year when you briefly touched on the time you were fifteen and ran away from your mother's? Can you tell me more about that, please?'

I was hoping I didn't look as sick as I felt. 'What did you want to know?'

She looked at me, offering a sympathetic smile. 'I want to talk to you about Terrence.'

I tried my best to disguise my shock while I shifted several times in my seat.

'You brought him up with me before you went back to Canada last year. Do you remember that?'

I nodded, recalling the session where I talked about running away from home and being that terrified fifteen-year-old staying in a shelter and meeting Terrence.

'Do you remember how you told me he was very good to you and that you spent a lot of time together? How you constantly had to convince Tami that he was a good guy and she didn't have to worry?'

Again, I nodded. The lump in my throat prevented me from joining in on the stroll down memory lane. I was growing agitated, and Yvonne could sense it too. She took a deep breath before speaking. The suspense was nearly unbearable.

'How long into the relationship did you find out that Terrence was a pimp, Carrie?'

The tears I'd held back initially fell in a steady stream down my face and onto the front of my shirt. The shame I felt was immense. But what surprised me most was the relief I began to experience as I shared the one significant piece of my life I had left out since I'd started my sessions with Yvonne.

My body was shaking, and I felt as if I was going to throw up. 'I don't know where to begin, Yvonne.'

She smiled and looked at me with a mixture of care and concern. 'Why don't we start from the beginning?'

'I started seeing Terrence while I was staying at Avenue 15. He would convince me to skip school and we'd meet at the indoor stadium in the city to play basketball. He always bought me lunch, would take me to movies and tell me an uncomfortable amount of times how amazing I was. I didn't believe him, of course, but I did believe he believed it and during the months we spent together, he wormed his way in and I trusted him completely.

I explained that I was pretty much an open book. Once you had my trust, my natural disposition was to wear my heart on my sleeve. I couldn't hide my feelings well, nor could I lie to save myself. My strengths as well as my weaknesses were apparent. He knew about everything that had caused me shame. Terrence was able to alleviate a good deal of the shame my father had ingrained in me. He told me he would never let anyone hurt me again, and I believed him.

Yvonne's expression held no hint of shock.

'Looking back, I can see how incredibly stupid this all sounds. I mean, God, how hard was he working to get close, earn my trust and somehow make me believe that I was valuable to him? I should have known it was too good to be true. How could I have been so stupid?'

My tears began to flow again.

'Carrie, listen to me. You were a fifteen-year-old girl with a lifetime of severe abuse behind you. When are you going to give yourself a break?'

I leaned forward, staring at the floor, my tears splashing on to the lap of my old, worn jeans. Fighting my shame, I couldn't bring myself to continue. I checked my watch, relieved that the hour had nearly passed.

'Tami never trusted him,' I told her. 'I spent months defending him but her mind was already made up. He was bad news and she didn't want me to see him. I eventually stopped trying to convince her and started sneaking out to meet with him.'

I glanced at Yvonne for assurance that I was still doing okay and that she was fine to hear more. She was hard to read but something told me not much rattled her. I didn't know how to find the words for what I needed to share.

'He hurt you badly, didn't he, Carrie?' she whispered. 'Please tell me what he did to you. It's okay, I promise.'

Keeping my eyes fixed on the window, I summoned the courage to go back and revisit a time I wished more than anything I could forget.

I was introduced to a side of Terrence I hadn't seen before on a cold January evening when one of his girls was caught stealing money from him. We would sometimes hang out at this pizza place in the city that had a living area out the back. It was old and run-down, but at the same time it provided shelter from the cold.

I was in the back room watching music videos with a few

of Terrence's boys when I first heard the muffled screams coming from behind the closed door. Two of the boys got up and headed in that direction. The door swung open, and I could see a young girl inside, naked and bound. I'd noticed her hanging with Terrence earlier when she seemed to be having a good time.

Now she had burn marks on her chest, and her arms were tied tightly behind her back. Terrence pushed her through the bedroom door, and she landed with a thud on the floor right in front of me. I couldn't take my eyes off the cigarette burns covering her chest. Terrence charged out of the room behind her, fuming. Shocked by what was happening, all I could do was stare as the girl continued to cry and beg them to let her go. They did not. Terrence then kicked her in the ribs as she lay on the floor curled in the foetal position.

'Terrence,' I screamed. 'What are you doing?'

The girl looked over at me. Her face was swollen and her tears had caused her mascara to run down her cheeks. She met my eyes, pleading with me, as if believing I was the one with the power to call the whole thing off – if only I could have.

'Help me, please?' she begged in desperation.

I wanted to, but not one part of my body was capable of moving. My limbs were lead, my thoughts frozen. One of the guys slipped out the back door. For some reason, I assumed he was going to get help. When I tried to run after him, Terrence grabbed me by my hair and dragged me back to where the girl was lying on the floor. One of his friends was undoing his pants and climbing on top of her. She tried to fight and screamed at me to get help. For all the use I was, I might as well have been bound myself.

As Terrence forced me closer to the assault, he growled, 'I want you to get a real good look at what happens to whores that try and fuck with me.'

Just then the door opened up, and the guy who had left moments earlier returned. Terrence threw me toward him and said, 'You let her get a good look at the action, ya hear?'

While Terrence and his friend took turns brutally raping the girl, I slumped in the corner and wondered how playing basketball just hours earlier could have led to this.

The girl's eyes still searched mine hopelessly long after she'd lost the ability to speak. I cried as they continued to beat and rape her to within an inch of her young life.

She began to lose consciousness, and her screams ceased. But it seemed I had been doing enough screaming for both of us. Terrence got off the girl and charged toward me. I stared up at the man I once thought I loved. His eyes were dark and snake-like. There wasn't a trace of mercy in his expression. I saw my father in his black face.

'Keep on screaming, bitch, and I will do you like I plan on doin' this bitch.' His breath was hot against my face. 'You understandin' me, girl?'

I nodded.

Throwing me back into the wall, he climbed back on top of the girl and continued to assault her.

Later, I heard through the streets that the girl had somehow survived the attack. After that, I was determined to remain silent and not ask questions. One quickly learned that the less one knew, the better. Nobody had to tell me a damn thing.

I was trapped in a situation that I saw no way out of. A few days after that girl was attacked, I was given my first client. I cried the whole time.

Yvonne remained silent while I was speaking. I found myself unable to stop once I'd started. Eventually she asked me questions, and I answered every single one as truthfully as I could. Sometimes shame prevented me from being completely honest. But for the most part, I shared with Yvonne events that no one else knew about.

'Carrie, did Tami know what was happening to you?'

'Yeah, she suspected,' I said. 'There were times when Terrence or a client would rough me up a bit and Tami would see the bruises or scratch marks. One time she even took me to a vice detective and tried to make me talk. But I was too scared.'

My worst encounter with Terrence happened one February afternoon. I had been lying low for quite some time. I knew he would be looking for me, but as the weeks passed, luck was on my side. My avoidance tactics were proving successful, and I managed to keep out of his way for three months when I went back to the east coast to meet my birth mother.

But on this day, I happened to run into one of Terrence's girls. She was seven months pregnant with bruises all over her face.

'My God, Amber,' I said. 'What the hell? Girl, you gotta get out of there before he kills you.'

She looked at me with a pained expression. Her eyes were void of life. 'He's crazy,' she said. 'He's been beating all of us and everybody is too scared to do anything.'

'The baby,' I said, looking at her swollen belly. 'Is it his?'

'I don't know.'

'Amber, you have to get away. You've got a baby you have to think about.'

She was fifteen, into drugs and didn't seem to be at all bothered about the welfare of her unborn child.

'I don't know how to get away.' She was crying.

My heart went out to her. I agreed to meet her at the place she'd been living. Somehow, between the two of us, we were set on coming up with a plan. Without cops.

The following day I arrived on her doorstep. She opened the door, and I was shocked at the terror in her eyes.

'What's the matter?' I asked her.

No sooner had she whispered 'sorry' than the door swung open. Terrence stood there, furious. He dragged me into the house; three of his boys were there as well. There was a pile of cocaine and weed on the coffee table, and they appeared as high as they had ever been. I couldn't believe Amber had set me up.

Terrence ripped off my clothes while two of his thugs held me down. They all took turns raping me. I didn't fight, knowing from experience that it only made him crazier.

'Yo, man, pass me that cigarette,' Terrence called out to the guy who was nearly passed out on the couch. 'We gon' teach this here bitch a lesson.'

One of his boys held my arms above my head while Terrence straddled my bare torso. I can only recall the pain of the first burn, as he held the cigarette to my breast. It sizzled like bacon in a pan. As I screamed out in agony, he laughed in my face. The same man who had just several months before kissed the scar my father left, was now leaving his own.

'Imma give you a little reminder 'bout who you think you too good to be,' he said, sneering.

When he had finished, he simply let me go.

I somehow managed to make it back to my mother's place that night. Sneaking upstairs, I got in the shower and scrubbed away the filth I felt was covering me. I stepped out of the shower and wiped the steam off the mirror with my towel. Then I stood and stared at what had been burned into my chest.

The letters spelled out *WHOR*. I can't say for certain if he had run out of room before it was finished or if he was just too stupid to spell, but I wasn't about to go back and have the word corrected. Even with the 'E' missing, the message was clear. I was a whore – at least that much had been decided.

I spent the following two or three days in bed, telling my worried mother I was sick. It was the first time in my life she didn't believe me. She saw that I was in pretty bad shape, so she rang the only person she knew I would confide in.

Tami came to pick me up immediately. The burns on my chest were torture, so on the ride back, I was forced to pull the seatbelt away from my body and try to hold it there without her noticing.

I lay on the couch watching TV while Tami banged around in the kitchen preparing dinner. She knew something wasn't right – she just didn't know what. Tami came over and sat with me on the couch. Lifting up my head, she placed it in her lap. She began stroking my hair and putting the back of her hand on my forehead. She told me I was warm.

'Carrie,' she suddenly shrieked. 'What is that on your neck, behind your ear?'

I panicked. 'I don't know.' I reached behind my ear to feel a sore scabbing over.

'It looks like a cigarette burn!'

I sat up and tried my best to come up with an explanation as to what else it could be. Seeing the tortured look on Tami's face made me dissolve into tears. She held me in her arms and continued to ask me what had happened, while all I could do was cry.

'Carrie,' she began. 'Do you have any more of those marks

on your body?'

I didn't answer.

'They're cigarette burns, aren't they?'

Met again with silence, Tami stood up and stormed over to the coffee table, which was covered with papers and books. She picked them up one by one and began throwing them across the room. Screaming words I couldn't make out, she continued ranting and raving until she was spent. She fell into a heap on a chair and began sobbing uncontrollably. I walked over to her and placed my hand on her shoulder.

'Why, Carrie?' she cried. 'Why don't you tell me what's going on in your life and let me help you?'

I didn't know what to say.

She pleaded for hours to get me to tell her what had happened, and I eventually broke down. She cried as she heard how I was held down and burned with cigarettes.

'Where did he burn you, Carrie?'

'All over my chest.'

She put her hand back on my forehead. I was feverish, and she asked me if there was a chance that they could be infected, but I didn't know.

'Carrie, we need to take you to hospital.'

The thought of a hospital made me stop breathing. I told her no.

'Can I at least see them, then?' she asked.

I reluctantly went into the bathroom and carefully removed my shirt. She stared in disbelief at what had been done to me. Several of the burns had become red and were oozing angrily.

'That bastard.' It was all Tami could bring herself to say as she read what had been burnt into my chest. She knew they were scars I would likely carry for the rest of my life.

Tami bought an expensive healing cream, used to

diminish scarring, and an antiseptic spray that stung as badly as the burns themselves. She sprayed my chest several times a day, as I was unable to inflict the pain upon myself.

'Are you still badly scarred, Carrie?' Yvonne's voice brought me back.

I checked my watch and realised I'd lost a couple of hours.

'Most of them have faded completely,' I said. 'A few are visible but not enough to make out that horrible word.'

We sat in silence.

'Yvonne, I can't ever go back to Canada. In those three months I was back, I feared for my safety on a daily basis. How can I let go of the life I've always wanted when my only other choice is to return to the hell I left behind?'

I could see she agreed with me. The answer was simple, really – I couldn't.

It was evening when I left Yvonne's to begin the walk through the University of Melbourne to my room at Deanne's. The air was crisp; the Australian version of winter was on its way.

When I arrived, I remembered that I had wanted to do something about the disgusting state of the carpet. Five people were living in the house and not one of us owned a vacuum. I decided to try to borrow one from our neighbour. Why I'd been hit with the desire to become a domestic goddess on a Friday night was anybody's guess, but there I stood in front of the house next door, ringing the bell.

Carlo came to the door and invited me in out of the cold.

'Hey, Carrie,' he said. 'What can I do for you?'

In spite of knowing he was probably going to laugh when I told him, I bit the bullet and asked politely for the vacuum.

Sure enough, he laughed. 'It's Friday night, you do realise?'

'I do,' I replied. 'So ya gonna give me your vacuum or stand here and make fun of me?'

'Carrie, you can't really want to stay home and vacuum on a Friday night. Listen, I've got a friend coming to pick me up any minute. Why don't you put off the cleaning until tomorrow and come out with us?'

I thought he was crazy. I had just spent most of the afternoon disclosing secrets about myself that people would die if they knew. I had a large carpet burn under my left eye from a flashback earlier in the week, and my hair looked as though I had spent the day test-driving convertibles with Michael Schumacher.

'Carlo, do I look like I want to go anywhere tonight?'

'Well, it would beat the hell out of vacuuming.'

While that was probably true, all I wanted to do was grab the machine and get home. As luck would have it, while I was struggling with the vacuum and going back toward Dee's front door, Carlo's friend was blocking my way. I kept my head down while I fought to carry the heavy bloody thing around him.

'You sure you won't reconsider?' Carlo yelled after me.

'Positive,' I said, slamming the front door behind me. I could still hear them laughing.

The following morning, there was a tapping sound at the back door. I could make out Carlo's voice on the other side. He and his housemates shared the same backyard as we did. I went outside to speak to him.

'My friend from last night wants your number to ask you out to dinner tonight,' he told me.

'My number?' I said. 'Carlo, is this friend of yours particularly desperate?'

Carlo laughed, but he assured me his friend had never done anything like this before. The last thing I was looking for was a relationship, but a free meal? Even I'd be crazy to turn that down. I had absolutely no money; I'd been on a strict diet of air biscuits and water for more months than I cared to remember, telling Deanne when she'd ask that I had already eaten. Maybe dinner wasn't such a bad idea.

'So does this friend of yours have a name?' I asked him.

'Chris.'

'Chris, huh? Well, you tell Chris to ring me in an hour from now.'

I don't know why I chose an hour. Maybe I needed that amount of time to get my head around what I was about to do. It had been ages since I had even looked in the direction of a man, so my accepting a dinner date from a total stranger was completely out of character. But there I was, back inside the house, with what seemed to be an invitation to a free meal that would fill my empty stomach. I figured helping myself to a couple of Dee's Vodka Cruisers before going out wouldn't hurt either.

Exactly an hour later, the phone rang. I picked it up, still unable to believe what I was doing.

'Hi, is this Carrie?' the voice on the other end asked.

'It is,' I answered, shocking myself with confidence. I forgot to put on my no-Carrie-live-here foreign accent. 'You're Chris?'

'Yeah. I feel really strange doing this,' he said. 'I've never done anything like it before.'

'Well, you mustn't have been able to stop thinking about that beautiful scrape on my face and my gorgeous wild hair.' My sarcasm was showing.

'Yeah, you're so tiny I bet your hair weighs more than you,' he said and laughed.

'Very funny, smart-ass. And I don't remember you being particularly tall.'

We both laughed.

'That thing on your face looked sore,' he said. 'How did you do it?'

'Playing basketball,' I lied.

'Ah, Carlo tells me you are quite the ball player.'

'Oh, does he now? And what else does Carlo have to say about me?' I was surprised by how much I was enjoying our conversation. He was so easy to talk to that it almost felt as though I'd known him forever. The rest of our conversation went really well. When we finally hung up, the plan was set in motion. He would swing past at seven and we'd head off to a good Italian restaurant on Lygon Street – apparently the place to go when you're in the mood for Italian food. He told me he was looking forward to my company; what I failed to tell him was that I was mainly looking forward to the calories.

Our meal could not have been lovelier. We talked easily, and my two vodkas disappeared with little effort. I'm sure that aided the flow of amiable conversation. I learned that he was ten years older than me and had separated from his wife the previous year. It certainly looked like we were well on our way to a beautiful friendship. After everything I had been through, there was no way I was ready for a serious relationship, though there was something in this man's deep brown eyes I felt I could trust. Sometimes chemistry is inexplicable and this seemed to be one of those moments.

'Jeez, it's too bad I picked a backpacker to start dating.'

I smiled. 'Oh, I'm not going back to Canada.'

He laughed. 'You like it that much here, do you?' His smile faded when he caught a glimpse of the fear on my face.

182

'I can't go back, is what I meant to say.'

'What do you mean?'

I thanked him for dinner and left. The explanation was definitely a story for another day.

12

DESPITE MY WITHDRAWN state, I kept an appointment with Yvonne I'd booked the previous week, when I was still clutching at straws and living in hope. She had grown to know me rather well during our year and a half together, so she could see that I was desperate without my having to say so.

'Carrie, are you suicidal?'

'Suicidal?' I asked with a contrived laugh. 'No, Yvonne, I'm not suicidal. That would require energy that I just don't have anymore.'

'Have you been eating, Carrie?'

'No money, Yvonne. Can't really eat without money. Can't get money without a job and don't really have anywhere to live now either. Have I mentioned that my luck is most definitely the best it's ever been? I'm thinking of buying a lottery ticket.'

Deanne had been worried sick about me. I'd decided that it would be best for everyone involved if I just moved out. Not that I had anywhere else to go, but given all the problems I was facing, I no longer cared.

Yvonne left the room to make a phone call. She returned with guilt written all over her face.

'Come with me,' she said. 'We have an appointment to go speak with someone.'

'Yvonne, no amount of talking is going to change the fact I can't stay in Australia.'

She looked at me and sighed. 'Just humour me then.'

We caught a cab from in front of CASA House and drove to another office a few suburbs away. We were greeted by a nurse of some sort and a male psychiatrist.

I turned to Yvonne. 'I'm not talking to him, just so you know.'

'Humour me,' Yvonne said again.

We followed them through the building to an office that was too bright for my taste. I can't recall much of what happened in the session, but whatever it was, the shrink felt the need to continue our conversation in a hospital.

'I'm not going to any hospital,' I whispered to Yvonne.

When we walked outside, a car was waiting for us. Yvonne had her arm around my shoulders, squeezing me hard against her. She had never touched me before because she knew I didn't like it. Feeling trapped, I began to panic.

'Yvonne, could you let go of me, please?' My breathing was noticeably faster.

She acted as though she hadn't heard me as we made rapid tracks toward the car. Without a plan, I instinctively bent down, as if to tie my shoelaces.

'Carrie, what are you doing?' she asked. 'Don't run off.'

'No,' I said. 'I was just …'

I took off so fast that none of them had a hope in hell of catching me. I hadn't a clue where I was headed, but the hospital would never be my final destination if I had anything to do with it.

Hours after I'd fled and still no clearer about where to go, I found myself alone in the dark of that winter's night, crouched on the landing of some random building. I went over the crazy events of the day. It felt surreal. Had I really just run away from Yvonne? I felt a twinge of guilt remembering how I had abandoned her on her own with some shrink and a nurse. This guilt was soon replaced by anger as I replayed the set-up. Were they out looking for me? I stared at the ground three storeys below and then off into the distance, listening to the sound of Melbourne's peak-hour traffic.

Growing cold and hungry, I climbed down the fire escape and started to walk back through the north end of the city toward my home. The weather was damp and miserable, but I loved how the reflections of the streetlights danced upon the wet road. As I approached the house, I was struck with panic. I began to fear who might be waiting for me there and started laughing almost hysterically at the mess I was in. I turned toward the sound of the trams. Before realising what I was doing, I stepped into the middle of the tram tracks and stood there. Maybe I should just end it. But would a tram really be the way to go? Leaving the tracks, I continued heading for home.

I don't recall the rest of the walk back, but the next thing I knew I was on the opposite side of the street from my North Melbourne home. I couldn't see any suspicious vehicles, but since the house was on one of the main roads in the inner city, spotting a suspicious car wouldn't be easy.

As I got to the door, a male voice called out my name.

'Carrie, are you alright?'

It was Chris. He seemed a little freaked out, so I turned around, found the energy to smile, and attempted to replace crazy anxiety with something in the ballpark of expected social behaviour.

As I spoke with Chris, Deanne arrived looking tired and visibly stressed.

With Paula in October 1996 at the Melbourne Botanic Gardens.

Mom on her first visit to Australia, January 1997.

*Feeling free at twenty-one while visiting the beaches
of northern Queensland, after nine months in Australia.*

*Cathy (bottom left), the manager of the Young Women's Project,
with some of the other workers.*

Cuddling Jordan when she was three months old.

Jordan at eighteen months old.

The Hon. Philip Ruddock MP
Minister for Immigration and Multicultural Affairs
Minister Assisting the Prime Minister for Reconciliation

Parliament House, Canberra ACT 2600
Telephone: (02) 6277 7860
Facsimile: (02) 6273 4144

Ms Sherron Dunbar
Springvale Community Aid and Advice Bureau
PO Box 312
SPRINGVALE   VIC   3173

Dear Ms Dunbar

I refer to my letter of 22 December 1999 in which I advised you that I was considering the exercise of my power under section 417 of the *Migration Act 1958* to grant a visa to Ms Carrie   .

I am pleased to advise you that I have decided to intervene in Ms   's case and grant her a Class UK/Subclass 820 Partner (Temporary) (Spouse) Visa.

The Subclass 820 Visa is a temporary residence visa only. In order to obtain permanent residence she must apply for a Spouse Visa Subclass 801 and pay the appropriate fee. An officer of my Department will be contacting her shortly with further details about evidencing the visa grant.

May I take this opportunity to wish Ms   and her family well in the future.

Yours sincerely

Philip Ruddock

2 8 JUN 2000

*Philip Ruddock's letter confirming that I had been granted
a visa as a result of his Ministerial intervention.*

My husband, Chris, with three-year-old Jordan.

Chris and the girls in the first home we owned together.

With Rhian when she was two.

Chris and Megan having a drink and a laugh at my thirtieth birthday party.

At my thirtieth party with Deanne and Tami. It had a 1970s theme,
which I'm using as an excuse for the bad taste in clothing.

With Chris and Rhian, who was two. I shaved my dreadlocks off two months later when I returned to Canada to care for my dying mother.

Tami at Rhian's christening during her second trip to Australia to visit me.

Alma, Deanne's mom, leader of the garden gnomes. She really is a character.

With Deanne doing what we do best: laughing.

Performing 'Sold', my spoken-word poem, at an event for St Kilda Gatehouse.

'I've got to go, Chris,' I said. 'It was good to see you again.'

Deanne didn't say a word to me, but I remained behind her as she fumbled through her bag, looking for her keys. Just then, one of our housemates let us in.

Dee said hello to the housemate and proceeded up the stairs to her bedroom, still not speaking to me and slamming the door with reasonable force. I assumed Yvonne had rung her at work to pass on that I had gone crazy and AWOL. I flopped down on the mattress in the back laundry and began to cry as I recalled the laughs and great times we used to share. I hated myself for causing her such distress. Perhaps giving up was the most selfish thing I could do. Deanne wouldn't forgive me if I did anything stupid. Yvonne must have been incredibly angry as well. I couldn't even entertain the thought of what Deb would do to me if she found out I'd fled from Yvonne and the doctors.

When the phone rang, I heard Deanne answer it. She yelled down for me to take it. It was the hospital, and they wanted me to come in for an assessment.

'Look,' I said to the nurse on the other end of the line, 'I'm not going to kill myself. I just need a damn break for a while.'

'Yes, Carrie, we understand what you are saying,' she replied, in a somewhat condescending tone. 'But it would be great if you could just come in and we could have a chat.'

'A chat,' I said. 'So you're not going to be waiting for me with a straightjacket and one of those blue gowns with no back?'

'Of course not,' she said and laughed. 'The doctor only wants to talk to you.'

'So can I come in tomorrow?'

'It would be best if you came tonight.'

While I was on the phone, Deanne passed me in the hallway and headed out the front door. I heard an engine start and a car drive away. I knew my downward spiral and selfish behaviour could destroy our friendship. I walked across to Carlo's house and asked if Chris could give me a lift to the hospital.

'What's going on?' he said.

'Oh, the short answer? Everyone seems to think I am going to kill myself. And who knows, maybe if the opportunity arose … well, I'd consider a quick and relatively painless death. The hospital wants me to go in and have a chat to them. What I need is a lift to and from the hospital. Deanne just took off and I was wondering if you …'

Before I could finish my sentence, I began to cry. Chris put his arm around me and led me to his car. He opened the passenger door, and we drove to the hospital. A nurse was waiting to escort me in to the doctor. As the nurse whisked me away, I turned around in a panic and said to Chris, 'Please wait for me.'

He nodded.

It didn't take me long to figure out that the doctor had no intention of letting me leave the hospital that evening. While I sat there, locked in a room with strangers, I felt my rage begin to build.

'You can't just lock me up,' I screamed. 'I have nothing with me. Nobody knows where I am.'

'Calm down,' the nurse said.

'Calm down? How can you say that? You tricked me into coming here.'

'Carrie, you're at risk right now and people are worried about you.'

Leaning my head against the wall, my knees started to buckle and I began to slide toward the ground.

During my first few days in hospital, I was stuck in an observation room. No privacy – just a room with dirty white walls and a big window facing the nurses' station. I wasn't allowed out unless I ate. But I'd stubbornly decided that I wouldn't eat or drink a thing unless they let me out. Several nurses had been in to try to draw blood from my arm, but because I refused to drink anything, my veins had collapsed. After four failed attempts, a doctor came to see what he could do.

He looked at the inside of one arm and followed it down to my hand. Running his fingers over the backs of my hands, he let out a sigh.

'They're right. Your veins are nowhere to be found.'

'Have you tried the big, pulsating one sticking out of my forehead?' I muttered.

He looked up at me and laughed. 'I never would have picked you for a comedian.'

'Oh yeah? Well, get me the hell out of here and I promise front row seats to my hilarious next gig.'

He sat down on a chair in front of me. 'Look, I know this must be a difficult time for you, but you're not making it any easier for yourself. All you need to do is have a bite to eat and something to drink and you can move on to, well, a less secure ward.'

I knew he was right. Being stubborn and mad at the world was not going to get me anywhere. I agreed to eat a sandwich and drink some apple juice. The doctor smiled and promised to do his best.

'It's a hospital,' I said as he got up to leave. 'Warm apple juice and stale sandwiches are really all you guys have.'

After choking down the sandwich, the doctor held up his end of the bargain and had me moved. I wasn't sure being relocated to the 'less secure' ward was an improvement. Yes,

I would be permitted visitors and be allowed to take the odd supervised stroll outside, but the company of the other patients left something to be desired.

Deanne stopped by to see me. She brought me shampoo and some clothes.

'Thank you for coming,' I said. Neither of us was speaking much. 'Dee, I'm sorry for putting you through this.'

She looked at me for the first time since her arrival and began to cry. 'Every day I would leave for work and pray I wouldn't find you dead in your bedroom when I got back.'

'I'm so sorry, Dee. I love you so much and the last thing I ever intended to do was hurt you.'

'I know that,' she said. 'You just need to get yourself better, okay?'

She gave me a hug and promised to visit me again during the week. I watched her walk down the corridor until she turned a corner and disappeared.

After several days of shuffling around the hospital in runners with the laces removed, I eventually worked up the courage to go to the nurses' station and ask for my laces back.

I waited patiently, knowing that I was being deliberately ignored. I coughed ever so subtly.

'Yes, Carrie,' said an older nurse, opening the window. She always seemed to look down on her patients through the rectangular glasses that rested on her long, skinny nose. 'What can I do for you?'

I pointed down at my feet and asked if I could have my laces back.

'And what were you planning to do with your laces, Carrie?'

Unable to take her condescending manner, I replied, 'Well, I was thinking of tying them together and going back to my bedroom to skip for a while. When I got bored, I thought I'd hook them around a doorknob and hang myself.'

She stared at me a while, eyebrows raised with a smirk painted on her face. She shook her head and slid the glass window closed. It seemed my toes would remain scrunched up, and I'd have to continue to shuffle just so my damn shoes would stay on. My chances of walking down the corridor in a normal and comfortable fashion were dashed.

After nearly two weeks in hospital, the psychiatrist handling my case told me the reason I was still there was because there was nowhere else for me to go. By then, everyone was aware of my predicament and knew I wasn't prepared to go back to Canada. They were all relatively sympathetic to my situation. My cooperation and willingness to cut down on the sarcasm had worked wonders.

The day before I was finally allowed to leave, Yvonne came in to visit. I hadn't seen her since that day I'd left her standing on the street with the doctor in front of a cab.

'Hello, Carrie. How are you feeling?' she asked.

'Much better. Thank you, Yvonne,' I said as we made our way to the hospital's visiting room. 'Sorry I ran from you that day.'

She laughed. 'I knew you probably would. They tell me you are leaving tomorrow.'

'Yep. Off to some place called the Young Women's Project.'

'I've heard of them,' she said. 'They are in Oakleigh, yes?'

'No idea. As long as they are a long way from this place, I'm not complaining.'

She looked at me as though she was trying to read where I was at emotionally.

'I've had a lot of time to think in here, you know?' I said.

She smiled. 'So what's different?'

I went on to explain that, externally, nothing was different. My situation was still the same. Before landing in hospital I was consumed by my anger and frustrations. I let myself slip back into that victim mentality. I'd forgotten how far I'd come and how blessed I truly was.

Yvonne nodded.

'So,' I added, 'I'm not wallowing in my own self-pity but choosing to focus on my blessings. That's the difference, I guess.'

It was a Sunday afternoon in late July when I was finally able to discharge myself from hospital. Being a Sunday, things were pretty quiet. I sat outside on one of the picnic tables and waited for my ride to show up. It was an unusually mild winter's day. Sitting in just jeans and a t-shirt, I closed my eyes and lifted my face toward the steady stream of sunshine that spilled through the leaves of a large eucalyptus. The birds were chirping, and I caught myself humming my own tunes. I hadn't felt hopeful in a long time. It was a welcome relief to have some of that feeling back. I was nervous as I awaited the next adventure with no clue what to expect. I took comfort in knowing Yvonne had at least heard good things about the refuge I was heading to. But anything other than a psych hospital would be a vast improvement.

Lost in thought, I hadn't noticed the enormous red hippy van that pulled into the car park. When I did, I watched a slim woman in her late twenties slide out of the driver's seat and walk toward the hospital. Massive sunglasses covered half of her face. Even from a distance, I could tell I was going to like this girl. She had spunk – wild crazy curls like mine, but red with streaks of bright blonde. As she came closer, I saw her lip ring. She seemed laid-back, and I relaxed. If this was my ride, I didn't care if she'd come to take me to the

Australian version of Woodstock, as long as she got me away from this place.

'Are you Carrie?' she asked.

'That's me.' I stood up to shake her hand. She told me her name was Emily.

'Do I need to sign anything to get you outta here?'

'No experience with busting people out of mental hospitals, huh?' I said, and she smiled.

Just to be sure of the procedures we went back to the office. After everything was good to go, I thanked the nurses for their lovely care of me. Nurse Ratched reached into her top drawer and handed me my laces. I smiled at her and quickly stuffed them in my pocket.

Although grateful to Emily for getting me out of the pscyh ward, I said very little as we drove south, to the other side of the city. My calm exterior was a false front for my thoughts, which continued working overtime. I knew I should have been used to the unknown by then. But for whatever reason, I was struggling to breathe. Chaos was nothing new to me, but convincing myself I was in control was the only way to trick my mind into a calmer state.

As soon as Emily and I arrived at the shelter, we headed out back to have a cigarette. During my two-week stay in hospital, I'd picked up a smoking habit to get me a pass out into the fresh air, ironically. All patients were allocated certain times of the day to go outside – unless, of course, they were a smoker. Then they got more. This sounded far too good an opportunity to ignore. Before I knew it, I was hooked.

'So tell me, Carrie,' Emily said, pausing to take a long drag of her ciggie. 'What brought you all the way from Canada?'

I wasn't in the mood to get into the specifics. 'I just

needed to get away before I went absolutely mental.' Then I remembered where she'd just picked me up from. 'A lot of good that did me, huh?'

We both laughed.

We spent around an hour at the centre, getting acquainted and filling out paperwork. She told me that the house I had been allocated was empty, and asked whether being on my own would be a problem.

'Um, no. That definitely works after the company I've kept recently.'

When we were done, Emily and I drove to the 'secure location' that I would call home for many months to come. Helping me with my bags, Emily walked to the front door and handed me the key. As I unlocked the door I was suddenly hit with an overwhelming sense of relief. For the first time in weeks, I had a place to call home.

Emily quickly showed me around the small two-bedroom flat and allowed me to get settled before she left.

'Thank you for taking me away from that place.'

'No worries. I will see you sometime tomorrow.'

Suddenly, with Emily gone, I began to feel terrified. Images of the past began flashing in my mind. Before I had the opportunity to talk myself back into the present, the past took hold of me. I was nine again, standing behind my father as he opened the front door of his house to the man with the German shepherd. My twenty-two-year-old legs trembled as badly as they had the day I watched helplessly as my father accepted money from the man he had sold me to.

'Daddy, I don't want to go over there,' I said in barely a whisper. My father showed no indication of hearing me.

'I'm not going,' my voice became strong, and I fixed my eyes on him.

He stared at me in disbelief, and I held his glare. He said nothing for a long time then eventually roared a wicked laugh. His laughter stopped as quickly as it had started, and a familiar expression crept across his hardened face. It showed me, in the most cunning of ways, how very little power I actually had over my life. But this time I was determined not to go down without a fight.

While my father was in the bedroom, I took a steak knife out of the drawer in his kitchen and carefully placed the weapon down the back of my pants before the man arrived. Recalling what had happened to me the last time I was in his basement with the dog, there was no way I would be leaving there in the same shape as I had last time.

'Have her back by tomorrow morning.' My father's words echoed in my ears as he pushed me forward.

With my hand in the tight grip of the stranger, we made our way toward his car. My terror mounted and panic struck.

The drive back to the basement was very long – maybe a few hours, though it's hard to say. Not only was I a terrified child, but when you're young, time always seems to move more slowly. Fear has the same effect. The last part of the journey was a long stretch of dirt road riddled with potholes, which made the car bounce every few metres travelled. When we hit that section, I knew we were close. That explains why even today I get anxiety attacks if I have to drive on dirt roads.

Pine trees and telephone poles lined the side of the road. Other than a few houses spread far apart, not much else existed. I was feeling less vulnerable than I had two weekends before. I may have initially brought the knife as a means of protection, but as we grew closer to that dilapidated house, the desire for revenge struck and spread as quickly as wildfire. A person can only be pushed so far before breaking. At nine years old, I had broken. My soul carried the scars while my mind harboured the memories. My body still ached from the brutal encounter with the man two weekends before. It was his turn to learn that his lack of compassion for me would be reciprocated. Mercy would be the last thing I offered.

I was left alone in the basement to undress while he went outside to fetch his dog. Standing naked in the corner of the room, I used the few minutes I had left to try to calm myself down. Soon there would be two bodies bleeding on the cold cement floor – neither of which would be mine.

I heard the terrifying sound of his heavy footsteps, accompanied by the scurrying scratches of a large dog on floorboards. My heart was beating hard in my ears as I stood helplessly in the corner during their descent of the basement stairs toward me. I waited, gripping the knife behind my back. The closer they came, the smaller the room appeared to become. It would only be a matter of seconds before that terrifying beast was within life-threatening distance.

Although I saw the German shepherd growling, I don't remember actually hearing its frightening sounds. My mind was racing, yet my thoughts were frozen. The beast finally lunged, and I instinctively held out the weapon.

A strange silence filled the room. The knife had plunged deep into the dog's neck and remained there as he fell to the ground, where he lay in a crimson pool of blood. The hush was soon replaced by the cries of the wounded dog and the screams of the enraged man.

'What have you done?' He grabbed my face, pushing it into the dog's wound. The man removed the knife and held it firmly against my own neck. Shaking with fury, he continued to yell. Once again I could hear nothing. It was as though I was watching a horror movie with the volume turned off. For my own self-preservation, I can't allow myself to share what happened next. To this day, it is something I have never spoken of.

After a restless sleep in my new bed, I awoke early and walked down to the shelter for a meeting with Emily and the rest of the team. I was pleased to find out that all the workers were women. Each had plenty of experience dealing with young women in similar predicaments to my own – minus, of course, the Canadian accent, the flashbacks, and my complete lack of entitlements to help lift me out of my homeless situation. But like the other young women at risk, I too needed a secure environment and the space to feel safe again. Though I wasn't entitled to any of the benefits the local girls received, the supervisor managed to get me thirty-dollar weekly food vouchers. At least I wouldn't starve to death.

My flashbacks became an almost daily occurrence. I didn't leave my place much, and if I did, it was only for a brave ten-minute walk to the office. There was no way of hiding these flashbacks from people. They were becoming horrendously embarrassing, and there were numerous times when I fought to regain composure only to learn later that I had failed miserably. It was a constant struggle to maintain what little dignity I had left. Although my successes were few, and the cuts and bruises on my face told their own story, I refused to surrender. My blackouts were also increasing significantly. I lost hours at a time – sometimes days. Often workers referred to conversations we'd had that I couldn't recall at all. Too scared to admit this to them, I managed to find a way around it, as I had for most of my life, by pretending I knew what they were talking about.

But then workers began finding me on my knees on the office floor drawing disturbing pictures. I'd have no memory of doing that but I knew it must have been me who had drawn the pictures, because I had seen similar pictures before.

The first time I found such artworks was when I was sixteen and living with my mother. Rushing to make the bus for school one morning, I got stuck wrestling with my sock drawer that appeared to be jammed. After struggling for some time, I lost patience and ripped the drawer open with such force that I fell backward with a crash and my mother yelled up to see what the commotion was.

What I discovered between the bottom drawer and the slats was a red binder that I never knew existed. I got up and carefully closed my bedroom door, listening to make sure no one was coming. With the binder close to my chest, I leaned against the door and slid down to the ground.

I took a deep breath and slowly opened the cover. What I found inside disturbed me terribly. Drawn mostly in pencil were graphic scenes of horrific abuse. These were the same images that haunted me in my nightmares.

13

SPRING WAS NEARING an end and another scorching summer was on its way. I stayed at the Young Women's Project because there was nowhere else for me to go. My twenty-third birthday passed without notice – there wasn't much to celebrate. Deanne rang me to see whether I would like to meet her for a drink. Not wanting to be alone, I forced myself out of the house and caught a train into the city.

'So how goes the illegal-immigrant-trying-to-stay-in-the-country battle?' she asked.

'I'm still here.'

'I can see that, idiot. I meant have there been any more developments?' It was nice to see the smile on her face.

'Not yet,' I said. 'But I do have an appointment tomorrow afternoon.'

'Can I ask you something?' Deanne's voice became serious again.

'Sure. Ask me anything.'

'How do you do it?'

I laughed at the question. 'How do I do what?'

At first, she didn't reply. But finally, she said, 'How do you keep going when everything always seems to turn to shit?'

I smiled at her. At that stage in my life, I didn't really know the answer. 'What's the alternative?' I asked

'True,' she said.

We both sat in silence for a while.

Then I spoke. 'We keep pushing forward because it is the only acceptable direction. No one else is going to do it for us and there is so much to be grateful for. Life is a blessing, girl, and it helps having friends there to remind us that this too shall pass.'

'I'll drink to that, girlfriend,' she said, and I lifted my glass to meet hers. 'And vodka,' she added. 'When there is nothing else, there is always vodka.'

'I'll drink to that, too.'

And we did.

I stayed over at Dee's that night. I remember leaving her place the next morning and getting on the train to go to my afternoon appointment at the Project. Then the next thing I knew, night had fallen, and I was nowhere near anything familiar. Panicking, I walked around, hoping to find a recognisable landmark. No luck.

Eventually I found another train station, one suburb out from where I should have been. I had no money and no more energy to walk, so I slipped onto the train without paying and prayed I would make it to the next station. People were staring at me. At that stage I didn't realise why. I turned toward the window. It wasn't until I saw my reflection that I felt the warm sensation making its way down my forehead and over the edge of my eyebrow. I watched as it trickled past the corner of my eye. Brushing the back of my hand across my face, I glanced down and saw blood. I remained with my back to the train passengers and looked out the window. All I had to do was make it to the next station.

When the train stopped, I jumped onto the platform

and ran. I finally made it to the Project office and banged frantically on the door, hoping that someone would be there to let me in. One of the workers I was close with, Sarah, came to my rescue. Shaking and unable to speak, I fell into her arms.

'Carrie. Oh my God. What happened to you?' she asked, pointing to my head.

'I can't remember. Can you take me to the hospital?'

She sat me down and went to look for a cloth to stem the bleeding. Terrified of what may have happened to me, she began grilling me for information. I was unable to give her any answers. We both felt as if we were in way over our heads and decided to wait until the other worker came back from her errands before we went anywhere. Sitting there holding the cloth to my head, I tried my best to account for the missing hours.

The other worker arrived shortly after, and by then my bleeding had subsided, and the wound turned out to be relatively superficial. I sat with them quietly, hoping that my memory would return in time.

The workers had called Cathy, the supervisor of the Young Women's Project, and as we waited for her arrival I started to feel strange again. I rocked back and forth, hoping the sensation would pass. The workers' voices sounded further and further away as I slipped into the past. Scenes of a basement flashed before me.

I was standing in the storage area below my father's house, awaiting punishment. The walls were made of large wooden sleepers, like those found at old railroads. The smell of oil was so strong, I tried not to breathe through my nose. I stood alone in the middle of the room on a hard dirt floor. Above my head were low rafters. The furnace was loud as it kicked in, and I shuddered remembering the big mound of earth I'd once discovered in the adjacent room. It always looked to me like a freshly dug grave.

'That's where the last little girl who told is buried,' my father would say to me. Unless I was willing to risk my life, or that of my mom and sister, telling was never an option.

The door at the top of the stairs opened with a screech, and I could see my father's trouser legs as he made his way down with my little dog, Toby.

'Don't hurt him, Daddy,' I pleaded through my tears.

Saying nothing, he dragged the dog toward me. On an old and very broken black barstool was a yellow rope. My father picked it up and pulled out a dishtowel that had been tucked into the back of his pants.

'Lie down,' he commanded. I had only seen him this crazy a few times. I dropped onto the cold dirt floor without arguing. Swearing under his breath, he took the dishtowel and wrapped it around my ankles. I knew from experience that the rope would come next. Once he had the rope tightly secured around the bottom of my legs, he threw the other side of it up over the rotting rafters. Terrified of the unknown, I would have been more than grateful to escape with at least an expected punishment. Instead of securely looping the rope around the rafter several times, he left it hanging loose. It dangled inches from my face, just above the ground. I began to panic. Something different was lurking in his mind.

Closing my eyes, I tried to prepare myself for what lay ahead. My blood ran cold as I heard my dog yelp. Winding the rope around my dog's neck and through his collar, my father began cursing my existence.

'Daddy, no!' I screamed. 'Don't hurt him.'

'You shut up and remember you brought this on yourself,' he hissed, tightening the collar around Toby's neck.

'Please, Daddy. I'm sorry.' I began to cry. 'Just let me go clean it up. I want to clean it up.' I tried to stand, but he brought his foot down hard on my chest.

'Say something else,' he screamed at me. 'I dare you.'

Holding Toby under one arm, he hoisted me up off the ground with a single pull of the rope. Quickly realising this to be a two-handed job, he dropped my dog and pulled until I was suspended in the air.

'Please don't do this, Daddy. I'll eat it. I promise I'll eat it.'

Ignoring my pleas, he continued to make the necessary adjustments in the rope, looping the remainder of what was left around Toby's neck. My dog let out a pained cry as he soared up to the rafters. I dropped down, my head nearly hitting the floor.

'No!' I screamed, struggling to get free. 'Daddy, let him down.'

Placing my hands on the dirt floor, I pushed myself up, trying to lessen my weight. Toby lowered, but only a few inches. Between whimpers, he began to make horrendous wheezing noises. I stared up at my little dog and the look in his eyes matched the terror in my own. His tongue slipped in and out of his mouth as he frantically licked at his nose.

'No, Daddy, please,' I screamed. 'He can't breathe.' I made drastic attempts to free myself so that I didn't kill my friend.

'Daddy, please,' I begged again, staring at my father's upside-down image as he leaned against the far wall. 'I'll do anything you want if you just let him down. He's going to die.'

Pushing himself off the wall, my father slowly walked over to where I was hanging. Getting down on his knees, he tilted his head and leaned into my face. His breath reeked of Scotch.

'You should have thought of that before your fuckin' dog shit on my carpet.'

I was on my knees in the middle of the refuge as two workers tried to restrain me.

'Toby!' I screamed.

They held me tight as I tried to free myself. Struggling to form the words through my sobs, I pleaded for them to let me go. I fell in a heap onto the pillows they had put out for me. I stayed on the floor, covered in my own blood and vomit. There was someone kneeling before me, and I looked up to see who had come to comfort me.

'I was too heavy, Sarah,' I said, crying. 'I was too heavy.'

She opened her arms to hold me. I continued to sob as she rocked us both back and forth.

'It's okay, Carrie,' she whispered. 'It's okay.'

After some time, another worker handed Sarah a wet towel so that I could clean myself up. I held it in my hands and looked around the room. Cathy and three other workers were staring on in horror. A couple were crying and the other two appeared too shocked to do anything. I placed the towel over my face and continued to cry.

Cathy organised a meeting a few days later. I sat around a table with all the workers who were with me during the flashback. With my stress levels at an all-time high and my future in Australia looking impossible, my flashbacks were very frequent. And personal trauma aside, it was also taking an obvious toll on those around me.

Cathy opened the meeting by saying that we had to do

whatever was necessary to get the flashbacks under control.

I hung my head and tried to keep from choking on my shame. 'I am so sorry for all the trouble I have caused you,' I said. 'Maybe I should put myself back in hospital for a while.'

'Carrie, don't be silly,' one worker replied. 'You don't belong in hospital.'

'This is not your fault,' Cathy said. 'Don't you feel guilty about any of this. I'm looking after my staff and will give them the support they need so that they can all continue to support you.'

As the weeks passed, the flashbacks and blackouts grew worse still. Unable to cope with what was happening to me, the workers made the decision to seek professional help. The problem was, I had absolutely no money to offer and no right to medical assistance from the government.

Sarah was studying psychology and she discussed my situation with her university professor. The professor explained my situation to some of her colleagues, and a female psychiatrist agreed to have a chat with me. Dr Helen Driscoll specialised in severe trauma and was willing to see me free of charge and give me some advice on how to cope with the debilitating flashbacks.

The following week I was sitting in Dr Driscoll's waiting room with Sarah.

'Carrie, hi, I'm Helen Driscoll.' The voice quickly brought me back to reality.

I jumped to my feet. The doctor smiled and extended her hand. Not entirely comfortable with shaking hands, I reluctantly did so. She was younger than I had expected – probably mid-forties.

Dr Driscoll showed us to her door, allowing me to go

through first. Her office was cosy. I noticed a box full of toys in the corner and assumed that this was for her smaller clients to play with – perhaps her adult ones as well. At first, I said very little and only listened as Sarah and the doctor discussed the intimate details of my life.

Dr Driscoll took notes. Every time she stopped writing, she would look at me over the top of her glasses and smile. I could tell her mind was working overtime. She turned away from me and stared out the window for a minute. Then she got up and walked over to her filing cabinet.

She handed me a small booklet. 'Now, Carrie, this is a questionnaire from Harvard University on dissociation and post-traumatic stress disorder. I want you to take a look at it and tick on the scale where you believe yourself to be with each symptom.'

Taking the booklet, I started to look through the pages. A cold, familiar fear began to grow inside me, and I wasn't sure how honest to be. I didn't want to come across as a complete basket case, but on the other hand I knew she'd be unable to help unless she had as accurate a depiction of my mental state as possible. I decided to meet her somewhere in the middle; I'd be as honest as my fears would allow.

Picking up a pen, I began to mark where I believed I fit on the 'dissociative scale'. Halfway through the exercise, I was distracted by a barrage of familiar voices flashing through my mind. Just as they subsided, images of my past began flashing before me at a rate I was unable to control.

'Stop it,' I whispered under my breath, trying to calm down.

Dr Driscoll looked concerned. 'What's happening for you, Carrie?'

I managed to keep the memory away and focus on the present moment.

'I guess here's as good a place as any to go crazy.' I laughed as I shot Sarah a sideways glance. She smiled nervously.

'It's not crazy, Carrie,' Dr Driscoll explained. 'You are under a lot of stress right now and your brain is looking for a way to release some of that tension.'

She then explained the complexities of the human brain and how the mind copes when it has been traumatised. Dr Driscoll's knowledge of trauma and its effects on an individual's psyche amazed me. I could relate to everything she said, and for the first time ever I actually felt as if I understood what was happening in my mind.

When the hour ended, I thanked her for her time.

'Carrie, would you be willing to come back next week? We have a lot to discuss and if you are willing to do the work, I am happy to work with you on an ongoing basis.'

Overwhelmed, I turned to Sarah, who was furiously nodding at me like a bobblehead.

'But I don't have any way of paying you.'

'That's okay. You have been through so much. Don't you think you deserve a break?'

The tears ran down my cheeks. I couldn't believe my luck. Just a month earlier I had nearly lost all hope and considered ending my life as I believed there was nothing to live for. To have the opportunity to work with such a brilliant doctor was a dream come true. Before leaving her office, I offered my hand without hesitation.

'Yes, Dr Driscoll. I would be honoured to work with you.'

'The honour, Carrie, is mine.'

I began seeing Dr Driscoll on a weekly basis, and she was amazing. Each time I went, she validated my fears of returning to Canada and agreed that if I was to be successful in healing the trauma of my past, I would need the safety of

207

distance to do so.

'Feeling safe, Carrie, is crucial to your healing,' she told me.

But how would I stay? I didn't have the desired migrant skills, nor any company or family willing to sponsor me. How could I be seen as a refugee? I came from a peaceful, democratic country.

'Carrie,' she said. 'Tell me what life is like for you back in Canada.'

I looked at the floor and shook my head. 'There is no life for me in Canada, Dr Driscoll. I would honestly rather be dead than go back there again.'

I told her of the terror I faced on a daily basis. I laid out my experiences with Terrence, but barely touched on my agonising fear of what my father would arrange to have done to me for informing the local authorities of the abuse.

'You can't go back there,' Dr Driscoll said.

'But it doesn't seem like I have any choice.'

Passing the box of tissues closer, she looked at me sympathetically. 'No, Carrie, that's where you're wrong. There is something we can do.'

I listened intently to what she had to say but couldn't fathom how she would pull it off. She explained how the life I lived in Canada was comparable to that of someone coming from a war-torn country. With the help of trusted allies, respected officials and humanitarians, I was going to attempt one of my hardest battles yet. With Dr Driscoll leading the charge, we were going to take on the Australian government and fight for my right to remain in this country as a refugee.

Having no money for lawyers, we had to find a place that took on humanitarian cases pro bono. We found an agency called the Springvale Community Aid and Advice Bureau and were told to speak to Sherron Dunbar. She was a tough-looking woman, who was neither easily impressed nor particularly friendly. She had more than twenty years' experience as a social worker and registered migrant agent.

For several hours, she listened to my story. The more I spoke, the more her demeanour softened. I knew she was going to be a hard one to convince as she was already overloaded with 'politically legitimate' refugee claims. All I could do was tell my story and await her decision.

'Your father sold you into an organised paedophile ring in Canada?' she asked.

I nodded.

'Were there other children involved in this operation as well?'

Again, I nodded.

For a while she said nothing, and I grew uncomfortable.

'I'm not going to lie to you,' she said finally. 'If we go through with this, it will be a long shot. You're from a country that is not recognised by the UN as a politically unstable or war-torn area.'

I swallowed hard and said, 'Then of course on the other side of the country where my adoptive mother lives, there's a pimp who wants me dead.'

She leaned back in her chair and placed her hands on top of her head. 'Have you ever met your natural mother?' she asked.

'Yeah, I met her,' I said. 'But it ended in disaster.'

'Why's that?'

There was no beating around the bush.

'She walked in on me dressing one morning and saw a scar on my body.'

'You have scars on your body?'

'Most of them have faded quite a bit.'

'But you can still see them?' she asked.

'Yeah, you can see them.' I showed her faint cigarette

burns I still had on my right hand and wrist.

'That's great,' she said. 'Would you be willing to go to a doctor and have them all documented?'

I was slightly bothered by her enthusiasm but replied, 'I'm willing to do whatever it takes to build a solid case.'

'Carrie,' she said, 'I am truly sorry these things have happened to you. I'm not going to make any promises. I will tell you right now, going up against the Department will be the toughest fight of your life.'

'I survived my father,' I said quietly. 'With all due respect, I've fought that fight already.'

Sherron leaned back, smiled and said, 'I guess we'll never know unless we give it a shot now, will we?'

I brushed away tears, stood up and offered my hand. She came to be one of many dedicated people working tirelessly for me as I began my journey as an asylum seeker.

Sherron informed all of us of the proper steps to take and the legalities involved. Our best bet was to apply for refugee status. Since I was fleeing my home country this was the only category that applied. Given that Canada was a stable, peaceful country, my chances of being accepted on these grounds were slim. Once we were knocked back for that, she said we could then apply for a humanitarian visa. We submitted an application for a protection visa with the Department of Immigration in December 1998. Although a long shot, it was the only option we had.

As suspected, the Minister's delegate refused our application. We sought a review of the rejection and appealed on humanitarian grounds through the Refugee Review Tribunal. Our plan was to go in hard and use the connections Sherron had built up through her long career as a migration agent to help push my case forward. She also knew a female lawyer willing to meet with us and discuss my case, again without charging a cent. Everyone who agreed to work on my case was wonderful, going beyond the call of duty and offering their services free of charge. I felt incredibly blessed to have that team working for me. At times, I was overwhelmed with the support I received and was struck by a debilitating sense of unworthiness. I had always struggled with shame and found it hard to accept when good people wanted to help me. However, there must have been a part of me that knew I had every right to feel safe and free, because when they reached out, I reached back.

Dr Driscoll also used her contacts and reputation to our advantage. Being as highly respected as she was, people listened when she spoke. Once the relevant authorities took up my case, it would then be up to me to provide the necessary documentation to substantiate my claims. I would do this through contacting the people who knew me well. Letters from these contacts supporting my cause would be crucial.

I had applied for refugee status and so we had to prove that my intense fear of returning to Canada was well-founded. I had to convince the Tribunal that there was a real chance of me being persecuted if I returned home. In their letters of support, both Dr Driscoll and Sherron Dunbar emphasised the tremendous suffering I had experienced as a child. Dr Driscoll wrote:

> ... It is difficult to adequately present the depth of the traumatic impact on an adult who has been through what Carrie has. Hence, the consequent difficulty for Western countries and associated social and bureaucratic agencies to respond to the desperate plight of such individuals. There is a need for a safe environment, removed from the physical proximity of the trauma. Only in such a removed place, can an effective therapeutic treatment process

begin to facilitate the psychological and emotional healing process. Carrie has experienced gross violations of her human rights as a child. Such gross violations occur in all countries and have been recently referred to in the trauma field of studies as the 'Hidden Holocaust' and the 'Invisible Refugees'.

To meet the criteria for refugee status I had to prove that I was a member of a particular social group and that, because of this, I'd experienced persecution and violation of my human rights. The United Nations Executive Committee recognises women and children as specific social groups with innate, unchangeable characteristics. Women are socially, politically, economically and physically vulnerable, and children share these traits, but with even less power. Since I was a traumatised female child, we all believed I met the criteria.

I woke up on the day of the Tribunal hearing with a sickness in the pit of my stomach. With only an hour to present my case to a member, I feared they would be harsh and unforgiving in their decision. It didn't seem fair that my life would rest in someone else's hands. My father had controlled my entire childhood, and once again it seemed that one person had the power to shape the course of my destiny. All I wanted was the opportunity to finally live a life of freedom and dignity. The one thing I felt I had going for me was that a woman would make the decision.

Dr Driscoll entered the building shortly after the rest of my supporters had gathered inside. She was the star witness, and as she walked toward me with her briefcase and kind smile, the gratitude I felt for her was immense. So many of my supporters came to rally around me. I didn't know what would happen inside the walls of that hearing, but I knew in that moment I mattered.

The Tribunal doors finally opened, and we were invited in to take a seat. The number of professionals in the room only made the butterflies in my stomach worse. Dr Driscoll was the first person called to speak on my behalf. She confidently made her way toward the microphone, leaning in to begin her speech in my defence.

'I was contacted by staff from the Young Women's Project in September 1998, requesting a secondary consultation regarding assistance for Carrie. The concerns were relating to the sequelae of severe childhood trauma, which in particular was being experienced by Carrie as depression and episodes of flashbacks and associated dissociation.

'Since being in Australia, Carrie has been able to develop a social support network that has been assisting her in her first sense of dignity, and the possibility of life without abuse and with healing.

'Carrie has only been able to give a statement to the police regarding the abuse she had suffered since experiencing safety in Australia. This statement is as detailed as possible, given the severity of childhood trauma, and the associated re-traumatisation experienced in giving such a statement. Although Canadian police have a copy of her statement, she understands they will not investigate unless she goes back to Canada. This would appear to be the usual requirement that the witness must be present, however, Carrie becomes deeply distressed at any thought of going back to Canada.

'A summary of the abuses experienced by Carrie include: severe sexual and physical abuse perpetrated by her adoptive father from the age of about four years until fourteen years of age; torture, rape and child prostitution; and being made the subject of depraved child pornography.

'Her adoptive father has threatened to have her killed if she were to disclose the abuse. She said she knows what he is capable of. Carrie also knows that he can easily get someone else to kill her. He is aware that she has gone to the authorities and made a statement.

'At the first session, it was clearly evident that Carrie was experiencing significant dissociative functioning as part of severe post-traumatic stress. Professional staff at both the Young Women's Project, as well as at CASA House have witnessed Carrie having flashbacks. They have described to me that Carrie is like a terrorised young child being orally raped and sexually assaulted in a basement by men. Staff have found it traumatising to them to see the degree of trauma that this young woman has experienced as a child and young teenager. Staff have said that the episodes are extreme and can last for twenty or thirty minutes. Carrie can inadvertently injure herself during these episodes, as I have observed carpet burns on her face.

'The diagnosis for the symptoms that Carrie experiences is that of a complex post-traumatic stress disorder with depression. The more severe and repetitive the trauma, the more complex the PTSD that can result. This particularly is now being recognised in the follow-up studies of children who have been severely abused. The impact on the developing child who has been objectified, abused and tortured by a parent is immense. A disruption of the integration of the developmental parameters – physiological, emotional, psychological and social – occurs, with the whole focus of the child's coping strategies and resources being on survival.

'The Witness Protection Program is not sufficient protection, as paedophile rings are highly secretive and often well-organised. The children become a possession of the group and are expected to be loyal. There is an ownership these men believe that they have over these children. Even if the child has been discarded from the group as they grew older, the men still believe these children to be their possessions. They have been known to kill group members who informed authorities on them. And their victims, like Carrie, are vulnerable because they do not know the identity of most of the people who have abused them.

'Carrie's prognosis is good. She is a remarkable young woman to have survived as she has. She has high intelligence, is creative, and has a degree of integrity and empathy toward others. Like some other victims of such grave abuses, she defies the defence of others that abuse is their excuse for perpetrating the same onto other children.

'Carrie has much potential to yet realise, but she needs to have safety, both physical and psychological, before she can sufficiently heal and have some quality of life. She can only be treated for the complex PTSD and associated depression in a safe living situation. If she is living in fear, she will constantly be in a state of heightened PTSD and dissociative functioning. She will be living under siege of the past. Additionally, she has the very real threat that she will be killed by one of her perpetrators.

'Like other young adults who have survived sadistic abuses involving a perpetrator group engaged in the making of depraved child pornography, the global fear is all-encompassing. This is seen most of all when the principal perpetrator has been in a parental role. The betrayal is extreme.

'Carrie cannot know who all the perpetrators are. She does not know who will see her and fears coming into contact with an abuser through any male in her country of origin.

'Her prognosis is good if she is able to remain in a safe place. Carrie will always carry scars, and will be vulnerable to resurgence of PTSD in the future with any re-traumatising and multiple triggering events. However she can progressively experience a diminution of the intensity of the PTSD and the depression. With trauma-based treatment, she can also experience a decrease in the dissociation, and progressively develop more integrative functioning.

'Carrie shows ability to use treatment well, and has made gains already in the more overt intensity of symptoms. However, it is not possible for her to continue to make gains while she lives in uncertainty and fear of the future.

'Carrie has experienced gross violations of her human rights as a child. There is a social need for recognition of individuals such as Carrie who have had these rights taken away.

'As stated in the Universal Declaration of Human Rights: "Everyone has the right to an effective remedy by the competent national tribunals for acts violating the fundamental rights granted him by the constitution or by law."

'Everyone has the right to liberty and security of person. And everyone has the right to inherent dignity. I ask you to act compassionately when making your decision.'

The room was silent after Dr Driscoll finished speaking. I only hoped the Tribunal member felt the impact as deeply as I had. I turned to face my supporters in the back row. They nodded, acknowledging that what Driscoll had put forth was a very moving and accurate account of the trauma awaiting me if I was forced to return.

The Tribunal member addressed me. 'Ms Bailee, is there anything you would like to add?'

For the first time in my life, I had the opportunity to speak

216

on my own behalf in relation to my childhood experiences, although I didn't like having to follow Dr Driscoll's articulate speech. Leaning toward the microphone, I reached into my back pocket and unfolded a piece of paper.

'I have spent my entire life living in fear. It has only been since coming to Australia that I have experienced what it is like to live as a human being. When I am in Canada, I don't experience one waking moment where fear is not a part of my life. I have been tortured, abused and used in the most degrading of ways. I know that Canada is not looked upon as a war-torn country, but I've been at war since the day I was born. I believe the fear I have of returning to my home country is well-founded.

'The Department of Immigration manual lists several situations that are considered well-founded fears of persecution: these are threats to life and liberty. I believe the threats made to me by my father and members of the paedophile ring do, in fact, fall under this clause. It also mentions torture or cruel, inhumane treatment. Again, I believe that I have suffered this, and therefore fit into this particular category.

'The men involved in this operation have not been apprehended for their actions and I fear they would kill me if I ever went back. I reported the abuse to Australian authorities who have since passed this on to the relevant people in Canada. I can't have them find me again. I am confident the distance living in Australia provides me is a deterrent to them and a saving grace for myself.

'The Human Rights and Equal Opportunity Commission is responsible for ensuring Australia's compliance to create a durable solution for the refugee. If I am recognised as a refugee, then I ask you to exercise your powers to enable me to stay in the country in which I first sought asylum.

'I have been able to build a life for myself I never dreamed possible. Like Dr Driscoll has asked of you, please act compassionately toward my plight. And once again, I know that Canada is not recognised as a war-torn country, but sometimes war doesn't have to exist to cause a similar suffering to that of individuals who are unfortunate enough to find themselves in a country where violence has turned their lives upside-down and has stripped them of their dignity and human rights. I know this because the suffering I have experienced in Canada is comparable to that of many refugees on your country's shores begging for your intervention. Thank you.'

'Thank you, Ms Bailee. I will take all that was presented before me under close examination and you will hear from me when my decision has been reached.' The Tribunal member stood up, and we were all dismissed.

After a gruelling few months of extensive research, intrusive questioning and medical checks, my case for claiming asylum as a refugee had been presented. My future rested in the hands of that one woman. While my destiny hung in the balance, I went on with my life at the Project and continued to dream of the future I would build for myself in the unlikely event that I was granted protection.

14

SEVERAL MONTHS PASSED while I awaited the Tribunal's decision. I continued to see Dr Driscoll on a weekly basis, and we began the process of gathering more support letters from overseas. My police statement was the property of Canadian authorities in my home town – the city in which my father still resided. My stomach churned whenever I allowed myself to imagine what he was capable of.

I continued to play basketball at the University of Melbourne. It was the only normal thing I had in my life. None of my teammates knew of the fight I was involved in to stay in Australia. They also didn't know I was homeless and living in a shelter. In the months I stayed at the Project, I lost track of the number of young women who lived with me – each struggling with their own personal crisis. Although I was grateful to have a space to live in, I never really felt completely safe. Not all of my housemates were trustworthy and some of them had drug habits. Not that I owned much, but often my belongings would go missing. Sometimes I got them back, but mostly I didn't.

Once again, basketball became my haven, just as it had been when I was a kid. I found solace the minute I'd lace up my sneakers. And on the odd occasion when even basketball couldn't cut it as my therapist, I had Yvonne just around the corner from the university, and a weekly spot on Dr Driscoll's couch.

Deanne and Chris were the only friends who knew what I was going through. Chris and I had become very close in the time since he'd dropped me off that night at the hospital. I would often joke around with him, saying that times must be tough if he was choosing to spend his nights with the girl who got herself sectioned in a mental ward. It turned out that the night I was locked up, no one bothered to tell Chris I wasn't going to be released. He sat in that waiting room for hours expecting my return. I was so grateful for his ongoing support. And for whatever reason, despite all of my baggage, he was more than happy to continue seeing me.

We caught up at least twice a week. Chris and his former partner shared the care of a three-year-old boy named Xavier. Chris was recovering from the separation, and the laughs we had helped ease his mind.

Many of the girls I lived with were facing family violence situations and so our residence was considered a secure location. We were not allowed to have people over or give out our address under any circumstance. I didn't mind the rule, but many girls ignored it, and there were plenty of times I rang Chris or Dee to come and get me as I didn't much care for sharing with drug-affected and drunk individuals with anger issues.

One evening I walked the block and a half to where Chris and I always met. When he pulled up, I jumped in his car and leaned over to kiss his cheek. We drove back to his place for drinks, and the conversation grew unexpectedly deep and heartfelt.

'Carrie, I have to tell you something. From the moment I saw you I knew that you were the one for me.' He slowly reached over and stroked my face.

'What do you mean?'

'I don't know exactly, I can't explain it. Nothing like this has ever happened to me before.'

'No kidding,' I said. 'Damn, that day you saw me, I was looking like something that had washed up on shore.'

He laughed. 'No, it wasn't a physical thing. It was almost a spiritual connection. Something was definitely drawing me to you.'

He must have been able to tell he was losing me.

'I'm serious. The pull I have toward you is strong, even with everything I know about you. To be honest, I should just run in the opposite direction, but here I am, and I think I am falling for the most unusual girl I have ever known.'

Feigning offence, I said, 'Wait a minute. I'm not that unusual, am I?'

'Well, I would say you are one in a million. After all you've been through in your life, that crazy sense of humour of yours is wicked. I've never met anybody with the positive outlook you have and the strength you possess despite everything. I can't shake the feeling that you and I were meant to meet, and will probably be in each other's lives forever. I feel so protective of you, Carrie. I know, given all you have been through, that you probably want nothing to do with men. I just want you to know I will always be here for you. That's all I'm trying to say – in a really clumsy way.'

I laughed nervously, not knowing what to say in response to his honesty. For some reason I was getting emotional. I swallowed hard to clear the lump in my throat. I was generally so scared of men, but I felt safe with Chris. I raised my eyes to meet his. For the first time in the eight months I had known him, I was seeing him differently. I leaned toward him, and we kissed for the first time.

221

We ended up spending the entire weekend together. Lying in his arms had awakened emotions in me that I had never before experienced.

A few weeks after spending that weekend with Chris, I was over at Dee's place telling her, with uncharacteristic animation, all about the man I was falling for.

'Dee, I think I'm in love with this guy.' I was unable to hide the happiness in my voice.

'And you thought you were gay,' she said and laughed.

It was something the two of us had always joked about, given my strong aversion to men.

I blushed. 'Hey, I still might be. Let's see how this relationship pans out first, alright?'

We talked all evening, catching up and laughing about the times we'd shared over the three years we had known each other. Given everything we had been through together, those few years felt like a lifetime.

'Remember that time you had a flashback when we were coming home from the pub in a taxi?' she said, laughing.

How could I have forgotten that one? I couldn't recall jumping out of the taxi and Deanne having to chase me through the city in the pouring rain, but I certainly remembered coming to and finding both of us sopping wet, Dee pinning me against a building. Her hair, which she took such care to straighten each morning, was a big, wet afro plastered to her face. She was less than pleased, and I was so ashamed that I was ready to jump in front of the next oncoming cab.

After a night of reminiscing, I woke the following morning extremely unwell. I walked downstairs and found

Deanne already dressed and ready for work. Dragging myself over to the couch, I dropped in a heap.

'What's wrong with you, Miss Carrie?'

'Don't feel so good,' I mumbled.

'How long have you been feeling like this for?' she asked.

'A few days, I guess.'

'Really? You seemed fine last night.'

'Yeah,' I said. 'It seems to get better as the day wears on.'

Deanne winced. 'Carrie, could you be pregnant?'

That question sat me straight up. 'Pregnant? Hell, no. Surely my luck isn't that bad.'

'Well, did you guys use protection?'

'Which time?' I laughed nervously.

Pulling me to my feet, she said, 'Let's go to the chemist and I'll buy you a test.'

We arrived at the pharmacy across the road, but I was too embarrassed to choose a pregnancy test.

'Oh, for godsake,' Dee said, grabbing a test from the shelf and taking it to the counter. As we walked out of the shop, Dee handed me the test and told me to ring her as soon as I'd reached home and peed on the stick. She was already late for work and hopped on the next tram.

Unable to wait until I was back at my place, I went into one of the toilets at the train station. Taking the little stick out of the wrapper, I held it in front of me as I read the directions.

The two-minute wait was a killer. Thoughts raced through my mind. Do I look now? Do I wait for the two minutes to pass? What if it is positive? What if I did it wrong? Finally, fed up with my paranoia, I grabbed the stick and looked at it.

Fuck. Two lines: positive. I was certain I was seeing double. There was no way this could be happening.

The twenty-minute train ride seemed to take about as long as the initial plane trip from Canada. Back home, I found my new flatmate passed out on the couch. She was a prostitute, addicted to heroin, and when she wasn't getting high, she was getting sick. I crept past, making my way to the privacy of my room and ducked under the bed covers. As I lay there, I told myself I should go and see a doctor. If I really was pregnant, it was best I found out early.

God, I wondered, what was I going to do? What would Chris say? Would I even tell him?

Before I drifted off to sleep, Deanne rang.

'So, what'd it say?' she asked, impatiently.

'I don't think it's right,' I told her.

'Oh my God, you're pregnant!'

After a ten-minute argument over my maternal status, I managed to end the conversation, saying I had a doctor's appointment to get to. I'd decided to make an unexpected appearance at the practice that I had been introduced to through the Project.

Thankfully the doctor had time to see me. She took me into her office, ordered a blood test and gave me a cup to pee in. When I handed her the specimen I crossed my fingers and hoped for the best.

After testing my samples, she turned and said, 'It's positive.'

I don't remember what she told me afterward, nor do I recall the walk back to the Young Women's Project. I only remember my fear.

One of the workers rushed out of the centre when she spotted me. 'I'm glad you're here. We've been trying to ring you for the last hour and a half.'

I went inside and there was Cathy standing in front of me waving an envelope in my face.

With little enthusiasm, I asked, 'What is it?'

'It says it's from the Refugee Review Tribunal.'

As Cathy handed me the thick brown envelope, every worker crowded around, anticipating good news.

'Just remember, Carrie, this is only the first stage. No matter what is in that envelope, this is not the end.'

Taking a deep breath, I opened it and read aloud.

'I regret to advise that the Tribunal has decided that you are not a refugee, which means you are not entitled to a protection visa. I enclose a copy of the Tribunal's decision and reasons. The Tribunal's file on your case is now closed.'

Cathy placed her arm around me, urging me to read on. I couldn't see the point but she persuaded me I should see where my case had faltered under the Refugee Convention. It stated as follows:

THE LEGISLATION

A criterion for a protection visa is that at the time of the decision the Minister, or on review the Tribunal, is satisfied that the applicant is a person to whom Australia has protection obligations under the 1951 Convention relating to the Status of Refugees as amended by the 1967 Protocol relating to the Status of Refugees. Australia is a party to the Refugee Convention and the Refugees Protocol and, generally speaking, has protection obligations to people who are refugees as defined in them.

Article 1A(2) of the Convention defines a refugee as any person who:

> Owing to well-founded fear of being persecuted for reasons of race, religion, nationality, membership of a particular social group or political opinion, is outside the country of his nationality and is unable or, owing to such fear, is unwilling to avail himself of the protection of that country.

CLAIMS AND EVIDENCE

The applicant has applied for refugee status on the basis that she was abused from age 4 until age 14 by her adoptive father and used in a paedophile ring. The adoptive father was described as a sadistic paedophile. She was sexually abused, raped, tortured, physically scarred, held in bondage, subjected to bestiality and various other forms of abuse. Photographs were taken of her at various stages of these activities. She could identify only a few of the men who abused her, apart from her father.

The Tribunal discussed with the applicant's advisor the issue of whether the applicant constituted membership of a particular social group, and the issue of state protection.

One of the applicant's witnesses stated that '... because information about victims of paedophilia was only beginning to come to light, Amnesty International has established a special group to look at this matter in relation to the Refugee Convention.

FINDINGS AND REASONS

I accept the applicant's evidence in its entirety. I accept that the applicant has a chronic subjective fear of return to Canada. I also accept the material submitted by her supporters, including her adoptive mother and her counsellor in Canada, about her experiences there. I also accept in large part the information provided by the applicant's witnesses about the effects of such trauma on a person, the need for feelings of safety and the need for effective treatment.

As I outlined at the hearing, the issue in which I need to consider is whether the applicant's claims of harm and persecution are Convention related. In order to be so, they must be committed for one of five reasons: a person's race, religion, nationality, membership of a particular social group, or political opinion.

From the applicant's claims, it seems to me that the only Convention category the applicant could fall under is membership of a particular social group.

I now turn to an examination of this case.

I accept that people who are abused by paedophiles may have a number of common experiences, and may face similar difficulties as a result of those experiences. However, the common element of these shared experiences and characteristics appear to me to arise from the persecution of the individuals themselves, not in anything inherent about them.

From what I have read of the literature and of the individual stories, these people were chosen, not because of any inherent characteristic about them, but because the opportunity arose in individual circumstances, family or otherwise, for an individual adult to take advantage of individual children. This appears to me to be the situation in the applicant's case. I therefore do not accept that she belongs to any particular social group …

I am satisfied that the applicant has a very real fear of return to Canada, and that that fear is chronic. I can find no Convention reason for that fear, however, and therefore her claims do not bring her within the protection afforded by the Refugee Convention.

In coming to this decision I in no way discount the extent of the applicant's fear of harm. The applicant's witnesses presented compelling evidence about the pervasive and corrosive effect such fear has on a person's life, and the necessity of finding a place where the applicant herself feels subjectively safe before she can begin to rebuild her life – the search for, as one witness put it, an 'effective remedy' for the applicant. I accept that the most effective remedy and the best chance for the applicant to rebuild her life may indeed be for her to live in another country where she herself feels safe and appears to have developed a supportive and more stable environment. However, I cannot see that the concept of effective remedy applies to the Refugee Convention. It may be that such a concept applies in humanitarian consideration of a case such as this.

However, I have no power in relation to humanitarian claims for stay in Australia. This power resides solely with the Minister for Immigration and Multicultural Affairs.

CONCLUSION

Having considered the evidence as a whole, the Tribunal is not satisfied that the applicant is a person to whom Australia has protection obligations under the Refugees Convention as amended by the Refugees Protocol. Therefore the applicant does not satisfy the criterion set out in section 36(2) of the Act for a protection visa.

DECISION

The Tribunal affirms the decision not to grant a protection visa.

I was numb. I handed Cathy the envelope and made my way toward the door.

'Are you okay, Carrie?' someone asked.

Without so much as turning around, I mumbled under my breath, 'Never better.'

Being in the midst of a fight to remain in the country, the timing of my pregnancy couldn't have been worse. Once you apply for one visa and get turned down, you aren't allowed to apply for another kind. Now that I had already been rejected for refugee status, if I wasn't accepted under the humanitarian clause, I'd be forced to leave the country. Pregnant or not, there was no going back and changing my status to 'spousal visa' even if Chris and I did wish to marry or ended up living together. I was, in a word, screwed.

I decided it was best not to tell Chris about the pregnancy. No sense both of us stressing over something so completely out of our hands. So there I was, living in crisis accommodation with a prostitute on smack, while Chris was staying with his boss, trying to get his head above water after his separation. Without question, news of a baby was the last thing either one of us was in a position to celebrate.

15

DR DRISCOLL WAS made aware of my situation. Concerned for me and the welfare of the baby, she said it was critical that we received as much help and support as was possible. She didn't know if my pregnancy would increase the urgency of my case in the eyes of Philip Ruddock, but we had to make sure we had the right people on our side. I was twenty-three, facing deportation, with a baby on the way.

'Are you still getting medical treatment, Carrie?'

I told her about the female doctors at the practice who were seeing me outside of regular hours. They would sneak me in for appointments when their boss took his lunch breaks, and sometimes, if he left early, one of them would stay back to see me. Dr Driscoll told me to focus on keeping well for my pregnancy and leave the political matters to her.

I continued to spend time with Chris after learning I was pregnant. He suspected something wasn't right, but I just said it was the disappointment of the refugee decision.

Because I was suffering terrible morning sickness, as well as being hormonal and emotional, two months into my pregnancy, in a moment of weakness, I decided to tell Chris about my predicament. I was so terribly alone and frightened that I could no longer hide my desperation. And given he was the father, I decided he had a right to know.

Chris actually handled the situation far better than I anticipated. I had assumed he would react violently, because my history with men had taught me that was the most likely outcome. When I first told him, he just stared at me in shock. Finally he whispered one word: 'Fuck.'

And, though seemingly directed more at himself than me, he said that word probably twenty more times. He wasn't angry. He was just shocked. And I couldn't blame him, really. I felt the same.

Over the next few days, we discussed our options at length. Philip Ruddock's intervention as Minister for Immigration and Multicultural Affairs was my only hope. Despite the fact that Chris and I were expecting a baby, I would be deported if the Minister decided not to intervene. In the interim, Chris said we had to find a way to get me out of the shelter I had lived in for the past nine months. While I was grateful for the time I had spent there, under the circumstances, I needed more stability.

As the months slipped by, my belly began to show. Though still incredibly thin, I was at least able to hold my food down again. The stress of uncertainty wasn't helping, but Dr Driscoll took on a great deal of that burden, exhausting every contact she had. She wrote to humanitarians, members of parliament and anyone with political influence who might be interested in helping with my plight. My case landed in the hands of dozens of people who could have at least tried to use their influence. Sadly, we never heard back from most of them, or if we did, the standard response was: 'Although we empathise with your situation, there is nothing we can do.' It was difficult to not lose hope.

Over the coming weeks, we continued to run into dead ends, until Dr Driscoll's letter arrived at the Canberra office of the Independent Senator Brian Harradine, who was known for his compassion for asylum seekers – especially women and children. Harradine looked at my case, and instead of throwing it into the too-hard basket, he saw its importance.

Doctor Driscoll's letter read as follows:

Dear Senator Harradine,

Following much consideration, I regard it as important to provide you with the following information, of an introductory nature, concerning this young woman, whose case has failed at the level of the Refugee Tribunal in February 1999. She is now awaiting an outcome from the Ministry of Immigration regarding the request for the Minister to grant her leave to stay on in Australia on compassionate grounds.

Ms Bailee is a survivor of a paedophile perpetrator group, which included her being used for depraved child pornography. Few children survive such a profoundly abusive childhood. They either meet their final demise at the hands of another, or from drugs/suicide.

While there are the beginnings of social concern for the availability of child pornography, the identification and humanitarian response to the children so devastated by such depravity has essentially eluded any protective, let alone therapeutic, endeavours.

As a clinician specialising in the field of childhood trauma and abuse, I know something of the enormity of the suffering and the total inadequacy of system responses on all levels for such children.

She went on to give my history and the reasons why I did not fit the criteria as a refugee. Dr Driscoll continued:

It is relevant to state that the Refugee Review Tribunal did not question the validity of what has happened to Ms Bailee. An additional factor for Ms Bailee now is that she is twenty-four weeks pregnant to a young Australian man. He is the first male with whom she has had any relationship, and he has been very nurturing, even though it is very difficult for her to trust. He wishes to marry her, and has put in a letter of support of her to the Department of Immigration.

However, this young man has been told by an immigration lawyer that because of her situation, he cannot marry her. Moreover, that the Department may either exert the option of returning her to Canada before she is seven months pregnant. Or, the Department could send her back to Canada after the baby is born, with the baby being allowed to stay while she is not.

The effect on Ms Bailee due to this ongoing uncertainty is a deep and perpetual suffering. That she is just a commodity and has no legitimacy in her own right as a human being. She has no eligibility for any human rights considerations anywhere, as she does not slot into any acceptable criteria.

Ms Bailee gave me $200 last year. It was all the money she had. She said she could not use my time unless she contributed in some way. Although I refused this money initially, she left it at my consulting rooms, and said that she could not come back if it was not accepted. She hence has continued to see me weekly, never missing a session no matter how she feels. I have never been paid so much, Senator Harradine, for help.

She is not asking to be kept. She wants dignity. She wants to have an opportunity for a life.

A GP is providing medical care pro bono. I think it is not necessary for me to say anything further. But I do welcome any input you may have to offer.

Respectfully,

Dr Helen Driscoll

A few months later, we received word that Driscoll's letter asking Senator Harradine to intervene in my case had been acted on. Senator Harradine had written to the Minister for Immigration, Philip Ruddock. Dr Driscoll handed me the letter. She sat silently while I read.

Dear Philip,

I know I have made a number of requests to you for your humanitarian intervention in some pressing cases recently, however I hope I may put to you one more compelling case, recently brought to my attention.

The Springvale Community Aid and Advice Bureau and a psychiatrist, Dr Helen Driscoll, have written to me on behalf of a young Canadian woman, Ms Carrie Bailee, and provided significant documentation on this woman who was subjected to serial sexual assaults, including by men in a paedophile/pornography ring. This record of abuse is contained in a Federal police report.

Ms Bailee has an intense fear of having to return to Canada. She suffered ten years of sexual abuse from the age of four to fourteen by her adoptive father and other men. Those involved in her sexual persecution threatened to kill her if she revealed the abuse – which she has, to authorities both in Canada and Australia. While the Canadian authorities want Carrie to return so charges can be laid, she fears for her safety if she were to return.

Ms Bailee lodged an application for a protection visa with the Department in December 1998. Your delegate refused to grant a protection visa and on 17 December 1998 the applicant sought a review of that decision.

While the RRT could not find a Convention-based ground for granting a protection visa, the Tribunal member stated, 'I accept the applicant's evidence in its entirety. I accept that the applicant has a chronic subjective fear of returning to Canada.' She continued, 'The applicant's witnesses presented compelling evidence about the pervasive and corrosive effect such fear has on such a person's life, and the necessity of finding a place where the applicant herself feels subjectively safe before she can begin to rebuild her life – the search for, as one witness put it, an "effective remedy" for the applicant. It may be that such a concept applies in humanitarian consideration in a case such as this.'

Dr Helen Driscoll informs me that Ms Bailee is now expecting a child to an Australian man – the first man with whom she has had a caring relationship. Dr Driscoll says, however, that the ongoing uncertainty about her future is causing 'deep and perpetual suffering'. I am informed that this case is similar to a case in which you intervened.

Minister, I ask you to act in the best interest of this young woman and her baby.

Yours sincerely,

Senator Brian Harradine

Upon reading the letter, I looked up at Dr Driscoll and my eyes filled with tears of unworthiness. 'I don't deserve this support,' I told her.

'And you don't think you're worth it?' she asked. 'Carrie, one day you will see in yourself what others see in you.'

'Mom sent me a copy of the letter she sent Ruddock,' I said. 'I brought it with me if you'd like to read it.'

When I'd asked my mother for a letter, I wasn't confident her words would be all that powerful, considering how unwilling she was to give much thought to the past. Her ability to move on seemed to rely heavily on denial. My father had made life hell for both of us. Mom was his prisoner for so many years. Just the thought of the terror inflicted upon her made me shudder.

However, when the letter arrived, I was reminded of something I had once heard on *Oprah*: 'When we know better, we do better.' My mother learning to 'know better' could not have come at a more appropriate time. With my life hanging in the balance, she came through for me when I needed her the most.

With shaking hands, I reached into my bag and took out the letter Philip Ruddock would soon be receiving from my mother. I couldn't say for sure which letter would be the most persuasive for my case, but the one I held in my hands at that moment meant more to me than anything ever had.

My mother's letter to the Minister read as follows:

Department of Immigration and Multicultural Affairs

To Whom It May Concern:

I am writing with regards to Carrie Bailee's application to the Immigration Department to remain in Australia. She has a very valid reason for not wanting to return to Canada. Perhaps some background information may help you understand the reasoning. My ex-husband was a very abusive man. Before I married him, I had no knowledge of his problems. A few years into the marriage, I found out there were many.

His mother died when he was approximately fifteen years of age, and he and his two sisters were left to live with his alcoholic father. His father at that time had many live-in girlfriends that made it very uncomfortable for him and his sisters. Not knowing what condition they would find their father and these women in when they returned from school, they would never bring friends home.

When George was eighteen, his father left him to be responsible for his two younger sisters, one thirteen and the other fifteen. Both girls were continually running away from home due to the severe beatings George would give them. He had to always be in total control. He was angry at his mother for dying and leaving him with his father and angry at his father for leaving him with his two sisters.

Problems began to arise in our marriage after the second year. His temper flared over the least little thing. He had to be in control of everything: the family car, money, my time, what I cooked. If I didn't watch everything I said or did, he would lose his temper. One night I disagreed with something he had said and, for that, he choked me. I was almost to the point of passing out before he stopped. I managed to get away. It was the middle of winter, snow on the ground and I ran to the neighbours. Bare feet, no coat, and they drove me to my mother's.

I had always wanted children but found out after years of trying that George was unable to have them. It was then that we decided to adopt. After the kids were adopted he became worse than ever. The fact that he was unable to father his own child had questioned his manhood. As I had found out later, two priests abused him as a child. As a result, I guess he was always trying to prove his manhood. As he became worse, my full attention went to my girls. They were the most important people in my life.

Realising this, he then knew how to get to me was to hurt my children. The only thing was I didn't know he was hurting them. I'm sure he derived much pleasure in this. There were times I would have to lock myself and the two girls in the bathroom until he either went out or cooled down. Because of the hollering and violence, we were all so scared of him.

When the girls were four and two, I developed breast cancer and had to have surgery in a hospital out of town. He had a friend who happened to be a priest and he invited us to stay at the priest's residency, which was along the way. I went off to bed and George and the priest stayed up to have a few drinks. I awoke in the night and went into the room where they had been before. I walked in on my husband and the priest while they were having sex. They did not see me and so I went off to bed, saying nothing.

On the drive home fifteen days later, I confronted him about it and he admitted that it wasn't the first time. I told him that it was over. He said he didn't care because I was going to die and he would then 'get' my girls.

I'm sure it was this statement that had given me the will to live. I was determined that there was no way he would ever get my girls.

We stayed in the same house together for a few years after that incident. I was too sick to work and he had me backed into a corner. It was constant threats and abuse from then on. I believe that it was around that time that he had started sexually abusing the girls. Looking back, I remember the change in them, especially Carrie. They would both cry when I left them with him, even if it was just for a short time to get groceries. He blamed their crying on the fact that I spoiled them.

Because of the constant threats and abuse, I obtained a court order to remove him from the home, and he was given visitation every second weekend. Carrie started school shortly after that. There was a big change in the girls. He would pick them up for their weekend and about an hour later I would get a phone call from Jillian telling me she felt sick and wanted to come home but that would leave Carrie alone with him.

Carrie became more and more scared and quiet and one day her teacher called me and suggested I take her for counselling. I made the appointment immediately. The child psychologist told me the problem was she was having difficulty dealing with the separation and divorce. Believing that if her father and I were on friendly terms it would help, I started encouraging her visits, thinking that would help.

After the divorce, George started drinking heavily and with that, his personality changed. According to Carrie, this was when the abuse became more horrific. My concern was that he would drink and then drive with the kids in the car. I even told them to ring me if that was the case, not realising that this was the least of their worries. He had threatened Carrie with so much, she was scared for her life, and she was only a child.

The girls mentioned that their dad had a lot of X-rated books around his house and they didn't like them. I called a social worker with Children's Aid Society about this concern and was told there was nothing I could do about this. It was his home so he could have whatever books he wanted.

Carrie continued to be depressed and was starting to be an angry little girl but she would not talk to me, and I believe she protected her sister from her father by taking all the abuse herself. Carrie was in and out of psychology appointments throughout her teen years. She has also tried to take her own life twice. When she was fifteen she eventually ran away from home.

She continued high school and graduated, but it certainly wasn't without problems. She tried going to college but was having so many flashbacks she could not function. She was living on campus and one night she could not be found. My daughter and myself went to her apartment and we found her all curled up on her closet floor. She was having a flashback. When she came out of it she did not know who we were or where she was. She could not control the flashbacks; a lot of times it was fear that brought them on. She then had to leave college and come home.

She was eventually hospitalised for a suicide attempt. She told me in hospital that she was tired of being scared all of the time and couldn't bear having one more nightmare or flashback. She had officially given up.

It was after she came out of the hospital that someone talked to her about Australia. She started making plans. She came to work with me, and she saved enough money to go. It was really scary for me knowing that she was going so far away, and I couldn't be there if she needed me. But the distance for her meant safety from her father, knowing he could not reach her there, and she could leave some painful memories behind.

I kept in touch over the phone and every time we spoke, she sounded better and better. She sounded happy for the first time in eighteen years.

She came home after the year was up. She was really happy at first, but week by week, I could see her getting lower and lower. I got her a job with me, that helped a little until one day I went down into the basement where I work and Carrie was having a flashback. During these flashbacks she relives the abuse, and it's like it is happening all over again. She is a nine-year-old child again, crying, 'Stop it hurts, Daddy. Please stop.' This lasts for about an hour. It just broke my heart seeing her in pain like this and not being able to do anything to help her.

If she is to return to Canada, my fear is that I will lose her and I just cannot bear to think about that. I miss her so much but I am willing to let her go so that she will have a chance at happiness.

Please give her that chance.

After Driscoll finished reading Mom's letter, she handed it back to me and said nothing. She didn't have to. Her expression said it all.

I knew writing that letter would have been incredibly painful for my mom. Her level of honesty shocked me, and I was moved to tears by the fact her love for me was greater than I ever imagined. She had been willing to let me go so that I would have a chance to live the life she had been unable to provide for me as a child. Holding the letter in my hands, I cried, realising for the first time that I could truly understand the depth of my mother's suffering.

When I was six months pregnant, Chris rented a small two-bedroom house in Blackburn for us. When I first met him, he was working as a financial controller for a big firm in the city. He worked long hours but loved what he did and had an amazing knack for business. While we were renting, Chris was being head hunted on a fairly regular basis. He was offered the position of Chief Financial Officer at a leather company that supplied luxury cars with leather interiors. We were saving plenty of money, and he often told me that once the Minister intervened, we would buy a place of our own.

While awaiting the Minister's decision, I gave birth to a baby girl. She arrived on 31 October 1999. Exactly sixty-one years after the birth of my father. I named her Jordan. At first I looked upon the date of her arrival as an unfortunate event. Of all the days for me to give birth to my first child, I couldn't believe it had fallen on my father's birthday. After all, there were 364 other days to choose from. But looking into the eyes of this precious soul, I realised how miraculous her birth was. I couldn't believe that something so beautiful had come from someone so broken. Never in my wildest dreams had I believed I was capable of creating such perfection. I always viewed my body as something vile and disgusting, in no way capable of carrying the miracle of life.

The midwife handed the baby to Chris as soon as she came out because I had lost a considerable amount of blood and needed urgent care. Jordan was so calm that Chris at first thought there was something wrong with her. The moment Jordan was given to her dad, she just stared at him quietly, as though she was assessing the situation. Chris said it was like she was challenging him and saying, *You'd better look after me.* As if she somehow knew of her mother's past experience with fathers and, from the very beginning, this little soul would make certain her journey would be the polar opposite of mine.

Jordan became another source of love that carried me when times seemed too difficult. She had this beautiful way of looking into my eyes and showing me that I was the most important person in her life. Her vulnerability taught me that it was not a weakness, but an opportunity to be cared for and protected. Her innocence gave me a glimpse of my own. To be innocent and vulnerable was not weakness on the part of the small child, but a precious gift to be cherished by all those around. My daughter's presence proved to me that growing up as a little girl needn't be a shameful or dangerous experience. Rather, the sacredness and fragility she possessed was to be treasured. I spent countless nights lying awake watching as my baby girl slept peacefully beside me. I fell madly in love with this little being. She reminded me of the possibility of angels on earth.

It took six months for the Minister for Immigration to reach his decision. Finally, in June of 2000, when Jordan was almost eight months old, I received the news I had been waiting for. After carrying a baby for nine months without any entitlements to healthcare or insurance, or money to receive assistance in delivering my daughter, my fight to remain in Australia was over. The Minister had intervened and, at his discretion, granted me a spousal visa on humanitarian/ compassionate grounds.

The day after I received my passport with the permanent residency visa glued onto the thirteenth page, Chris, true to his word, took Jordan and me out, and we started looking for a house to buy. Only weeks into our hunt, we found the perfect home. It was quaint, with three upstairs bedrooms and a newly renovated bathroom. A lower-level extension had recently been added, which was quirky and perfectly suited to our tastes. There was a courtyard made of large stones you had to walk through to get into the house. A man-made waterfall ran along the right side, and the water flowed into a fish pond. Chris loved the fish, and I loved the sound of running water. It was perfect. We had found our family home. Two months later, we moved in.

And two years later, Chris and I got married in this house, when Jordan was two and a half years old. She was our flower girl, and Chris's son, Xavier, accompanied her down the stairs of the courtyard as part of the ceremony. My mom had flown over from Canada, and Dee was my maid of honour. As I looked around at the faces of the ones I loved, I became overwhelmed with gratitude. I had been given a second chance. I could barely believe, on that day, how different my life was from the life I'd left back in Canada.

At one point in the evening, Constable Debbie Schultz came up to me with tears in her eyes. I looked at the toughest woman I'd ever met in confusion and wondered if there was a dust storm in the smokers' section that had blown through.

'Deb, what's wrong?'

In all the years I'd known her, no matter what we had been through together or the number of horrific stories she listened to me disclose during the police statement, I never once saw her cry.

Placing her hands on my shoulders, she stared directly into my eyes and said, 'Carrie, I am so proud of you.'

'I know that, Deb.' I didn't really, but I was so shocked I didn't know what else to say.

'No, I don't think you do. You did it. Look at the beautiful life you have created for yourself.'

It was the first time she had ever revealed her true emotions with me. I sat quietly as I learned how much the woman I respected, respected me in return.

'Can I ask you something, Deb?' I said.

'You bet.'

'Well, you went on long service leave immediately after finishing my statement, right?'

She nodded, and we both reached for our drinks.

'That was five years ago and you haven't been back.'

'And you're wondering if my leaving the job had anything to do with that?'

Relieved I didn't have to ask the question, I nodded and stared into my drink. I had thought that for years but felt too guilty to ask. Being the prickly, unapproachable person she was, I never seemed able to summon the courage. But this was the most vulnerable I had seen her. Maybe alcohol really was a magical truth serum. I held my breath while awaiting her response.

'Don't be stupid,' she shot back.

It was all I would get. Tough Deb had returned.

'We've come a long way together, you and me,' I told her. 'Thank you for being there with me every step of the way.'

'It has been my absolute pleasure.'

We raised our glasses and spent the rest of the night celebrating my new life.

16

AFTER THE WEDDING, I made the decision to go back to school. Growing up, I had always wanted to be a police officer. My mom's brother was a detective sergeant in a town outside of Toronto, and the idea of a career that helped the vulnerable and put away the criminal appealed to me. I had actually been accepted into a criminology degree in Canada after high school, but with the stress I was under, I lasted little over a term. Not ready to take on university as I settled into Australia, I found a justice course I could finish in two years and come out with a diploma at the end. If I did want to pursue a degree, I would be able to transfer and receive credit for the study I had completed.

My TAFE lecturers told me I didn't belong there. The exams and papers I submitted were all given A grades, and I was often told I could easily excel at university. But after that first year, I fell pregnant with our second child and decided to defer my final year as the pregnancy was a rough one and took its toll. I was sick more often than not and spent a good deal of my time getting acquainted with the toilet bowl.

By then Jordan was three years old. Often she would crawl into my bed at nights. Usually I would wake before her and watch her as she slept beside me. The perfection of her features always astounded me. Her brown curls framed her tiny face and fell around her, resting on the pillow. Her thick black lashes were like caterpillars on her closed lids, so extraordinary, they almost appeared false.

One morning I was watching my baby as she began to stir and flutter her waking eyes.

'Good morning, angel.' I brushed the hair from her brow.

'Hi, Mama.' She smiled. 'Did I stay on my side of the bed?'

I smiled, remembering how her every limb had poked and prodded my body throughout the night. I was exhausted and in desperate need of a good sleep. But looking into those big brown eyes always melted my heart.

'Yes, baby,' I lied. 'You did a remarkable job.'

She threw her little arms around my neck and giggled in my ear. 'I love you, Mama.'

'I love you too, baby,' I said as I kissed her on the cheek. 'Let's go have breakfast, shall we?'

'Mama,' she began. 'What do you think God eats for breakfast?'

I was intrigued at my child's fascination with the breakfast habits of the Creator.

'Definitely pancakes,' I told her.

'With blueberries on top?' she asked, her eyes as wide as dinner plates.

'Of course!'

For the past several weeks, Jordan had begun speaking about God. Not in the story out of the Bible way, but more as if she personally knew the guy. I had no idea where she came up with half of the things that emerged from her mouth.

'Tell me, baby,' I said. 'You speak about God as if you

know Him. Have you ever seen God before?'

'Yes,' she answered, without hesitation. She looked at me as if I was the innocent toddler and she the all-knowing mother. Feeling incredibly silly, and with nothing to lose but perspective, I enquired further.

'When did you see God?'

'I used to live with him,' she replied.

'When did you live with him, baby?'

She smiled gently at my ignorance. 'When I was waiting to be born, silly.' She continued, 'Before we choose our parents, we have to wait with God and the angels.'

'Before you choose your parents?' I repeated. 'What do you mean?'

'Well,' she replied, 'I had to wait up with God and the angels until the right mama came along.'

I couldn't believe what she was telling me. She spoke with such confidence when she described me as the 'the right parent' that my role as her teacher seemed reversed. When I fell pregnant, I was homeless and on the verge of deportation. I lived in fear of my future and battled severe flashbacks and blackouts. If her story carried any validity, it made no sense to me that I was the 'chosen one'. I hadn't even been able to look after myself. If there was such a thing as a miracle, it occurred when my child made me her hero. It was a role I felt far too insignificant to fill, but was determined to do my best.

'Well, then, why on earth did you choose me?' I whispered.

Her eyes softened and seemed to age in a matter of seconds. Her innocence was replaced by infinite wisdom and she gently replied, 'Because you needed me, Mama.'

I took her into my arms as my eyes filled with tears, and I began to rock my precious gift. It was true. I did need her. I didn't know where I'd be if it hadn't been for my little girl.

I was home alone on that February morning when the phone rang, totally unprepared for the news I was about to receive.

'He's dead.' Those were my mother's words.

From thousands of miles away, her voice had never sounded clearer, and yet the meaning of her words seemed to echo down the line. I knew exactly who she was referring to, and I fought to keep the receiver in my hand. Could it really be true? Was the bastard actually dead? It felt like I was dreaming. This was the same man who used to remind me that the only reason I was breathing was because he allowed it. Not once, in all of these years, had it occurred to me that I would be the one left standing. I reached down to hold my pregnant belly.

'They found him alone in a chair in front of the TV, with scriptures in his lap and the rosary in his hand,' she told me.

'What happened?'

'He had a heart attack. Which I suppose is strange because you'd think you'd need a heart to have one of those.' She laughed at her own joke.

I was stunned. My legs began to give out from under me.

'He's dead, Carrie. That bastard will never hurt you again.'

The idea was difficult to grasp. As the room began to spin, I hung up the phone and staggered like a newborn fawn toward the kitchen table. Jordan was at day care, and I wasn't expecting Chris home for hours. The table was covered with an array of Jordan's artwork. I searched the mess on the table in front of me in an attempt to find something familiar – anything to make sense of the insanity beginning to resurface in my mind. I hadn't felt this unbearable cold, trembling deep in my bones, since before I'd had Jordan. Pushing aside the mess of papers, I spotted one of my baby albums my little girl had dug out the previous day to see if there was any resemblance between the two of us. There was not. She was her father all the way through.

I reached for the album and rested my hand on the cover for some time. I took a deep breath and slowly opened the book that held evidence of my early life. Stopping at the first page I stared at the photo of my parents and me, the six-week-old baby at the adoption agency. My father's face had been cut out of every picture by my mother on the day I had run away from home. Not one photo of that man's face existed in our world. Examining the picture, I traced the missing gaps and found myself drawn to the one thing more important than his face that needed chopping – his hands. Then I had a chilling thought: how would life have been different if this baby had ended up with a different couple?

A sharp, stabbing pain ran through the side of my head. I did what I could to calm down and made myself believe I was okay.

'It's just a memory,' I said out loud.

Another familiar pain tore through my insides. The kitchen walls transformed and the warm terracotta tiles beneath my feet faded away to reveal the floor of my father's basement.

Sometimes during the weekends with my father, we would spend time visiting family friends who were good people. I didn't care how boring it was going to be or how long both my sister and I would have to sit patiently in the background while he went about his business. None of that mattered. When we were in public, surrounded by the decency of others, my father became the man I no longer had to fear.

Before we left home, he would put on his 'nice guy' disguise and off we would go – the perfect family. My father had mirrors throughout his house, but the only time I ever noticed him really study his reflection was just before he headed out the door to visit people. Perhaps he was making sure no one could see behind the charade. He would fix his curly silver hair with a quick sweep of his hand and practise several of his best smiles before stepping away from the mirror and out the front door.

I didn't care what phoney smile my father decided upon. We were going out for the day, and for the next few hours, my father would be forced to find what little humanity he possessed and pretend to be the all-loving and adoring dad he wanted everyone to believe he was.

It always surprised me that his disguises worked so well in the outside world. Could they not see the monster he actually was? I couldn't understand how grown-ups would fall for his smiles, when all I had to do was look up into his cold blue eyes. In my experience, a person's eyes were incapable of deception. But as I got older, I noticed that adults rarely searched one another's expression for truth or meaning. Perhaps they feared that the other person would look back and also find whatever it was they were hiding from the rest of the world. I suppose children, in all their innocence, have nothing to hide. Whatever the reason, I knew then that when we reach a certain age, we become unwilling to share who we really are with others and slowly begin to live a lie.

One day, during one of these outings, we arrived at

Frank and Margaret's shortly after lunch. They were an older couple, and friends to both my mother and father. My sister and I once spent a week or so with them when my mom had cancer and was in hospital having surgery.

Frank was a funny old man who had lost his voice to cancer years before. I must admit, he sounded a lot like Donald Duck, and Jillian and I always laughed when he spoke to us. He would also put on these smashed-up coke-bottle glasses that made his eyeballs bulge out like a fish on a hook. He jokingly stumbled around, pretending to have survived a train wreck. We really liked him.

While our father chatted with Frank and Margaret, Jillian and I were free to play on the stairs. After a while, we decided to continue our fun down in the basement. It was cold and untidy, but there were plenty of things to play with and numerous places to hide.

I don't remember where I found Frank's old rifle, but before I knew what I was doing, I had a loaded weapon in my hands and was heading up the stairs. It was the first time in my life that I was the one in absolute control.

As I came around the corner, I spotted the back of my father's head. No one seemed to notice me at first. They were all deep in conversation and no doubt taken in by my father's lovely smiles. With both hands, I brought the barrel to the back of my father's silver curls.

I could hear a voice in my head speaking to me. *Just pull the fuckin' trigger.* My hands were surprisingly steady and the weapon felt nowhere near as heavy as it should have. Placing my finger on the trigger, I heard the voice again. *Come on now, you're gonna pull it, aren't cha?*

Frank and Margaret were facing me and could only stare in disbelief. My father must have seen the fear on their faces and realised what was pointed at the back of his head.

'Alright, Carrie,' Frank said in a whisper. 'Now I'm going to come toward you slowly and you don't move, okay?'

Since my father had become aware of his predicament, he had begun cursing with both fury and anxiety.

'Damn it, girl, you better put that fucking thing down,' he hissed at me with his jaw tightly clenched. But there wasn't a lot more my father could say. He was still trying to hide behind his stupid smiles all while he had a gun aimed at his head.

Ignoring the voices urging me on, I lowered the rifle and handed it to Frank, who at some point had come over to stand beside me. It had been obvious to me who'd had control while I held that weapon. For only a few moments I got to watch my father tremble with fear. But I decided that, unlike him, I didn't much enjoy the feelings that came with causing terror in another. I couldn't derive pleasure from his pain. Yes, I did have every right to pull the trigger, and I believe that if people had known the truth about him, no one would have blamed me. In the eyes of the law, I would have been an eight-year-old child who could not be held accountable for her actions. However, even at that age, I knew better, and decided that what I was doing was wrong.

Frank rested the rifle against the wall and pulled me close in a hug. I didn't want to let him go because I knew that when I did, my father would hurt me in a way that would have me wishing I had pulled that bloody trigger.

For the embarrassment I'd caused him, I spent the night alone, hanging from the rafters of my father's basement. There was a thick cloth around my wrists so the rope wouldn't cut into me and the punishment I received would go unnoticed, leaving no visible marks. He knew my fear was enough to keep me silent.

Hanging there in the basement, my pain lessened as I remembered the look on my father's friends' faces when he'd shown his fury and a side to himself few other people saw. His image and how he was perceived was everything to him. I smiled, knowing the victory was mine – even if only for the briefest of moments. Neither Frank nor Margaret had ever witnessed my father's evil temper in all their encounters with him over the years. For just one split second, he had lost control and his disguise had fallen away. Maybe he did get the last laugh, but in my mind, I'd won.

When the flashback ended I found myself curled in a tight ball on the smooth tiles underneath my kitchen table. I instinctively touched my stomach to ensure my baby was okay. The chair I had been sitting on had fallen on its side. The phone was ringing as I struggled to remember where I was. Getting up off the floor, I felt a sharp pain in my head. Reaching a hand to the source of the pain, I discovered a warm, sticky wetness seeping from my hairline and knew it was blood.

The phone continued to ring. I decided to let it go to voicemail. I grabbed a cloth lying on the counter to catch the blood. My head was sore, but I knew the knock I'd taken wasn't serious. Over time, I'd become a master of inadvertent injuries. I groaned in frustration because I hadn't had a flashback in over three years.

I went outside into a beautiful summer's day and hoped the warmth of the Australian sun would alleviate the chill that had crept back into my bones. The news of my father's passing had caused conflicting emotions. For so long, I had dreamed of nothing but his death. I shuddered just remembering my recurrent fantasy of his execution. It looked like the bastard ended up taking his last breath in a chair after all, I thought as I picked the dried blood from under my nails. It's just too bad it had to be the one at his home in front of the damn TV set. I had always assumed with such certainty that his death would allow me to close a terrifying chapter in my life.

The phone rang once more. The news of my father's death made me reluctant to pick up. I listened, waiting for it to ring out for a second time, but then thought what shocking piece of news could possibly top that last one?

I made myself answer it. It was Chris. Upon hearing his voice, I began to cry.

'Baby, are you okay?'

The worry in his tone only made me cry more.

'My father's dead, Chris. I can't believe the fucker is actually dead.'

'I'll be home straight away. You just sit down, fix yourself a hot drink, and I'll be there as soon as I can.'

Hot drinks were a huge deal in Australia. I had no idea why, but a hot drink was the answer to every Australian problem, no matter how big nor how disgustingly hot the weather.

'No, baby, don't come home. I'm okay – and besides, I've got an appointment with Dr Driscoll in half an hour.'

I had continued to see her every few months even though things were going well for me. After I was granted permanent residency, and with Jordan to look after, the flashbacks had stopped, but I occasionally suffered from anxiety and nightmares. We both knew I would likely always be affected to some extent, but I sure had come a long way.

Sitting in her waiting room that day, preparing myself to tell her the news, I was surprisingly calm.

'Carrie, hi,' Dr Driscoll said to me. 'Come through.'

Falling onto her comfy black leather couch, I placed a

pillow in front of me, put my head back and stared up at the ceiling tiles. I sensed myself beginning to shake.

'Dr Driscoll, do you ever get the feeling that if you let go for just one second, your life would come crashing down?'

'Is that how you're feeling, Carrie?'

'To be honest with you, I don't know what I'm feeling,' I whispered.

I managed to waste a whole hour talking about nothing in particular. I didn't know why, but I hadn't the words to tell her about my father. With the session nearly over, I stood to leave. At the door, I told her my news.

'My mom rang me before I came here, doc. My father's dead.'

'Oh, Carrie, how do you feel about all of this? I'm assuming you have a number of emotions coming up right now.'

'I don't really feel anything,' I told her. Images of the past were clouding my thoughts. I quickly laughed. 'I mean, it's not like anyone will miss him, right?'

She looked at me and pointed to her couch. I sat down again and gathered my thoughts.

'I mean, God, after everything he did to me, there is no way I am ever going to shed a tear for that asshole. He has always been dead to me so now that he actually is, why the hell would I care? It's not like he gave a shit about me ever. Look at everything he did to me. He hurt me so badly and still I loved him. Like really loved him. Can you believe that? And he didn't care. You know what? Fuck him. He doesn't get my tears. He doesn't.'

'Oh, Carrie,' she said.

Thanking her for seeing me, I jumped off the couch and headed to the door again. Just as I reached for the knob, I felt Dr Driscoll's hand on my shoulder. In all the years I had been going to her, she had never done this before.

'Can I give you a hug?' she asked.

I turned and stood with my back against the door and my head down for what seemed forever. At last I managed to nod and step into her arms.

'Carrie, it wasn't you who was unlovable,' she said. 'Your father was so damaged and sick that he was incapable of loving.'

She pulled back and gripped my arms, holding me at a distance where she could see my face.

'You understand that, don't you?' she said. 'It was never about you.'

As soon as she said those words, something huge shifted inside of me. Walking to my car, the tears spilled down my face. These tears were different to any I had ever cried before. She was right. He was so damaged that he had no ability to see past his own hatred of himself to the love I had for him as a child. He was blind to it, and it had nothing to do with me being unlovable and everything to do with his inability to love himself, and therefore unable to accept the unconditional love I represented. And on the car ride back home, I forgave my father. Only I didn't do it for him. I did it for me. I did it so that I could let go of my hurt and anger. I didn't want to be the bitter woman who let life pass her by because she held on to a belief that destroyed her future when it wasn't even the truth. I allowed my compassion and forgiveness to be there so that I would be able to love wholeheartedly and be a person who had a strong sense of worthiness. Because, as Dr Driscoll said, it was never about me.

My mother came out to stay with us after the birth of our second daughter, Rhian. Having broken my coccyx during both deliveries, recovery took a bit longer than I'd hoped. Having my mom there was invaluable. She helped with all the practical stuff, like looking after Jordan and taking care of the meals and the dreaded laundry and housework. One of the amazing skills she had was keeping a spotless house 24/7 and doing so in ninja-like fashion. We all marvelled at the state-of-the-art, hospital-standard cleanliness, yet nobody ever witnessed Mom lift a finger. I could be drinking a glass of water, place it down for one minute, and when I returned, it had already been washed, dried and put away.

Mom and I never really spoke of the past, but I noticed after the death of my father, both of us seemed able to let go of it, if only a little. Chris would often say he found it difficult to look into my mom's eyes as that is where she visibly harboured her trauma. I saw her pain, but related more to that faraway look she often displayed. I understood it to be her only means of survival. Keeping busy was her way of coping. Staying one step ahead of the past while remaining loyal to the one rule keeping you going: looking back was never an option. Despite the two decades that had passed since my parents divorced, even in death, he'd managed to take the life out of her eyes and leave her a broken woman. As an adult, I finally understood her pain had less to do with what he did to her and more to do with what he had done to me. The sad reality of the situation was simply this: in the twenty-three years since leaving my father, she had never been with another man.

The night before my mom was scheduled to fly back to Canada, she was in the bathroom washing and getting ready for bed. Jordan followed her in, and I could hear the two of them chatting away. After I finished nursing Rhian, I went into the bathroom.

'Mom, thank you so much for helping me out.'

She turned from the mirror to look at me and smiled. 'I will always be here for you. You know that.'

'Yes, Mom, I do,' I said. 'But I am so grateful.'

Closing the toilet lid, I sat down with the baby and continued chatting to my mother. A few moments passed then both Mom and I turned toward Jordan to see why she had gone so quiet. Her chirping and singing had stopped, and she was staring into the tub. At first I assumed she must have spotted a spider, but after a while I became curious and asked her what she was looking at.

She pointed into the tub.

'What is it, Jordan?' I asked. 'What are you looking at, baby?'

'I can see your daddy,' she stated calmly.

Shocked by my daughter's response, I looked over at my mom, unable to pursue further questioning. My father had been dead almost nine months, and I'd never spoken about him to her.

After composing myself and intrigued as to what her response might be, I worked up the courage to ask, 'What does he look like, baby?'

She continued to stare into the tub. 'He has curly white hair and a red face.'

My mom and I stole a wide-eyed glance at each other. She was as stunned as I was. For as long as I could remember, he'd had wild white hair. The redness of his face was due to high blood pressure, psoriasis and years of alcohol abuse. But my daughter knew nothing about the man. I never mentioned him and didn't even own a photograph thanks to Mom's *Edward Scissorhands* job on the albums.

'What is he doing, Jordan?' my mom asked.

Jordan turned to me calmly, her eyes filled with sadness, and replied, 'He's crying, Mama.'

17

MY FAVOURITE MOMENTS have often occurred during those times that fall at the beginning and the end of a day. I love the stillness of my own company as much as I love the profound silence that can exist in moments shared with the ones I adore.

There's a park with a lake close to our home where Chris and I would take the girls after dinner sometimes. One evening we made our way over the hill toward the lake. The girls – now aged eight and four – ran ahead of us. Chris and I went to our usual spot under the willow tree near the edge of the water. He sat down first, stretching out his legs and resting his back against the trunk of the tree. Using his jumper as a rug, I laid it out beside him. Lowering myself down, I kicked off my shoes and rested my head gently in his lap.

'Babe,' he said with disgust, hitting the brim of my hat, 'when are you going to get rid of this ugly thing?'

There were two items I still owned that had made the journey from Canada. One was my baseball cap, once a beautiful deep blue, now turned a prison grey. Tami bought it for me at a garage sale near her place before my first trip to Australia. It was tatty and badly faded by the strength of the Aussie sun. The other was the pair of jeans I'd worn upon leaving Canada, which were torn and as thin and fragile as a piece of paper. I was not one to attach myself to belongings, but for some reason I had not been able to part with either.

I lifted my cap, met his gaze and replied, 'Never.'

He rolled his eyes and continued, 'Have you heard from your sister lately?'

Chris had flown my sister out a couple times to visit.

'Yes, we spoke on the phone the other day,' I said. 'She is dating some guy and just started a new job. She sounds happy.'

'You think she will ever settle down and have kids?' he asked.

I laughed. 'Who knows.'

She was only thirty so children were still a possibility, although I wasn't so sure the desire was there. I loved thinking about what life would bring my own children. Chris and I would often talk about how Jordan was definitely on her way to becoming a brilliant lawyer – she was driven and focused and never took no for an answer. But instead of throwing a tantrum, she relied on her extraordinary verbal skills to outwit others, along with her uncanny ability to read a play, which meant she always prevailed in the end. She did that better than I ever could.

'What about Rhian?' I asked him as we sat there.

We both looked over and laughed at the sight of our youngest sitting down surrounded by ducks and appearing to be deep in conversation with one in particular. Dr Dolittle, I thought.

'Rhian will be a gypsy,' Chris said. 'Probably making her way through India and other developing countries helping children find their passion.'

'And Xavier?' I asked.

Chris's son, a beautiful boy, lived with us every weekend. He loved to play sport and read books, and he wrote amazing stories. We glanced at each other and agreed: a writer. Mostly I just wanted them to be happy.

'Mama, what is that flower floating on the water?' Jordan came up and asked with Rhian following behind.

I sat up to have a look. 'A lily, I think.'

'No,' Chris said. 'Those flowers over there with the broad green leaves floating on the surface are waterlilies. I believe that, my girls, is a lotus flower.'

'Smart-ass,' I muttered under my breath through a smile.

He pushed my hat down to cover my eyes.

'Do you girls want to hear the story of the lotus flower?' Both girls nodded. 'Do you, babe?'

'Yes, please, O Wise One. Enlighten me.'

'The lotus flower always originates from the bottom of the pond. The strong stem stays rooted in the mud, and through the murky, putrid water, the plant begins to grow. Bursting its way up out of the muck as it rises toward the sun.'

Turning away from the water, he looked directly at me and continued. 'And only once the sturdy plant has journeyed up through the mud and the muck to the surface will its beautiful flower bloom. Untouched by the difficult journey, it stands high above its humble beginnings.'

He placed his arm around my shoulder, kissed my forehead and added, 'It is also said that the deeper and murkier the mud, the more beautiful the flower blooms.'

The kids, unbeknown to us, had grown bored of the story and gone back to feed the ducks. I remained staring at the beautiful flower with the closed petals. Placing my head on Chris's chest, I thanked him for telling me the story.

As night was falling, Chris and I gathered the girls and walked home. Before we reached the house, I stood back to watch the silhouette of my husband with our children. They seemed to disappear into the setting sun. Jordan was holding her daddy's hand while skipping happily beside him. Sitting on his shoulders, Rhian pointed inquisitively to the treetops toward the sound of the cackling kookaburras settling down for the night. The sight of my two beautiful, trusting souls, who will only ever know love and kindness from the most influential man in their life, made my eyes well up.

Later that evening, I stood as I often did in our courtyard beside our pond and asked Chris the same question I'd been asking for years.

'Babe, can we please get rid of these awful fish?'

He smiled and stuck out his tongue as he reached for their food pellets.

'Well, do you think we could get a lotus flower for the pond?'

'Yes, baby. We can definitely get a lotus flower.'

My dear mother fell ill during the Canadian winter of 2007. I was thirty-two years old. She phoned to tell me the devastating news. I'd seen her just a few months before that call. She had looked fine, at least a decade younger than her sixty-seven years, and still had more energy than anybody I knew.

Now she told me she had cancer, and that it had spread everywhere. If we were lucky, we would have her for a few more weeks – maybe one more Christmas.

'Looks like it has finally come back for me,' she said. 'Twenty-eight years ago they told me I probably wouldn't see you start school. All I wanted was to see both you and Jillian through your childhood years. I made a deal with God back then when they said I was dying. Get me through until my girls graduate and then you can do what you want with me. I have been given another fourteen years on top of that, and I feel like I have been living on borrowed time ever since.'

The tears streamed down my face as I sat silently on the other end of the line.

'I walked into the hospital two days ago and they haven't let me go home. They are talking about different options that will maybe give me a few more months, but will make me even sicker than I already am. I'm not doing it, Carrie. I have made my peace with everything. I think I am ready to go.'

I understood that. My mom had been fighting her whole life. She had an amazing job and great bosses who had become her everything. But I could tell from her tone that she was tired of fighting.

In the twelve years I had been living in Australia, she had been to visit thirteen times – usually in December so that she could stay with us over the holidays and escape the bitter Canadian cold. Our relationship had changed dramatically since Jordan's birth. I was no longer the wounded, angry teenager who hated her mother for not protecting her. The years and distance between us had brought me wisdom and perspective. My daughters had gifted me with compassion and forgiveness. I knew my mother's limitations, but I also knew her love.

'Mom, I will tell Jillian for you, if you want.'

We both knew that would be an emotional conversation. She agreed that it would be best for me to break the news to my sister. I told her I would tell her boss as well. I knew how Mom never wanted to burden anyone. Of course this news would be devastating for everyone who loved her, but even in dying, my mom wanted nobody's pity.

After getting off the phone with my mother, I rang Jillian.

'It's cancer, Jill. It's incredibly aggressive and has spread everywhere.'

Jillian let out a wail. 'Oh my God! She's not going to die, is she?'

Denial was something the three of us had become proficient at over the years.

'Is she dying?' she repeated.

'Yes,' I whispered. 'She only has a couple of months at best.'

Jillian was far more attached to my mother than I was. She had been offered a job on the east coast months earlier, and Mom convinced her to take it. I think she knew she was dying long before the diagnosis. In typical fashion, she quietly went about her business, getting her things in order and telling no one. I sat helpless on the other end of the phone and tried to console my sister as she wept.

Upon hearing the news, Mom's boss's wife, Nicki, organised flights to Canada for me and my girls. I was so grateful. In the fifteen years Mom worked for them, she was given a high-achievement award and trusted with basically everything. Their children, especially, loved her. They would miss her terribly. She was hardworking and fiercely loyal.

I returned to Canada three days after speaking to my mother. Nothing could prepare me for the state I found her in. She needed assistance getting in and out of bed, and used a walker to go to the bathroom. In just a few months, she had gone from being relatively the same height as me and weighing twenty pounds more to reaching just above my chin and weighing maybe seventy pounds. Cancer is evil. I haven't the words to describe the suffering it inflicted upon her body.

Every day my mother would lose the ability to do something she had been able to do the day before. It was devastating to watch her deteriorate. Not once did she complain. She remained practical the whole way through, even writing thank you cards to the entire staff at Rockyview General Hospital and lecturing me about the thank you cards I had yet to write for my wedding, seven years before. Point taken, I thought.

Christmas Day was the last time my mother would get out of bed. She was determined to sit on the couch and watch her granddaughters open their presents. Not wanting to remember my mother as a shell of her former self, but also not wanting to forget the last days of her life, I took a few photos of my girls as they walked their presents over to my mom, placed them on the floor in front of her and excitedly tore open the wrapping.

Lying in bed with her on Christmas night, I stroked her hair and thanked her for everything she had ever done for me. I wanted her to know that I didn't blame her. That I forgave her for not knowing.

I had begun writing my life story two years before my mom fell ill. She knew that I had, but we never really talked about it. My mother was fiercely private, and I respected that she probably wasn't comfortable with our life being so publicly displayed. The timing felt right to have the conversation I had been meaning to have with her two years before.

'Mom, if you don't want me to publish this book, I won't do it.'

She was silent for a long time. I had shown her bits and pieces of my writing on several occasions. Mostly the positive stuff. I knew she was aware of the extent of the abuse, but I still felt a strong desire to protect her from my suffering. I also felt guilty about documenting our rough relationship during my teen years. I just felt guilty full stop knowing the pain that my pain caused her. How funny it was, the way both she and I took on the shame that had never seemed to afflict my father. Had it not been for his abuse, our relationship as mother and daughter probably wouldn't have suffered in the way it had.

I looked down at her hollowed face and stroked her prominent cheekbones with the tips of my fingers. The last thing I wanted to do was cause her more pain. She was the most at peace I had ever known her to be. The pain in her eyes was no longer there. For the first time in her adult life, she knew she was going to be free. No more suffering. No more keeping busy to hold the demons of the past at bay. Comforting though it was to know she would finally be at peace, I felt devastated by the tragedy of her having to die to achieve her freedom.

Resting my head on the pillow beside hers, I held her hand, and we looked at the ceiling together. We lost ourselves in the shadows above us, cast by the dim lamp I had taken off the bedside table earlier and placed on the floor.

'You have to finish it, Carrie,' she said. 'If you can help one girl to realise what's happening is not her fault and lose the shame and tell someone who can help her, it is worth doing.' She turned to look at me. There were tears in her eyes. 'Please forgive me for not protecting you. You must believe me, I didn't know.'

'I know, Mom.' I could feel the tears forming in the back of my eyes. Swallowing hard, I cleared my throat and held her stare. 'It's alright. I'm okay now. I understand and I believe you, Mom. I do.'

She smiled. 'If you can help one girl escape fear and shame, Carrie, it is all worth it.'

'I love you, Mom.'

'I have loved you from the moment I picked you up and held you in my arms. I am so proud of the woman you have become and the mother you are to your girls. They love you so much, you know?'

'I know, Mom.'

'Thank you for cutting those awful dreadlocks out of your hair before you came to see me.'

We both laughed. I'd grown them down to my waist, and she had been pestering me for years to cut them. I figured that was the least I could do.

'Mom, do you have any cool ideas for a tattoo you would like me to get in your honour?'

'Don't you dare!' she scolded.

I burst out laughing. She did not this time.

'I'm serious, Carrie. I hate those too.'

'I know, Mom.' I smiled and began to stroke her hair again. 'I know.'

A few days later my mom slipped into a coma and passed away. The day after my mother died I walked outside onto a lawn blanketed with freshly fallen snow. Wearing jeans and my runners, I lay down in the cold and stared up at the sky. The one person I knew for certain loved me, who had always been the direction in which my moral compass pointed, was no longer in this world. Despite everything, I'd never lost the desire to make her feel proud.

Raising my arms above my head and allowing my legs to move to a childhood memory, I made my last snow angel on the lawn that day. I closed my eyes, ignoring the bitter cold, and felt the warmth of my tears as they trailed down my face. That first day without her made forever seem almost unbearable. I felt completely empty. She was the one person who knew the intimacies of my suffering, in a way no other soul could possibly understand. We never spoke of it. We didn't have to. Her agony swam in the blues and greens of her eyes. I related to her pain so deeply that it often prevented me from holding her gaze. It hurt too much.

Standing up, I looked down and admired my work. It made me smile – I had forgotten all about the times I had made snow angels as a child. Wherever there was a blank canvas of snow, they became my masterpiece. They surrounded my childhood home, and every other weekend, my father's place as well. Standing there, in what would most likely be my last Canadian winter, I took one final look at my angel and turned around to retrace my footprints in the snow.

Epilogue

… SOLD. I was nine years old
When I shoulda been playin' with dolls and skipping down
*   halls*
When my surroundings shoulda been fields of green lying
*   under a tree staring up at the blue*
Chasing raindrops and rainbows, laughing for no particular
*   reason*
Other than I was a child and that's what kids do
But my reality was a concrete slab with four concrete walls
*   and grown men in every direction*
My truth became the lies that echoed in the deafening silence
*   of compassion's painful rejection*
There was nowhere to run. Nowhere to turn for protection
Twelve steps to the bottom of that basement
And I still count stairs
Each step I take placing me in a hypnotic trance, an
*   imaginative dance that carried my mind to*
the safe enclosures of a hidden reality my body would never
*   have the luxury of escaping to*
Nine years old and maybe twenty-five kilos with fragile
*   bones that made a ballerina's frame look huge …*
*   comparatively speaking*

Nowhere to run and so I fought the dark while I imagined
    the light
Broken and bound, pleading they do right – by me
Daddy, please. I'm sorry. Can't we just rewrite this story?
Don't let them hurt me.
I love you, can't you see?
Pleading for a father's protection
Persistent prayers landing on deaf ears
Seemingly, bad connection
And even though he was worse than any other
I held faith in the face of a familiar stranger
Convincing myself when it mattered most, he would protect
    me from danger
After all, he was my father. And don't men protect their
    daughter?
Too scared to count the tears I never cry
All the pain I held inside
Or the times I thought I'd died
And all the times I wished I had
Beyond the childhood abuses sat my adult excuses
And so walking the line between heartache and grace
I stand proud in this world and step into my place
Using my life to be one that inspires
Speaking to others and lifting them higher
Igniting the fire that fuels their desire
Letting them know that in their darkest hour
Hope is the gift inside us all that catches us each time we fall
So I will rise up to be that voice and speak for the many
    million voiceless
Whose stories need to be told because bodies continue to
    be sold
I will stand tall in the freedom forgiveness gifted me
And be that reminder you can still fly on broken wings

And it matters not how hard we land but that we eventually
    stand
Rising to soar to infinite heights
I hope to shine a light as bright as that North Star in the
    Canadian wild
Diamonds in the night sky I wished upon as a child
Because society pleads ignorance, stays misinformed and
    comfortably numb
Well, may I submit to you this; are we really that dumb?
To think the slave trade and exploitation of young girls is a
    foreign issue
Domestic daughters' greatest stress education. Evidently no
    need for emancipation
Hiding behind the deluded excuses – our backyard's clean of
    gender abuses
And so what of the fourteen-year-olds in the five-inch pumps
    working that one-block stroll
Or the twelve-year-old runaway who believed the grown man
    who told her that daddy missed out on a precious angel
And so long as she does what she is told
    he will love her … UNCONDITIONALLY SOLD
Trading people for pesos. For pounds, francs and dollars
Rupees and rands for the purchase of our daughters
The currency generated non-discriminatory
Cambodian or Canadian – same criminal story
Maybe men need to step up and teach boys that girls are
    not toys
To be used and abused. That you come correct and treat
    a girl with respect
Or you don't cum at all
Maybe if men and boys knew that the first time they lay
    an unwanted hand on an unwilling soul
Life as she knows it, will never be the same at all

*And just maybe if that girl remains protected and connected
     and forever respected*
*She will grow up and show up and be a force to be reckoned
     with*
Her hopes and ambitions will come into fruition
Her sons and daughters beneficiaries of what life taught her
Pursuing solutions for the existence of an ideal world
No tolerance for violence against women and girls
*Public outcry sparks aspiration for an introduction to
     inoculation*
A powerful concoction, a collective immunity
Against degradation, abuse, rape and cruelty
By injecting empathy into the veins of humanity
Let's combat apathy – our conditioned insanity
*For apathy is the underlying current in a sea of silent
     observers*
Granting themselves permission to turn the other cheek
To issues far too dark and much too bleak
Empathy is the driving force of action
Its birthplace requiring but a fraction of one's compassion
*One's moral obligation to stand tall and catch others
     otherwise destined to fall*
For half the sky is held up by women and girls
And the slave trade is hardly exclusive to third worlds
You want further persuasion? Here's a basic equation
*Abuse plus degradation minus hope, equates to this common
     denominator*
A soul's death
Divide a person's rights with a fraction of their worth
And then multiply the perpetrators she's endured since birth
Take away her power in addition to her dignity
Expand this concept globally. It couldn't be more plain to see
That no world has immunity

When it comes to modern-day slavery
There were twelve steps to the bottom of that basement
And I will remember that walk for as long as I live

Shortly before I finished performing my poem, a man stood up in the middle of the room and his eyes locked with mine. He was tall and a fairly intimidating presence. My heart stopped for a second as I wasn't sure what he was going to do. But he was one of the few men who made eye contact with me, so I held his stare while I finished my poem and prepared myself for whatever was to come. I held my ground. Feeling incredibly vulnerable and exposed, but intent on showing courage, I waited. To my astonishment, he began to cry and started to clap. The whole room rose to their feet to acknowledge what I had just done, and the courage it must have taken. I was later told it was the first standing ovation ever given in that building for any person.

I remember thinking halfway through my performance it felt as though time had stood still. As though all of the air was let out of the room. No one spoke. No one moved. No one even appeared to be breathing. All the men seemed to prefer to stare at their hands resting in their laps, and many even closed their eyes. The women looked at me and some were crying. It seemed the impact of my message of hope was landing and truly resonating with people.

Many came up to me afterward to share their stories for the first time. Others told me how moved they were and thanked me for being so brave. Some, mostly men, just stood there, unable to say anything. They shook my hand with tears in their eyes and walked away, sometimes with a little girl by their side. The most significant moment for me arrived when the mother-in-law of a young woman approached me.

273

'My son and I always knew something had happened to her,' she said of her daughter-in-law. 'Just in the way she presents and sometimes how she regresses back to being like a little girl. You know, we kind of put two and two together and assumed she'd been sexually abused. We've tried to gently go there with her, but she just won't talk about it. She is here with me today and halfway through your poem she got her phone out, texted her father and wrote: *You lose. I'm done with you.*'

I became overwhelmed with emotion and was at a loss for words. We looked at each other and smiled.

'What you are doing is so brave and so very important for young women to hear. Can I give you a hug?'

I let her.

After the crowd around me dissipated, my family and friends came over to congratulate me. Deanne's expression was priceless. She was so proud.

'Carrie,' Dr Driscoll said, 'this is the first time I have known you to stand in a room full of people and own your power without any apology. It was stunning to witness.'

My girls wrapped their arms around me. Their faces beaming and their smiles reassuring me that they were okay.

'Wow, Mom, I'm so proud of you,' Jordan said. 'That was amazing.'

She was nearly my height now. I looked into her eyes and kissed her gently on the forehead.

Just as we were about to leave, a woman approached me. She introduced herself as a yoga teacher who used yoga therapy to help people use movement and breathing to connect with their emotions. She asked if she could have a word with me.

'You have found your dharma, haven't you?' she began.

I hadn't a clue what she meant. I had never heard that word before. She went on to explain.

'That just means you have found your life's purpose and not many people can say they have done so, and when we align to that, life creates opportunities for our truth to be realised and expressed. When you speak your truth from the heart others will hear and connect with their own hearts and their own truth. Your voice and courage will ignite the voice and courage in others. Your story of hope will become theirs.'

The year before, a series of events had made me decide to come forward with my story. Of course I was scared but I made a promise to myself to see how brave I was willing to be in order to inspire others to rise up out of their 'victim mentality'.

My journey officially began lying in bed one night with my laptop, watching a YouTube link a friend had sent me. Dr Brené Brown, an American social worker, was giving a TEDx talk on the 'Power of Vulnerability'. She described a select group of people in this world who were living life 'wholeheartedly' and were not afraid to be vulnerable and authentic. That resonated so much with me because my whole life I had always been told that my vulnerability and openness was my greatest weakness. And this woman was on stage telling millions that, in reality, vulnerability was 'our most accurate measure of courage', and that the actual definition of courage was to get up and tell your story with your whole heart.

A few months later, I reconnected with two friends I had played basketball with at the University of Melbourne when I first arrived in Australia, brothers Josh and Jarett. Josh then introduced me to his friend Elliot, who turned out to be the eldest son of Tim Costello, CEO of World Vision Australia.

Not long after our friendship started, Elliot took me to his parents.

We arranged to meet at the Costello home and head to a local cafe for breakfast. Once we were seated and our food was ordered, I began to tell them about my life. Mr Costello seemed to listen more intently when I spoke about my message of hope. He mentioned that he knew somebody who would love to talk with me. She was an advocate and activist who went around the country raising awareness about violence against women, sexual exploitation and human trafficking. Her name was Melinda Tankard Reist.

My mind immediately jumped back to the hundreds of refugee and immigration papers I still kept filed away at home. A copy of the letter that Senator Harradine had written to Philip Ruddock had been faxed to Dr Driscoll, and the covering note had been signed: *For your records. Regards, Melinda Reist.* I'd committed the last line of that letter to memory because it was the sentence I often shared with others when I told my story: *Minister, I ask you to act in the best interest of this young woman and her baby.* I was certain Melinda Reist would remember me. How often had she or Senator Harradine had Canadian refugee cases land on their desks?

Mr Costello immediately picked up his phone and called her. Not only did she remember me, she was actually the one who'd drafted the letter to the Minister for Immigration. She had forever wondered how my life turned out.

A few months later I was holidaying in Cairns with my family. Melinda was also there speaking at an international conference, and we arranged to meet. I picked her up, and we went back to where my family was staying. You can imagine her emotions when my then fourteen-year-old daughter opened the door for us and she met the unborn baby she had years earlier asked Philip Ruddock to protect.

Some months later I found out Brené Brown was giving a talk in Melbourne. My friend and I bought tickets just before the event sold out. I expected we'd be right at the back of the room near the toilets, and she would be but a dot on the stage. When I was shown to my seat, I couldn't believe it. Our table was right next to the stage and directly across from Brené Brown's table. I wanted to go over and tell her what her vulnerability talk had inspired in me. I tried a few times, but was too chicken. My friend told me that I would never forgive myself if I didn't speak to Brené. I knew she was right and so I let her drag me over. Like a small child reluctant to do something, but too embarrassed to cause a scene, I dug my heels in while she pulled at my arm. When I was five metres away, Brené turned to face my direction. She pointed her finger at me and motioned me to come over.

She was completely blown away by my story. When I was finished, all she could say was 'holy shit'. And then she found more words.

'What you are doing is the embodiment of *Daring Greatly*,' Brené said.

I told her how in the few times I had spoken about my life, it seemed to create an authentic space, so that others, often for the first time in their lives, followed suit and shared their stories as well.

'Because courage really is contagious,' she said.

To this day, doors continue to open. People continue to appear who want to assist me, and everything I do feels as though it is guided by something far greater than myself. This does not mean my struggles are over – my past still haunts me.

There is no question that the good I have experienced in my life outweighs the bad. When I think back to the number of people who have helped me along the way, who continue to come into my life at exactly the right moment, I sometimes feel unworthy. I have read that when you discover your life's purpose and set out on the journey toward your destiny, the road you follow becomes the path of grace.

I strongly believe we are put on this earth to love and to be loved. That to experience authentic connection with others is the reason we are here. And if we manage to live our whole lives never truly showing up, allowing our fear of being hurt to be greater than our desire to truly love another, can we honestly say there was ever any point?

These days I look forward to spring, the season that enables new beginnings for everything on earth: when the leaves are a brilliant green and the fragrance of blossoms hangs in the air. I sit quietly, surrounded by peace and tranquillity – not just in my outer world, but my inner world as well.

I often climb through an upstairs window and onto the roof to catch the sunset. I have always loved the Australian sky. The view takes my breath away. Soft white clouds breaking up the pinks and purples. The sun's final rays cast an orange glow before disappearing beyond the horizon. Taking in my surroundings, I breathe in the fresh air and look out over the distant eucalyptus trees. The cockatoos soar above, white against the vibrant backdrop. I turn toward the sound of the cackling kookaburras as they race to settle themselves before dark. They are another one of my favourites, and I can't help but smile when surrounded by all of Australia's natural beauty – a world away from where my life began. I am often overwhelmed with gratitude.

There will likely always be times when I remember how my life used to be. When my nightmares take me back to that cold, dark basement. Even as a child, I somehow knew that what I was experiencing was only temporary. If I could find a way to survive my father, I knew something greater than even I could imagine awaited me.

Just as I am about to go back into the house and start dinner, the bathroom window swings open, and my two girls climb out to sit beside me on the roof. They are laughing and want to show me some silly video they have discovered on YouTube. I enjoy watching them become confident young women. Through the love I give and receive from those in my life today, I pick up the shattered pieces of my childhood. My children are constant reminders of my own innocence. When my girls laugh, I am able to imagine myself at various ages in my own life, laughing along with them.

Rhian catches me wiping a stray tear from my cheek.

'Mom,' she asks, 'are you crying?'

'No, baby, not really,' I tell her. 'I was just thinking how lucky we are to have one another.'

Jordan looks at me, squints her eyes at the setting sun and smiles. Taking them both in my arms, I hold them closely and remember the advice given to me by my mother that day in the sun, all those years before.

'I guess good things really do come to those who wait,' I say.

'Wait for what, Mom?'

'Freedom, girls. I've waited for freedom.'

Acknowledgements

FIRSTLY I WOULD like to thank my beautiful friend/pseudo mom Tami. Your unwavering support and unconditional love forever inspires. I am who I have become because of you. To my amazing girls, you make being a mom the best job in the world. I am so proud of you both. Chris, what a journey. Thank you so much for standing by my side through thick and thin and for helping raise three amazing kids! Mom, I honour your memory and hold you in my heart forever. Deanne, you have been there since I arrived in this country, and I look forward to many more years of love and laughter with you, my best friend. Dr Driscoll, you gave me hope when mine had almost vanished. My freedom was possible because of the work you did for me. Yvonne Pilatowicz, you helped me take my power back and I am forever grateful. Debbie, I've not forgotten, and I thank you. Thank you to Natasha Silberberg and Susan McDougall from SECASA. To Senator Brian Harradine, thank you for your intervention. May you rest in peace. Gratitude to the Refugee Review Tribunal, the Department of Immigration and Multicultural Affairs, and every official who was involved in my plight. Minister Philip Ruddock, you made the right decision. My daughter and I thank you. Samar, *mektoub*, my friend. 2012 – I am forever grateful for your love and care. I would also like to pay tribute to the memory of Jill Meagher and Jyoti Singh Pandey. Their violent demises were the catalyst for me to shed light on the global epidemic of violence against women and girls. It needs to change. Mrs Adams, Mrs MacNeil and Mrs Wadden, you were the only teachers who suspected there was something wrong and encouraged me to talk. Sheila for being the first person I ever told all those years ago. And my high-school guidance counsellor, Lesley G, thank you for your care and intervention when the school wanted to suspend me for never showing up. Beverly, for loving that angry, lost teen I once was. The Lefer gang. Josh! You always believed in me, brother. Janne. Bronwyn – eternal gratitude!!! The girls from the YWP. RIP Sherron Dunbar. Your support and hard work will not be forgotten, ladies. Vicki, Mandi and Heidi for the many laughs we've shared. Catherine and the Maguire family for your love and support. The crew at YGAP. Sally Tonkin and St Kilda Gatehouse. Dur-e Dara for telling me, 'Carrie, you are not just a one-trick pony with a poem and a pretty face!' Ha! No, I'm not! Massive thanks to the team at Affirm Press. And a special thank you to Aviva Tuffield – your final edits! I am so proud of the end result. To my dear friend Eddie Duenas, whose bravery and support carried me in my journey to publication and whose friendship totalled twenty-three years (that number is no coincidence, Ed). I will hold you in my heart for as long as I live. West siiiiiiiide 4 life playa. RIP sweet friend. Morgan, thank you for your friendship since high school. Melinda, what a reunion tour! Gratitude forever, girl. Lisa, I am so grateful for your love and support. Let's keep laughing when we should be crying. Robin Cain for your guidance and the first round of edits, as well as Zoe Costis. Camilla, just thank you. You know what for. Christine and the Cucia clan, for accepting my girls and me into your family. Daphne, girl, I cherish you! You have always had my back through the good times and bad. Thank you for your true friendship and OMG the inappropriate laughs! Gabrielle, I love your authenticity and the safe space and support you continue to provide. To Nicki and Mogens Smed for their love of my mother and their support and kindness when she was dying. Carmel P for the laughs while working on my broken wings. Best physio ever.

Jordan Kyle and Brandy, forever in my heart. Jessica, Mom would be so proud. I know I sure am, sweet girl. At last, to my sister, J. It was my love of you and your love of me that pushed me through as a kid. I have only now realised this. I love you and I thank you for giving me purpose.

Finally, to every single soul who has crossed paths with me and made a difference in my life, be it positive or negative. You have planted the seed, and I thank you for the inspiration!

Author's Note

I TELL MY story to honour the capacity of the human spirit and to illustrate its remarkable ability to not only endure, but also rise above adversity in order to flourish and thrive. Last year I was made an ambassador to Gatehouse Young Women's Project and I am so grateful to my publishers for donating 25 per cent of profits earned from the sales of this book to this initiative. It is so important that young women who have suffered abuse and are at risk of further exploitation have a safe place to go. A place where they are encouraged and provided the opportunity to realise their full potential. If you would like to make a donation to this project or to one of the other organisations doing amazing work in this area, I feature some of them on my website: flyingonbrokenwings.com. There you can also find a list of resources on where to go for help, news on author appearances, and a booking form to contact me if you would like me to speak at your school, conference or event.